WILLIAM R. WILLOUGHBY, now retired, was formerly Professor of History and Government, St Lawrence University, Canton, New York (1946–1964), and Professor of Political Science at the University of New Brunswick (1964–1976). He is author of *The St Lawrence Waterway: A Study in Politics and Diplomacy*.

Joint governmental commissions, committees, and boards form an important part of the intergovernmental machinery which supplements the work of the embassies and the direct contacts between Canadian and American public officials. As the first book to provide detailed descriptions of the major joint institutions of the past seven decades, this is a significant contribution to the literature on Canadian–American relations; in addition, it provides information essential to any methodological analysis of the intergovernmental relations between the two countries.

The book gives some attention to the joint commissions created by Britain and the United States in the eighteenth and nineteenth centuries to resolve boundary and other types of disputes, and it considers briefly the joint economic committees employed by Canada and the United States during the years 1941–45. Primary attention, however, is given to the more important of the joint institutions currently available to the two federal governments including the International Joint Commission, the international fisheries commissions, the International Boundary Commission, the Permanent Joint Board on Defence and other bodies concerned with military matters, the Canada–United States Ministerial Committee on Trade and Economic Affairs, the Interparliamentary Group, and the Roosevelt–Campobello International Park Commission.

The author's approach to each agency has been to consider first the reasons and circumstances of its creation; then to examine its organization and operating procedures; and finally to assess its importance and effectiveness in the conduct of the intergovernmental relations of the two countries. The book will be of particular interest to students of Canadian–American relations, Canadian foreign policy, and international institutions in general.

WILLIAM R. WILLOUGHBY

The Joint Organizations of Canada and the United States

with a foreword by
JOHN W. HOLMES

UNIVERSITY OF TORONTO PRESS
Toronto Buffalo London

Canadian Cataloguing in Publication Data

Willoughby, William R., 1910–
The Joint organizations of Canada and the
United States

Includes index.
ISBN 0-8020-5453-6

1. International agencies. 2. Canada – Relations
(general) with the United States. 3. United
States – Relations (general) with Canada.
I. Title.

JX1995.W55   341.24   C79-094396-4

To
ROBERT A. MACKAY
HENRY REIFF
H. GORDON SKILLING
AMRY VANDENBOSCH

Foreword

The debate on Canada–United States relations is never-ending – in Canada at least. Unfortunately there has been much less attention paid to the relationship. In recent years scholars in the United States as well as Canada have been turning their attention to the habits and conventions, the unstructured ways and means of doing business across the border. A better understanding of how the North American system actually works should contribute to more clear-headed and soundly based prescriptions for improvement. The descriptive literature has, however, been much less plentiful than the polemic.

Although Canadians and Americans have been chary of institutionalizing their unequal relationship, we have produced certain institutions that cope ingeniously with this inequality. They have not been adequately understood or appreciated by North Americans or by inhabitants of other continents for whom they provide important examples. One reason is, no doubt, that they have been inadequately explained. Professor Willoughby has for the first time assembled a comprehensive description and analysis of these joint organizations which fills a serious gap for students of political science and provides the concerned citizenry with much food for reference and for thought. It is fortunate that this work has been done by a scholar who has devoted many years to studying the storied border and has done so from vantage points on both sides of it. At a time when increased attention is of necessity being directed to the continental relationship, this study of basic structures is to be warmly welcomed.

JOHN W. HOLMES

Contents

viii Contents

Preface

This study is a narrative overview of the binational governmental machinery that Canada and the United States are using, or have used during the past seven decades, in the management of their joint affairs. It does not pretend to be analytical; nor does it attempt to present any new approaches to the study of the Canadian–American relationship. It is, briefly stated, a descriptive, organizational book, the only one available covering in any depth or detail all of the major institutions. Thus perhaps it is not immodest to say that the study not only fills a gap in the literature of Canadian–American relations but also provides information essential to any methodological analysis of the intergovernmental relationships of the two countries.

The book makes only brief references to state–provincial organizations and to multilateral organizations of which both Canada and the United States are members, such as the United Nations, the North Atlantic Treaty Organization, and the International Commission for the Northwest Atlantic Fisheries. It gives only limited attention to the diplomatic apparatus of each country and ignores completely dozens of working groups and committees of secondary importance that the two national governments have created from time to time, such as the joint committees on international bridges, on St Lawrence Seaway tolls, and on water and energy resources. Some attention is devoted to the joint commissions created by Britain and the United States in the eighteenth and nineteenth centuries to resolve boundary and other types of disputes and to the joint economic committees employed by Canada and the United States during the years 1941 to 1945, but the primary focus is on the more important of the joint institutions currently available to the two federal governments, viz., the International Joint Commission, the International Pacific Halibut Commission, the International Pacific Salmon Fisheries Commission, the Great Lakes Fishery

Commission, the Permanent Joint Board on Defence, the Military Cooperation Committee, the Canada–United States Regional Planning Group, the Joint United States–Canada Industrial Mobilization Committee, the Joint United States–Canadian Civil Emergency Planning Committee, the North American Air Defence Command, the Senior Committee on Defence Production–Development Sharing, the Canada–United States Ministerial Committee on Trade and Economic Affairs, the Canada–United States Ministerial Committee on Joint Defence, and the Interparliamentary Group.

The amount of attention devoted to an organization has been governed by, first, the author's judgment as to its importance in the history of Canadian–American relations and its significance for the study of international administration, and, secondly, the availability of source materials (which, for some of the defence agencies, has been somewhat limited). In dealing with each institution the general approach has been, first, to consider the reasons and circumstances of its creation; then to examine its organization and operating procedures; and, finally, to assess its importance and effectiveness in the conduct of the transgovernmental relations of the neighbouring countries.

In the collection of data and in the writing of the book the author has received much assistance, which he acknowledges with deep gratitude. Through interviews and letters, some eighty-five persons – including members of the Canadian Parliament and of the American Congress, officials of many governmental departments and of the joint agencies, research foundation staff members, and university teachers – provided information, analyses, and insights which in some instances only they could have given. Most of these helpful persons are cited by name in the notes.

W.M. Johnson, R.A. MacKay, Peyton Lyon, William C. Herrington, William M. Sprules, Robert J. Myers, David Chance, J.L. MacCallum, Eugene Weber, David H. Walker, R.A. Tweedie, Jane Fenderson, Hubert R. Gallagher, Anthony Malone, Louis J. Walter, André L. Marcellin, M.R. Mackenzie, Ian Imrie, Albert C.F. Westphal, Norvill Jones, A.F. Lambert, Richard L. Herman, Clifford J. Pierce, and Marie A. Sheehy each read and critically commented on one or more chapters, and Gerald Craig, John W. Holmes, Hugh L. Keenleyside, and the late Thomas Allen Levy read the entire manuscript. My wife, Rudell, helped with much burdensome typing and proofreading. The Canada Council, the Canadian Institute of International Affairs, the American Philosophical Society, the Social Science Federation of Canada, the American Social Science Research Council, and the University of New Brunswick each provided financial assistance; during the academic year 1970–1, the Center of Canadian Studies of the Johns Hopkins University, then headed by Professor Dale Thomson, gave me an appointment as a visiting research associate and afforded me various types of assistance.

Finally, the author acknowledges the uniformly friendly assistance that he received from the library staffs of the University of New Brunswick, Harvard University, Yale University, the School of Advanced International Studies of the Johns Hopkins University, the Library of Congress, the Franklin D. Roosevelt Library at Hyde Park, the Department of State Archives, the National Archives, the Public Archives of Canada, the Canadian Institute of International Affairs, and the Canadian Embassy in Washington, DC.

This book has been published with the help of grants from the Social Science Federation of Canada, using funds provided by the Social Sciences and Humanities Research Council of Canada, and from the Publications Fund of the University of Toronto Press.

W.R.W.

THE JOINT ORGANIZATIONS OF CANADA
AND THE UNITED STATES

1

Pervasive interrelationships and joint institutions

There are several reasons why Canada and the United States have developed a highly complex network of intergovernmental agencies and arrangements, but two reasons have been of major importance: pervasive Canadian–American interrelationships and historical forces.

The two countries share a boundary of more than 5500 miles and are isolated from other countries, except Mexico, by three broad oceans. By its north–south land formations, North American geography has channelled both people and goods north and south across the border, 'creating many close cross-boundary regional affinities.'[1] Thus in recent years the border has been crossed an average of more than 72,000,000 times annually.[2] Equally significantly, in 1974 approximately 1,000,000 Canadian-born persons were living in the United States, while something like 400,000 American-born persons were residing in Canada.[3]

Upwards of 8000 miles of Canadian-controlled railroads in the United States are linked with their parent systems in Canada and more than 1500 miles of American-controlled railroad tracks are operated in Canada. Gas and oil pipelines cross the border at many points; and five Canadian provinces have hydro-electric power hookups with American states. The St Lawrence Seaway and Power Projects and the Columbia River Power Project were cooperatively developed by the two countries and are cooperatively operated in the interests of both.

At the end of 1978 trade between the neighbouring countries was approaching $70 billion annually. No less significantly, in 1975 American-owned direct investments in Canada were in excess of $32 billion, while Canadian direct investments in the United States were valued at $5.6 billion.[4] Add the fact that 47 per cent of Canada's unionized workers belong to labour unions with headquarters in the United States, and that for several years Canada has been an important supplier of oil and gas to the United States, while the latter country has shipped sizeable quantities of coal to Ontario, and one can then appreciate the truth of Gerald Craig's conclusion that 'there is literally no equivalent anywhere in the world, no economic and financial interrelationship between two national states that is so vast and so intricate.'[5]

Then there are the extensive defence ties that have developed since 1940. In fact, one-third of the major bilateral agreements between the two countries relate to defence.[6] Finally, there is the cultural interaction in its multifarious forms and the fact that the two peoples share many moral and ethical values and have a similar outlook on most questions relating to other areas of the world.

The above synopsis, however, is only one aspect of the complex relationship. Despite the innumerable links and mutual interests, there are significant cultural, ideological, and governmental differences. More important still, between the two countries there are immense disparities in population, in wealth and industrial development, in military strength and world power, and in the amount and kind of influence that each has upon the other. The population of the United States is somewhat in excess of 215 million; that of Canada, less than 24 million. Aside from Alaska, the population of the United States is fairly evenly distributed over its 3,615,211 square miles of territory; whereas, within Canada's 3,851,809 square miles, approximately 90 per cent of the people live within 200 miles of the border and 75 per cent live within 100 miles. This, of course, not only encourages extensive Canadian trade and social intercourse with the American neighbours, but lays the less populous, less affluent country open to the penetration of both American culture and American capital.

The gross national product of the United States is about thirteen times that of Canada. To a much greater degree than is true of the United States, Canada's prosperity is dependent on foreign trade. For example, in recent years exports have represented 25 per cent of Canada's gross national product, but only 2 per cent of that of the United States.[7] No less significantly, and distressingly in the opinion of not a few Canadians, Canada's trade is predominantly with its southern neighbour. Thus in 1974, 67 per cent of its exports went to the United States and 69 per cent of its imports came from that country. By contrast, during the same year 21 per cent of the exports of the United States went to Canada and 25 per cent of its imports came from that country. The American market absorbed up to 35 per cent of all the goods produced in Canada, while Canada bought less than 2 per cent of all the goods produced in the United States.[8]

Equally worrisome to many Canadians is the large percentage of Canadian mining and manufacturing owned by American corporations, posing the vexing problem of making sure that those corporations and their subsidiaries are amenable to Canadian laws and responsive to Canadian interests. Again statistics suggest the proportions of the problem. By the end of 1974 American investors controlled 58 per cent of the capital employed in the Canadian oil and gas industries, 43 per cent in other mining and smelting, 44 per cent in manufacturing, and 36 per cent in the pulp and paper industries.[9]

Another worrisome problem has been that of maintaining tolerable environmental conditions along the lengthy boundary. The 'artificial' boundary forces Canada and the United States to share waters, airsheds, game, and fish. Because of its greater population and industrial development, the United States does a great deal more polluting of the water and the air of the boundary area than does its northern neighbour. At the same time, Canadians derive only limited, indirect benefits from American industrial activities.

But the area in which the relationship is most one-sided is perhaps that of communications and culture. Because of the virtually open border for books, magazines, films, radio and television broadcasts, and other forms of cultural and intellectual activity, there has long been a dominant south–north flow – a flow so overwhelming as to have 'a stifling effect on Canadian aspirations to develop a distinctive Canadian culture.' Approximately 95 per cent of the magazines on Canadian newsstands are American in origin; best-selling books in the United States usually are best-sellers in Canada; and most Canadians choose American, rather than Canadian, television programs whenever they live close enough to the boundary to receive them. The distributing agencies for films, magazines, and paperbacks are largely owned in the United States, and the computer industry in Canada is 80 per cent controlled by American firms, which 'tend naturally to incorporate Canadian information storing and retrieval systems into continent-wide networks operated from south of the border.'[10]

In military power the United States ranks as one of the superpowers of the earth, with responsibilities and interests spanning the globe, whereas Canada is only a 'middle power' with modest goals, ambitions, and influence. More important still, since the advent of atomic weapons, if not before, Canada's defence, like that of the western powers in general, has been largely dependent upon the American Strategic Air Command and its arsenal of nuclear weapons.

Given the facts outlined above, it is not surprising that a Canadian government publication of 1970, entitled *Foreign Policy for Canadians*, affirmed Canada's two major problems to be maintaining national unity and 'living distinct from but in harmony with' its powerful and dynamic neighbour. For that neighbour a major concern has long been to obtain Canadian cooperation in exploiting the natural resources of the continent and in defending it from foreign attack. Understandably enough, the American objectives have usually been more easily attained than the Canadian. Even in the days when Canada could call upon Britain for military assistance, the cards were heavily stacked in favour of the more populous republic, which until well into the nineteenth century had no qualms about resorting to military force whenever other means failed to achieve its objectives. But, fortunately for Canada, most Americans were peaceably inclined, while those with warlike inclinations were restrained by respect for British–Canadian military strength. Thus at an early date the Canadians, the British, and the Americans – with their common language and traditions – cast about for alternatives to military force. These they readily found in negotiations, joint commissions, and arbitrations.

A pioneering move was the negotiation of the Jay Treaty of 1794 which, asserting as its main objective 'the promotion of a disposition favorable to friendship and Good Neighbourhood,' called for the establishment of three British–American mixed commissions to resolve longstanding boundary and claims issues.[11] Although the commissions were only moderately successful,[12] the commission approach had such obvious utility that it was used regularly in subsequent years. Thus ten additional arbitrations were conducted by Britain and the United States to 1865, one of them before a commission that disposed of 115 private claims.[13] Between 1871 and 1878 a number of other vexing issues were arbitrated in implementation of the Treaty of Washington.[14] In 1892 the matter of the killing of fur seals in the waters of the North Pacific was submitted to a tribunal of seven members, which rendered a prompt decision.[15]

Most of the arbitration settlements of the 1794–1893 period, it should be noted, were considerably more acceptable to Britain and the United States than to Canada. In fact, Canadian spokesmen – with justification – regularly complained that the British and the Americans seemed all too willing to sacrifice Canadian interests on the altar of Anglo-American understanding. They had even more valid grounds for such complaints after the Alaska Boundary settlement of 1903, which was organized and pretty well carried out along lines dictated by President Theodore Roosevelt. For the unsatisfactory settlements, however, the Canadian people tended to place more blame on the British authorities who had helped to set up the settlement procedures than they did on the procedures themselves. Consequently, instead of renouncing the use of mediatory and arbitral proceedings, they initiated discussions leading to the establishment of direct Canadian diplomatic relations with the United States. For various reasons the exchange of ministers was not effected until 1927.[16] But during the interim period three joint organizations were set up to deal with exclusively Canadian–American problems: the International Boundary Commission, the International Fisheries Commission, and the International Joint Commission. All of these proved highly useful, contributing, in time, to the growth of the tradition 'that Canada and the United States dealt with the world, and especially with one another, in a manner peculiarly their own.'[17] This tradition, in turn, predisposed the two countries to establish other joint institutions – a predisposition powerfully reinforced by the accelerated growth of the social, cultural, and economic interrelationships. The joint agencies were able to deal directly and expertly with a great variety of trans-border problems on a continuing basis, developing a degree of familiarity with the subject matter difficult, if not impossible, to acquire at the diplomatic level.

The International Boundary Commission was first set up on a temporary basis in 1908.[18] It was established after the authorities in Ottawa refused to continue cooperating with the individual American states in the repair and replacement of monuments along the boundary.[19] It did such an efficient job of marking the boundary and erecting and restoring monuments that the two governments signed a treaty in 1923 making the commission permanent and assigning to it the general responsibility for maintaining an effective boundary – a responsibility that it still discharges with competence and a minimum of publicity.[20]

The first organization to bear the name of the International Fisheries Commission was set up in 1908 and abolished less than six years later, after the House of Representatives failed to approve the fishing regulations recommended by the agency. When the individual American states (which have primary responsibility for fisheries) demonstrated an unwillingness to enforce conservation measures on the American side of the boundary waters, the two national governments in 1923 signed the Halibut Convention, creating a new International Fisheries Commission with the power to investigate and make recommendations for the regulation of the Pacific halibut fisheries. These powers proving inadequate, a second agreement was signed giving the commission itself regulatory authority – an authority it has used to establish closed zones, to fix the type of gear to be used by the fishermen, to limit the catch, and to regulate the licensing and departure of vessels to the fishing areas.

Like the International Fisheries Commission (renamed the International Pacific Halibut Commission in 1953), the two other bilateral fishery commissions that Canada and the United States utilize, the International Pacific Salmon Fisheries Commission and the Great Lakes Fishery Commission, were established only after decades of ineffective attempts on the part of the concerned states and provinces to regulate the boundary water fisheries. The Salmon Commission, established in 1937, has the regulatory authority to order closed seasons, to issue fishing licences, and to adjust the catch in such a way as to give each country an equal share. In sharp contrast, the Great Lakes Fishery Commission, created in 1958, has regulatory powers only with respect to the eradication of the lamprey in the Great Lakes system. As for the Great Lakes fisheries in general, the commission merely has the authority to formulate research programs and to coordinate research activities.

On the basis of results achieved, the Salmon Commission must be judged a decided success. In both total weight and volume, the average annual catch has more than doubled since the introduction of the agency's regulatory controls. As for the Great Lakes Fishery Commission, its lamprey control program has also been quite successful. In recent years it has likewise given considerable attention to the coordination of research programs for Great Lakes fisheries in general, but the formulation of research for such programs it has left largely to the various Great Lakes committees – created under the auspices of the commission – and to the riparian states and Ontario.

The Halibut Commission's record has also been a mixed one. Between 1931 and 1964 the halibut catch registered a steady increase; since 1964 it has progressively declined. Most observers are of the opinion, however, that the decline has not been due to any negligence or incompetence on the part of the commission but rather to such factors as the catching of increasingly large quantities of fish by Canadian and American sportsmen and – until quite recently – by fishermen of Soviet and Japanese trawlers.

The oldest, and certainly the most respected, of all of the permanent joint institutions is the International Joint Commission, authorized by the Boundary Waters Treaty of 1909. It was created largely as a negative reaction of public-spirited Canadians and Americans – particularly the former – to the frustrating delays involved in the use of the British Foreign Office and diplomats in dealing with a plethora of boundary water problems.[21] By the treaty it was assigned four categories of functions: (1) administrative: directing the measurement and division of the waters of the Milk and St Mary rivers; (2) quasijudicial: passing upon applications for permission to use, divert, or obstruct treaty waters; (3) arbitral: making binding decisions with respect to any questions arising between the two countries; and (4) investigative: examining and making recommendations on any differences arising along the common boundary. Since 1909 the commission's jurisdiction has been expanded to include, among other things, the monitoring of Great Lakes water quality standards and of air quality standards all along the boundary.

The administrative role of the IJC is fairly routine and its arbitration authority has never been used. Its others powers have, however, been widely used and are of great importance. Thus, under its quasi-judicial jurisdiction, it has approved applications, usually with specific conditions attached, for the construction of mammoth projects such as the St Lawrence Seaway and Power Projects. Under its investigative power, it has carried out comprehensive studies of air and water pollution control, lake levels, and many other matters, and has made recommendations that have frequently been incorporated into treaties – with its own boards often made responsible for monitoring the implementation of the agreements.

Four of the five joint organizations discussed above, it is important to note, were created between 1908 and 1937 – the exception being the Great Lakes Fishery Commission. This, no doubt, largely explains how each came to be entrusted with some policy-making responsibilities. The problems of the day seemed to call for joint agencies with such powers, and few persons in that three-decade period feared integration or the relinquishment of a bit of national sovereignty.

The Second World War provided the impetus for the creation of the Permanent Joint Board on Defence and five joint economic agencies. The economic agencies – set up to coordinate the Canadian–American war production programs, in implementation of the Hyde Park Agreement of 20 April 1941 – were abolished or ceased operations between October 1943 and November 1945.[22] By contrast, the PJBD survived the conversion from war to peace and still is very much alive.

The board's establishment was the climax of a series of confidential meetings between Canadian and American spokesmen that started in 1937 and culminated in the famous Roosevelt–Mackenzie King Ogdensburg Declaration of 18 August 1940, announcing the intentions of the two leaders to set up a 'permanent' organization to concern itself with 'the defense of the north half of the Western Hemisphere.'[23] The wording of the declaration was largely that of Roosevelt but the pressures that led to the creation of the board were mainly those exerted by Mackenzie King, concerned as he was for Canada's military security.

The board – whose composition, significantly, has always been a mixture of military personnel and civilians – was expected to concern itself largely with studies of defence problems and the making of recommendations to the two governments. In practice, during the entire period of the war, particularly after Pearl Harbor, it not only discharged those important functions but also engaged in planning, coordinating, negotiating, and expediting activities – making, in fact, a significant contribution to North American defence as well as to the combined war effort. In the postwar period, especially after the establishment of additional channels for defence consultation, planning, and coordination, the PJBD's usefulness suffered a considerable decline. It has, however, continued to serve as a valuable forum for the discussion of such questions as weapons testing, radar screens, and the future of NORAD.

One of the postwar organizations that has taken over responsibilities once discharged by the PJBD is the Military Cooperation Committee, created in 1946. Each national section of the committee consists of a chairman, a secretary, and six members from the defence services. It conducts studies on technical and strictly military questions and makes recommendations to the board for its approval. To date, its most significant activities appear to have been the preparation and revision from time to time of Canadian–American defence plans.

With the signing in 1949 of the treaty creating the North Atlantic Treaty Organization, another Canadian–American joint defence agency was created. This was the Canada–United States Regional Planning Group, one of the five groups set up to plan for the defence of the various NATO regions. Aside from the fact that it has a separate chairman, the group's membership is the same as that of the Military Cooperation Committee. Although the group has performed a useful function in coordinating the regional interests of both Canada and the United States in NATO, most observers are of the opinion that it has never been a particularly valuable agency.[24]

Undoubtedly, the most important, as well as the most controversial, of the postwar joint defence institutions is NORAD (the North American Air Defence Command), organized in 1957. Narrowly viewed, NORAD is simply a joint air headquarters structure, consisting of a central headquarters at Colorado Springs and various regional headquarters. At the outset its dual mission was to provide warning of an enemy bomber attack and 'to accomplish the four basic functions of air defense: detection, identification, interception and destruction of enemy bombers.'[25] Later, through its

BMEWS (Ballistic Missile Early Warning System) installations, it acquired the ability to maintain surveillance over any intercontinental ballistic missiles that might be launched across the northern part of the continent. It also acquired operational control over the American surveillance network for tracking satellites.

When first announced, the NORAD accord was denounced by Canadian critics on various grounds, but particularly because it, in effect, placed Canadian security under American control. Later the principal objection became that both NORAD and manned bombers had been made obsolete by the advent of intercontinental missiles. Despite the objections, the agreement was renewed in 1968, 1970, and 1975

NORAD has, undoubtedly, added significant strength to the American nuclear deterrent. It has also had beneficial political consequences, notably in demonstrating the willingness of the North American neighbours to share the burdens of continental defence. Furthermore, it is less expensive for both countries to participate in NORAD than it is for each to establish and operate its own air and water surveillance system. Thus, since NORAD is difficult to justify on purely military grounds, one suspects that Ottawa's reasons for supporting the joint command in recent years have been mainly political and economic.

Another joint institution spawned by the Cold War was the Joint United States–Canada Industrial Mobilization Committee. Created in 1949 – in response to vigorous Canadian insistence that the United States purchase more military items from Canada – it was authorized to promote the exchange of information and the coordination of Canadian–American views with respect to industrial mobilization planning.[26] But it received only minimal political and moral support from the authorities in Washington – particularly after Eisenhower and his cabinet of businessmen came to power – and it did very little to promote economic cooperation between the neighbouring countries. The committee was fairly active during the Korean War, but, with the ending of the war, it went into somnolence and has remained that way.

Successor to the Industrial Mobilization Committee was the Senior Committee on Defence Production–Development Sharing, with the responsibility for promoting and coordinating both the informal defence production agreements worked out between the two governments from 1958 to 1960[27] and the formal defence development sharing agreement signed in 1963.[28] All of the agreements had as their major objective a greater participation by Canadian manufacturers in the development and manufacture of the equipment and materiel needed for the common defence.

Originally the Senior Committee, composed of representatives at the deputy minister–assistant secretary level, from the departments concerned with defence and production, met twice a year; but it has not met since 1966.[29] For a time thereafter its responsibilities were handled by person-to-person contacts of the civil servants. With, however, the growth of American concern in the early 1970s over its unfavourable balance of trade with Canada in defence items, in 1972 the Joint Steering Group of the Senior Committee was revived and has been holding annual meetings.

As is indicated below, the production-development program has brought benefits to both countries. At the same time, it has created problems and has aroused bitter controversy – especially in Canada. The economic benefits, however, are so great that the program is not likely to be terminated in the foreseeable future.

Still another joint agency born of the fears and tensions of the Cold War era was the Joint United States–Canadian Civil Defence Committee, created by the Mutual Aid Agreement of 1951, which – typical of the cooperative spirit of that era – called for the coordination of the civil defence of the two countries 'for the protection of persons and property from the results of enemy attack as if there were no border.'[30] To 1956 the committee held annual meetings and discussed such topics as the exchange of people and equipment and the entry of doctors, ambulances, and civil defence forces of one country into the other. It drafted a number of mutual aid agreements and participated both in joint air defence exercises and in the discussions that led to the construction of the electronic screens to detect enemy bombers. But in neither country did the leaders of the government or the majority of the people reveal any real interest in either the activities of the committee or in civil defence in general, and after 1958 both the committee meetings and the civil defence exercises were discontinued.

In an effort to find a more immediately useful role, the civil defence officials began shifting their attention from population survival in a nuclear war to assistance to local communities during times of floods, earthquakes, and other disasters. This new emphasis led in 1963 to the substitution of a new agreement for that of 1951 and the replacement of the Civil Defence Committee by a new Joint Civil Emergency Planning Committee.[31] In 1967 still another agreement was signed, replacing that of 1963, but retaining the joint committee.[32] Its most distinctive feature was an annex setting forth planning goals for the two governments in the development of 'compatible plans for mutual support in the event of armed attack on either country.'

The new accord did little, however, to stimulate cooperative planning by the two countries, the gist of the problem being that neither in 1967 nor at any time since have North Americans been seriously interested in planning to deal with nuclear war. As for the authorities in Washington and Ottawa, they have committed themselves so completely to nuclear deterrence that they have had little time or money for civil defence. Under the circumstances, it is not surprising that the civil defence officials have oftentimes seemed inept, confused, and frustrated – more than moderately successful in dealing with natural disasters but largely lacking in worthwhile plans for dealing with a nuclear holocaust.

A joint organization of fairly recent origin is the Roosevelt-Campobello International Park Commission, created in 1964 by a Canadian–American agreement, supplemented by Canadian, New Brunswick, and American legislation.[33] Its establishment was prompted by an offer of the Hammer Family to turn over the former Roosevelt home and grounds on Campobello Island, New Brunswick, to Canada and the United States. President Kennedy suggested that the estate be converted into an international park in memory of former President Franklin D. Roosevelt. Prime Minister Pearson agreed and the transfer was effected.

The commission, a juridical personality, was given by the agreement all essential powers, including the power to acquire and dispose of property, to enter into contracts, to appoint a staff, and to charge admission fees. Under the competent supervision of the commission, new land has been acquired, buildings have been repaired, roads have been built, public visits have been promoted, and potential air and water pollution threats have been vigorously opposed. Most important of all, the park serves as a tangible symbol of friendship between the people of the two countries.

All of the joint institutions discussed thus far have been composed either of public officials or of persons with special qualifications from outside the governmental services. As members of their respective joint agencies, they have been expected to concentrate on technical administrative problems, and to give only incidental attention to issues of high policy. Quite different have been the backgrounds of, and popular expectations for, the people who have constituted the memberships of three joint institutions created in the 1950s, the Canada–United States Ministerial Committee on Trade and Economic Affairs, the Canada–United States Ministerial Committee on Joint Defence, and the Canada–United States Interparliamentary Group. The Canadian members of the three agencies have all been parliamentarians, regularly accustomed to concerning themselves with policy issues. The American members of the Interparliamentary Group have also, of course, been legislators; while the American contingents of the two ministerial committees have always been composed of cabinet members or their top assistants, all also accustomed to dealing with policy matters. In actual practice, as is indicated below, the policy role of the three joint institutions has been quite modest.

The exchange of notes of 1953 creating the Committee on Trade and Economic Affairs affirmed that the function of that organization was 'to consider matters affecting the harmonious economic relations between the two countries.'[34] In reality, the main objective that the Canadian authorities – who first suggested the committee's creation – had in mind seems to have been to try to influence the Eisenhower cabinet members to moderate their protectionist tendencies and to show a greater awareness of the importance of Canadian trade and natural resources to the American economy. To November 1970 the committee met on an average of once every fifteen months. Since that date there have been no meetings. As for its achievements, virtually all observers agree that the meetings were extremely useful. The discussions helped to anticipate problems and to deal with them before they reached crisis proportions; they afforded participants an opportunity to get acquainted; they provided each country with early access to the policy thinking of the other country; they laid the groundwork for new programs, such as the Auto and Auto Parts Agreement; they helped to resolve the vexing problem of American disposal of agricultural surpluses abroad; and they set up several useful joint working groups. Perhaps most important of all, they helped to educate the participants with respect to the problems, interests, and viewpoints of the people of the other country.

The Ministerial Committee on Joint Defence was created largely on the initiative of Prime Minister Diefenbaker. Although his reasons are not altogether clear, he appears to have been motivated largely by the belief that an additional joint agency was needed to guarantee civilian control over all activities relating to North American defence and by his desire to facilitate cabinet-level discussions of integration of defence production. The exchange of notes establishing the committee listed as its major objective 'to consult periodically on any matters affecting the joint defense of Canada and the United States.'[35] Although the authorizing agreement called for at least one meeting a year, the committee has, in fact, met only four times: in 1958, 1959, 1960, and 1964. Of the four meetings, the first three appear to have been quite useful. They provided an excellent forum for the discussion of such topics as defence production sharing, cooperative measures to improve the defences of the continent, ways of making NATO more effective, and progress in arms control. On the debit side, it should be noted that the committee did not even meet during the Cuban missile crisis; that it was unable to resolve the question of nuclear weapons for Canada; and that the meeting of 1964 seems to have been pretty largely a waste of the participants' time.

The reasons for the discontinuance of the meetings of the two ministerial committees are discussed at length in later chapters. Here it will suffice to say that one reason was the difficulty encountered by the cabinet members in finding time for the meetings, and a second was the consensus that developed among the authorities of both countries that, for dealing with some issues, the ad hoc, informal approach is more useful than the committee procedure.

Returning to the Interparliamentary Group, that unique institution, although in no sense a creation of the Cold War, was in truth born out of crisis – a crisis in Canadian–American relations. Both a House of Representatives fact-finding mission to Canada and Senate Foreign Relations Committee hearings in the 1950s had brought forcibly home to members of Congress the fact that relations with Canada were badly in need of attention. In both national legislatures influential voices called for the creation of an interparliamentary organization. An ad hoc joint committee worked out the details; each government passed authorizing legislation; and the first meeting was convened in January 1959. Although the interval between meetings has varied, the organization has continued to have regular meetings, averaging about one a year.

Each legislature normally selects twenty-four of its members as its representation, usually twelve from the American House of Representatives, twelve from the American Senate, eighteen from the Canadian House of Commons, and six from the Canadian Senate (all ministers of the Canadian government being excluded). Each conference usually lasts four or five days. Discussion sessions are free and informal, with occasional sharp exchanges. Prior to 1975 the leaders of the two national delegations prepared a joint report for release at the end of a conference; since that date each side has drafted its own report.

Although the group's organizing conference suggested that the organization should make 'recommendations' to the two governments, by the date of its second meeting this idea had been abandoned, the majority of the delegates concluding that its role should be limited to the exchange of information and the serving as a forum for the discussion of Canadian–American problems. This has continued to be its major role.

Although the record of the group is a mixed one, it is generally agreed that it has supplied members of Parliament with useful insights relative to American policies and opinions and American legislators with valuable information regarding Canadian interests and grievances. It has, likewise, made an impact on various aspects of Canadian–American relations, such as congressional rejection of Chicago water diversion bills and the clearing away of obstacles to the ratification of the Columbia River Treaty.

A point that should not be overlooked is that the joint institutions supplement, but in no sense replace, the other channels of contact between the national governments. The preponderance of issues requiring governmental attention, as well as the greak bulk of simple administrative matters, are handled by the embassies and foreign officers. Cabinet members of both countries, as well as civil servants, frequently telephone, write, or visit their opposite members; in recent years it has become a common occurrence for the prime minister and the president to exchange visits and phone calls. Ad hoc working groups are formed 'at the drop of a hat' and many complex problems are examined in detail at specially organized joint conferences. The joint organizations, in short, are simply additional devices for getting mutual problems before the civil servants, governmental authorities, and legislators of the two countries.

An additional point to bear in mind is that an overwhelming proportion of the trans-border relations are carried on by private individuals and groups. It is they who make the border the beehive of activity that it is and give it its unique qualities. The joint organizations, cabinet members, diplomats, and civil servants participate in the relationship on a fairly modest scale. But, for all of that, their policies, decisions, and actions can and do have a great effect on the two North American nations.

2

The IJC: organization and the administrative function

The first of the joint agencies to be set up on a permanent basis was the International Joint Commission, authorized by the Boundary Waters Treaty of 1909.[1] This treaty was negotiated to provide North Americans with the machinery, principles, and procedures needed to resolve promptly and equitably disputes involving the use of boundary and trans-boundary waters. Neither the regular channels of diplomacy nor specially appointed joint commissions had been even moderately successful in dealing with such disputes. Providing for direct Canadian–American dealings in a limited but extremely important sphere would, the treaty negotiators confidently assumed, result in improved Canadian–American relations.

The treaty's specific objectives, as set forth in the preamble, were to settle all pending Canadian–American disputes along 'the common frontier,' and to prevent, if possible, or 'to make provision for the adjustment and settlement' of similar difficulties in the future, even such as might not be frontier questions. To achieve this purpose, articles I, II, III, IV, and VIII set forth the principles that were to govern the use, obstruction, and diversion of 'boundary' and trans-boundary waters. Article VII provided for the creation of the Joint Commission, and individual articles listed the four categories of functions that the new agency was expected to discharge: administrative: directing the measurement and division between the two countries of the waters of the Milk and the St Mary Rivers (article VI); quasi-judicial: passing upon applications for permission to use, divert, or obstruct three classes of water, i.e., boundary waters, waters flowing from boundary waters, and waters flowing across boundary waters (articles III, IV, and VIII); arbitral: considering and handing down binding decisions with respect to any questions or matters arising between the two countries (article X); and investigative: examining and making recommendations on any questions or matters of difference arising along the common frontier between Canada and the United States (article IX). The scope of these functions and others that have been assigned the IJC over the years – including those given it by the Great Lakes Water Quality Agreement of 1972 – will be examined on subsequent pages.[2] Here a few comments may be in order regarding the IJC's record. Since beginning its operations in 1912, the commission has handled 105 cases. All but five of these cases were concerned with the use or diversion of waters along the international boundary. The exceptions consisted of four cases relating to air pollution along the boundary and one dealing with the problems of residents of Point Roberts, a small American enclave isolated by water and Canadian territory from mainland United States.

Both the originators and the first members of the IJC assumed that its quasi-judicial role would be much more important than its investigative role, and for three decades this assumption seemed well-founded.[3] Thus of fifty cases handled by the commission prior to 1944, thirty-nine were applications for approval of specific works under the quasi-judicial powers of article VIII, and only eleven were references for investigation under article IX. Thereafter the story was strikingly different. Thus between 1944 and April 1978 there were thirty-five references and only twenty applications. This change in the character of the IJC's activities has been largely due to the active entry of governments into the water resources field. In the earlier years much of the work of the commission consisted of passing upon the applications of private utilities requesting permission to divert water for use in developing power or in irrigating land; recently it has increasingly been called upon by the two national governments to undertake the economic and engineering studies that are essential preconditions to the launching of boundary water developments or remedial measures.

Although IJC members have some of the attributes of judges and conduct their proceedings in a quasi-judicial manner, the treaty of 1909 does not guarantee them tenure of office, and in practice for a number of years in the United States – and to a lesser extent in Canada – they were selected, and often removed, largely on political grounds. Since the persons chosen usually were 'lame duck' politicians, well along in years and frequently in poor health, the commission's performance was often characterized by delays and slow-paced proceedings that contributed to the growth of an unfavourable public image and a lack of confidence, in both Washington and Ottawa, in the joint agency.[4] But, fortunately, starting in 1929, the chief executive began selecting the American members with greater regard for their qualifications and in 1939 introduced the practice, adhered to until very recently of appointing two top-level civil servants as part-time commissioners, while reserving the third position for a political appointee, who was expected to devote all or most of his time to the work of the commission. Similarly, since 1950 Canada, while continuing to fill the chairmanship of the Canadian Section through political appointments, has been drawing one or both of the other members from employees, or former employees, of provincial governments.[5] This arrangement – while posing a potential threat to the traditional virtual immunity of the commission from pressures from the national governmental agencies – has greatly increased the efficiency of the organization, while at the same time enabling it to retain much of the political adroitness and sensibility that characterized its operations in earlier years.

The drafters of the original IJC rules of procedure appear to have assumed that the chairman of each national section would simply be the 'first among equals.' He would be chosen by his colleagues from their own membership; his pay would be the same as theirs; and, aside from presiding at meetings, his duties and influence would not be appreciably greater than those of the other members. But very quickly the chairmen emerged as the dominant members of the agency, with higher salaries,[6] more prestige, and many more duties than the other commissioners. This came about in part by their early assumption of many responsibilities relative to the organizing and operating of their respective section offices, the amassing of data, and the scheduling of hearings and meetings. It was helped along by the early insistence of the authorities in Ottawa and Washington that the chairmen assume active leadership responsibilities. For example, in 1920 the acting prime minister – having reached the end of his patience with the dilatory habits of Commissioner Henry A. Powell – in effect, called upon Charles Magrath, the chairman of the Canadian Section, to exercise closer supervisory control over the negligent member. The government, he explained, felt that the work of the IJC demanded 'the best ability and energy of the members of the Commission.' They looked to Magrath 'to see that the work of the Commission does receive the consideration which its importance demands.'[7]

Also contributing to the increase of the influence and prestige of the chairmen was the procedure that came to be established at an early date for their selection. Despite the statement in the rules of procedure that the commissioners of each section 'shall appoint one of their number as Chairman,' the governmental authorities soon indicated that they did not interpret that statement very literally. Thus in 1920 Commissioner Powell wrote to the acting prime minister: 'I am in receipt of your favor of January 11th and I notice ... the Government's request that Mr. Magrath act as Chairman of the Commission. I think it is very desirable that the Chairman should reside in Ottawa, and as Mr. Magrath is the only member ... residing there it follows that he should be appointed Chairman. The appointment of a Chairman is in the hands of the Commission, but I will be pleased indeed when we meet to move that Mr. Magrath be Chairman. The action is doubtless an oversight.'[8]

Nor were the American commissioners slow to learn that they should comply with the preferences, assumed as well as expressed, of the political leaders when a chairman was to be selected. For example, in 1933, following Herbert Hoover's failure to win re-election to the presidency, the secretary of the American Section advised the newly appointed secretary of state that O.A. Stanley, the only Democrat on the section, had been made section chairman in the place of J.H. Bartlett, who had relinquished the chairmanship but not his membership on the commission.[9] With the introduction of the practice of appointing top-level officials as part-time commissioners, it became a routine procedure for the appointing government to indicate that the full-time commissioner of the section was to serve as chairman.

To 1952 the office force of each section normally consisted of four persons: the secretary, the administrative officer, and two stenographers. In that year, however, the Canadian chairman, General A.G.L. McNaughton, was able to obtain for his office both a lawyer and an engineer. By 1972 the Canadian staff had grown to eleven persons, exclusive of the commissioners. By 1978 it numbered twenty-one persons (ten professionals and eleven supporting staff members). In striking contrast – in spite of vigorous efforts on the part of successive American chairmen to obtain increased congressional appropriations – to 1972 the size of the American office force remained unchanged. In that year a lawyer and an engineer were hired and the following year an environmental adviser and another stenographer were added. By 1974 the total staff numbered ten. Not surprisingly, this discrepancy in the size of the two office staffs has at times enabled the Canadian Section to go into joint meetings of the commission with more data and a better understanding of the issues at stake than the American Section, despite the greater population and wealth of the United States.

Since 1973 the two governments have maintained a jointly financed, jointly staffed permanent regional office in Windsor, Ontario, under the IJC's supervising control, to assist the Commission in the discharge of its responsibilities under the terms of the Great Lakes Water Quality Agreement. Although Congress has been niggardly in appropriating funds and Canada has been slow in recruiting staff members, by the spring of 1979 the office had thirty-two persons at work collecting and evaluating data relative to the quality of the lake waters and performing other research functions.

The establishment of the regional office, it is important to note, marks a significant departure from long-established IJC policies with respect to staffing practices. Unlike the International Pacific Halibut Commission and the International Pacific Salmon Fisheries Commission, each of which has on its own staff all the scientists, technicians, and administrators needed to carry out its assigned responsibilities, the IJC has traditionally looked to other agencies and governments for most of its technicians. These – borrowed from state, provincial, and local governments and the universities, as well as from the civil services of the two national governments – usually are organized as 'international boards,' Americans and Canadians acting as one body under joint chairmen. The boards – normally appointed by the IJC after consultations with the appropriate governments – report to the commission and may refer disputes to it for settlement.

The first of the joint boards, the Lake Superior Board of Control – consisting of one engineer from each national government – was established in 1913 to supervise the construction, maintenance, and operation of regulatory works on the St Mary River between Lakes Superior and Huron. Its operations proved so satisfactory that over the years other boards were set up – some to conduct investigations and prepare reports and construction plans; others to perform regulatory functions; others advisory functions; and still others monitoring functions. Thus in 1920, to aid the IJC in determining the most satisfactory plan for the construction and operation of improved navigation works on the St Lawrence River, a joint engineering board was created to collect technical data and to prepare outline plans with cost estimates. In 1952, as one of the conditions for approving the construction of power works in the International Rapids section of the St Lawrence River, the IJC requested, and was granted, the authority to establish an International St Lawrence River Board of Control to advise the commission regarding the maintenance of the waters of Lake Ontario and the St Lawrence River at the optimum level.[10] In 1972 the Great Lakes Water Quality Agreement empowered the IJC to establish not only the regional office discussed above but also a Great Lakes Water Quality Board, a Research Advisory Board, and 'such subordinate bodies as may be required to undertake specific tasks.'[11]

When setting up boards the IJC's traditional concern has been to make certain that each country provides roughly one-half the membership of both the boards and their working committees and that each board and committee contains 'so far as is practicable a member from the agencies ... which have the primary administrative responsibilities for the matter involved.'[12] Despite this IJC concern, to the date of the signing of the Great Lakes Water Quality Agreement the experts had not customarily been viewed as representatives of their own agencies or of their governments in general but rather as international civil servants with the single objective of finding problem solutions acceptable to all members of the board. The agreement, however, specifically stated that the Great Lakes Water Quality Board was to include 'representation' from the two national governments and 'from each of the interested State and Provincial Governments.' Accordingly, the board consists of eighteen members – one from each of the eight Great Lakes States, one from the government in Washington, four from the government of Ontario, one from the government of Quebec, and four from the Canadian national government. This arrangement, while highly attractive from the standpoint of involving the states and the provinces directly in the policy-making and administrative processes, could result in friction and recriminations if the state and provincial representatives start thinking and acting simply as spokesmen of their respective governments rather than as members of an international advisory board.

There obviously are disadvantages to the IJC in being dependent upon other agencies for essential specialists. The agencies could decline to provide personnel because of staff shortages of their own or because of inadequate appropriations for the purpose in mind. State or provincial agencies might be reluctant to cooperate out of a desire to retain their independence of federal officials. And something might be lacking in the way of direct control by the commission over the loaned officials who, in any event, have other duties to perform.

In practice, these disadvantages have remained largely potential. Because service on an IJC board is viewed as a mark of professional recognition, individuals or agencies seldom refuse proffered appointments. The state and provincial governments, no less than the national authorities, are eager to reduce water and air pollution and to assure effective utilization of the boundary water resources. After all, jurisdiction over such resources is primarily theirs and, under the aegis of the Great Lakes Water Quality Agreement, they are making sizeable monetary contributions to support water pollution control measures. More important still, they have learned from bitter experience that piecemeal, uncoordinated attacks upon such problems as water and air pollution and high water levels are largely ineffective. Thus they generally are happy to cooperate in tackling common problems under the leadership of the respected IJC.

Viewed from still other angles, the established procedures for recruiting the experts is highly satisfactory from the standpoint of the IJC. The commission can request the services of whomever it wishes, drawing upon those technicians best suited to its purpose, including senior civil servants holding positions of responsibility on activities related to the matter in hand. As a result of their experience, these senior officials are able to plan investigations soundly and, through their administrative connections, are 'able to bring the full resources of appropriate governmental agencies in both countries to bear directly upon the problem.'[13] If an assigned expert proves unsatisfactory, the IJC can request a substitution. The arrangement also enables the commission to meet large personnel requirements for engineers, hydrologists, economists, and other categories of experts while keeping its own staff very modest in size. Furthermore, by drawing on experts from both countries and then releasing them when the job is finished, the IJC 'avoids the rigidities that frequently accompany a large permanent organization.'[14]

For the two national governments, 'it has been extremely useful to have agency personnel in both countries working together on IJC boards. This has enhanced U.S.–Canadian cooperation outside the diplomatic arena' and 'has given all governments involved a greater awareness of what is happening along the boundary and has consequently improved the planning process.'[15] Furthermore, by having board members of one country working with those of the other the odds are greatly increased that the IJC will be able to obtain a basis for agreements, thereby greatly reducing the risks of its reports 'being pigeonholed on the basis of inadequate underlying data.'[16]

The arrangement does, however, have some serious disadvantages, one being that, because the civil servants are able to devote only part-time to board activities and the membership of a board undergoes frequent changes, investigative studies often take longer than they should.[17] No less significantly, the practice raises the very real possibility of a conflict of interest between a member's responsibilities to the IJC and his responsibilities to his own governmental agency. He can, no doubt, be depended upon to provide first-rate information and advice when serving on a board of investigation. If, however, he is asked to evaluate the progress of governments and industry in implementation of IJC recommendations, an entirely different situation arises. May it not be too much to expect him to be completely objective when sitting in judgment on his own agency? To perform that type of function, the IJC should be permitted to employ its own technical personnel.[18]

Each government pays the salaries and personal expenses of the commissioners and other office workers of its own section, while 'all reasonable and necessary joint expenses of the Commission' are paid 'in equal moities by the High Contracting Parties.' The salaries and other expenses of personnel assigned to the commission are, as a rule, paid for by the departmental agencies making the assignments. When a state or a province is participating in an investigation, the nature and extent of its financial and work commitments generally are spelled out in either a verbal or a written understanding between the federal and state or federal and provincial governments.

The two sections operate as a unit, neither having any authority to act independently of the other. Except for certain discretionary powers assigned the joint agency in the field of water pollution control (to be considered later), the commission cannot originate its own work. All matters come to it from one or the other of the governments, or from the governments acting jointly, or from private and corporative interests through their respective governments.

The commission's rules of procedure require that it meet at least twice a year, in Washington in April and in Ottawa in October. Additional meetings may be held 'at such times and places ... as the Commission or the Chairman may determine,' the number of such meetings depending on the volume and nature of the items demanding the agency's attention. Thus when the St Lawrence power project was under active consideration, 'the Commission met many times several times for several days running.'[19]

In addition to the provisions of Article II, discussed in a later chapter, the treaty affirms the following significant principles: with certain specified exceptions, no further uses, obstructions, or diversions of boundary waters affecting the natural level or flow of such waters shall be made without the consent of the IJC (article III); neither boundary waters nor waters flowing across the boundary shall be polluted 'on either side to the injury of health or property on the other' (article IV); except in cases provided for by special agreement, no dams or other obstructions shall be constructed except with the consent of the IJC 'in waters *flowing from boundary waters* or in waters *at a lower level* than the boundary in rivers *flowing across* the boundary, the effect of which is to raise the natural level of waters on the other side of the boundary' (article IV, italics added); the order of use for boundary waters shall be: (1) for domestic and sanitary purposes, (2) for navigation, and (3) for power and irrigation (article VIII); 'no use shall be permitted which tends materially to conflict with or restrain any other use which is given preference over it in this order of precedence' (article VIII).

Although other principles will be noted later, an additional one that should be mentioned here is that each country shall have on its own side of the boundary 'equal and similar rights' in the use of boundary waters (article VIII). Significantly, this broad, neighbourly concept – in the words of Root, 'declaring a rule not before existing'[20] – has two important qualifications: (1) 'any existing uses of boundary waters' shall not be disturbed; and (2) 'the requirement for an equal division may in the discretion of the Commission be suspended in cases of temporary diversions along boundary waters at points where such equal diversion cannot be made advantageously on account of local conditions, or where such diversion does not diminish elsewhere the amount available for use on the other side.'

The second qualification was, of course, an attempt to introduce some flexibility into the implementation of the 'equal and similar rights' clause in the interest of achieving what today would be called 'equitable apportionment.' The drafters of the treaty recognized that under certain circumstances it might be advisable to allocate more of the water of a particular lake or stream to one country than the other country, the second country being compensated in some other place or manner. Significantly, it was this general formula of equal rights modified in the interest of special local conditions that the treaty itself used in outlining an ad hoc solution for a problem that had long defied settlement, i.e., the division of the waters of the St Mary and Milk rivers.

Both the Milk and the St Mary rivers rise in Montana and flow across the boundary into Alberta. The former remains in Canada and finally sends its waters to the Saskatchewan; the St Mary, after flowing for more than two hundred miles in Canada, recrosses the boundary into the United States. From the late nineteenth century onward Canadian and American settlers living in the semi-arid region drained by the two rivers had quarrelled frequently and vociferously over the utilization of the precious waters. Thus the diversion of increasingly large quantities of water from the St Mary by Montana evoked strong objections from Canadian farmers, who feared that an insufficient amount would be left for their own irrigation needs. Similarly, a Canadian plan to divert a large volume of water from the Milk aroused vigorous protests from settlers in Montana. On both sides of the boundary irrigation interests were aggressive and very tenacious of what they viewed as their rights. Moreover, they had 'a feeling of helplessness' because the existence of the boundary made so difficult the formulation of a satisfactory solution.[21]

To deal with these vexing problems, article VI of the treaty specified that 'the St Mary and Milk rivers and their tributaries (in the State of Montana and the Provinces of Alberta and Saskatchewan)' were to be treated 'as one stream for the purposes of irrigation and power' and were to be apportioned equally between the two countries, but either might have more than half of one stream and less than half of the other, while during the irrigation season the United States was to have a prior claim on 500 cubic feet per second of the Milk, and Canada an equal amount of the St Mary, or in either case so much as should amount to three-fourths of the natural flow. The measurement and apportionment responsibilities were to be discharged by an official from each country under the direction of the IJC.

Although the duties assigned the two government officials were fairly routine, when an attempt was made to draft rules for their guidance it became immediately apparent that Canadian and American spokesmen had widely divergent views with respect to the meaning of several words and sentences of the treaty. For example, Canada contended that the statement 'the St Mary and Milk rivers and their tributaries (in the State of Montana and the Provinces of Alberta and Saskatchewan) are to be treated as one stream' meant all tributaries in the specified state and provinces; while the United States insisted that it meant only those crossing the international boundary.[22] In an effort to arrive at an interpretation acceptable to both sides, the commission held several public hearings between 1915 and 1921.[23] These, however, did nothing to end the deadlock. Quite the contrary, they interposed a new and vexing issue into the discussions. In a letter to the chairman of the American Section of the IJC, dated 7 November 1917, Secretary of State Robert Lansing challenged the authority of the commission to construe the disputed sentences and phrases of article VI, and even affirmed that the United States would not be bound by any decision that the commission might make under its interpretation of that particular article.[24]

Although the secretary undoubtedly had good legal grounds for his position, his negative stand not only left unresolved the problem of drafting guidelines for the civil servants but also had a very demoralizing effect on the IJC. If the commissioners did not have the authority to interpret article VI, then surely the two governments had the responsibility of providing the IJC with an agreed-upon interpretation.[25] When, however, no such interpretation was forthcoming, the commission took the significant initiative of bringing together, in Montana, representatives of the interested farmers. 'The Commissioners and the farmers talked the matter over as man to man, and in a short time they had reached a common-sense conclusion.' Without attempting to interpret the controversial treaty provision, on 4 October 1921, the IJC issued an order accepting the American contention that only streams crossing the boundary were to be divided and the Canadian contention that Canada should have priorities in the use of waters of the St Mary River and the United States in the use of the Milk River.[26]

Although it had surmounted one hurdle, the commission's troubles were not over. In July 1927, at the urging of Senator J.T. Walsh of Montana, Secretary of State Frank B. Kellogg suggested that the IJC be requested to reopen the apportionment matter and to issue a new order.[27] The reason for this request was that the records of the gauging stations set up by the IJC indicated that the order of 4 October 1921 worked to the disadvantage of the United States in the division of the waters of the St Mary River. The Canadian reply was a polite but firm refusal.[28] If the settlement of any given issue 'could be regarded as subject to be re-opened at any given time at the simple request of either party,' it seemed obvious that 'there could be no hope of finality or of certainty, and the integrity and usefulness of the whole [IJC] system would be gravely endangered.' Would it not be better, the note asked, for the two countries to act on a suggestion made by the United States in 1922 that a joint board of engineers be appointed to make a thorough study of ways of making more effective use of the waters of the two rivers? Canada was prepared to cooperate with the United States in the appointment of such a board, with, however, the definite understanding that the apportionment of waters was to continue on the basis established in 1921.

The United States welcomed the Canadian suggestion of a joint engineering board but continued to insist on a review of the order of 1921.[29] Surprisingly, it found the IJC willing to listen to its arguments. The question of the reopening of the apportionment was argued before the IJC in Washington, on 4 April 1928; in Ottawa, on 7 October 1930; in Washington, on 10 and 11 April 1931; in Ottawa, 6 and 8 October 1931; and finally in Montreal on 25 and 26 February 1932, when the matter was put to a vote. The outcome was a three-to-three division, strictly along national lines (one of the very few occasions when this has happened), with the members of the American Section voting in favour of granting the request and the Canadian members voting against it.[30]

The request having been rejected, the two governments promptly set up the St Mary and Milk Rivers Board – consisting of an engineer from each country – and turned to the working out of plans for the construction of reservoirs and other engineering works for the more effective storage and distribution of the waters of the two rivers.

The commission's principal duty with respect to the two rivers is that of providing the reclamation officers with precise rules as to the establishment of gauging stations, and as to the volume of water to be delivered to each country during particular seasons. They, in turn, must report to the IJC the measurements of all gauging stations. Any disagreements between the two officers are resolved by the commission, whose conclusions are final. Most important of all, the commission has full power to modify or withdraw its orders on its own motion.[31]

Both the issuance of the order of 4 October 1921 and the defeat of the American attempt to get the apportionment question reopened indirectly strengthened the IJC. Because of the bitterness engendered by the apportionment issue, the far from helpful attitude of the secretary of state, and the low public esteem in which the commission was held in the months immediately prior to the issuance of the IJC order,[32] the future of the joint organization was most uncertain. The solution of the apportionment issue, at one and the same time, demonstrated the resourcefulness of the commission, improved its public image, and gave it new life.[33] Similarly, the graceful acceptance by the American government authorities and the members of the American Section of the commision of the negative vote on the apportionment issue demonstrated the basic strength of the IJC and gave assurances of its continued existence. At the same time, both incidents contributed to the formulation of useful principles and procedures to guide the joint organization in the performance not only of its administrative responsibility but of its other functions as well.

3

The IJC: quasi-judicial and arbitral functions

The commission's quasi-judicial function is derived from articles III, IV, and VIII, which empower it to pass upon all applications – whether filed by governments or by individuals – for certain uses of three classes of waters: boundary waters, waters flowing from boundary waters, and waters flowing across the boundary.[1] It also has an important quasi-judicial function derived from article XI of the Lake of the Woods Convention, signed in 1925, which states that 'no diversion shall henceforth be made from any waters from the Lake of the Woods watershed to any other watershed except ... with the approval of the International Joint Commission.'[2]

The drafters of the Boundary Waters Treaty viewed the IJC's quasi-judicial powers as of basic importance. In fact, it is perhaps no exaggeration to say that they 'appear to have regarded the International Joint Commission as being primarily a judicial tribunal.'[3] They not only publicly affirmed their determination to create a tribunal that would enable Canada and the United States to dispense with The Hague Tribunal as far as their bilateral disputes were concerned,[4] but went on to provide, in article XII, that the IJC should have the power to administer oaths to witnesses and to take evidence on oath; that all interested parties should be given an opportunity to be heard; and that the two governments would enact legislation 'to provide for the issue of subpoenas and for compelling the attendance of witnesses in proceedings before the Commission.

The signatory powers did not, however, attempt to prescribe rules of procedure for the joint agency. Except for specifying that the procedures should be 'in accordance with justice and equity,' they left the commissioners free to adopt such rules as they deemed advisable. Being predominantly lawyers, the commissioners at their first meeting in 1912 chose to adopt rules that conformed quite closely to those normally observed in

Anglo-Saxon courts. Thus they provided for pleadings, pretrial conferences, hearings at which witnesses would be examined and cross-examined by counsel, and written disposition of applications.

Although for a decade or so the commissioners adhered fairly closely to their formal rules, they gradually introduced important modifications in the direction of greater flexibility and informality. Thus in 1920, without any explanation, they abandoned the practice of issuing a written Opinion with each Order of Approval giving the grounds upon which the Order was based; similarly, in 1923, again without specifying the reasons, they discontinued the practice of taking the testimony of all witnesses under oath.

These changes appear to have been in response partly to the commission's recognition that the needs of the day called for speed and flexibility, partly to a clear indication that witnesses, as well as applicants, preferred a minimum of formality, and partly – especially after 1939 – to the dominance in the IJC of men with engineering training and with backgrounds and experiences significantly different from those of the earlier influential members.[5]

In at least one important respect, however, the IJC rules continue to be quite restrictive – more restrictive, in fact, than those of a court. A court allows a plaintiff to file a direct appeal for an injunction, a writ of mandamus, or some other judicial action. By contrast, any 'person' (a term that includes any subsidiary division of government, as well as individuals and corporations) who wishes to use, divert, or obstruct boundary or transboundary waters must submit an application to the government within whose territorial jurisdiction the use, diversion, or obstruction is contemplated, and the government can, if it is so inclined, kill the project by refusing to transmit the application to the IJC. By contrast, either federal government may transmit its own application directly to the commission. The application must include all the facts upon which the application is based and the nature of the order of approval desired. If the application is from a private source, two procedures may be followed: the government in whose jurisdiction the proposed works are to be located may pass upon the proposed engineering plans, or the application may be passed along to the IJC without comment.

On the receipt of an application, the commission notifies the other government, and it publishes the application in the *Canada Gazette* and the *Federal Register* and, for three successive weeks, in at least one newspaper on each side of the border, together with an invitation to interested persons to appear and state their cases. Statements in response may be filed by the government other than the one making or authorizing the application or, with its consent, by any private person, and a statement in reply may be made by the applicant or his government or both. If the commission so decrees, supplemental applications and statements may be required. 'Where substantial justice requires it,' the IJC, with the concurrence of at least four commissioners, may allow the amendment of any application, statement, document, or exhibit.

The rules drafted in 1912 called for the holding of final hearings on the applications not less than thirty days after the time fixed for filing the statement in reply. The revised rules, adopted in 1964, give the chairmen of the two sections the discretionary power of fixing the time and place of the hearings. The hearings generally are held, not, as one might assume, in Washington and Ottawa, where the permanent offices are located, but near the scene of the proposed work, enabling private persons to state their case with a minimum of expense and inconvenience. All hearings are open to the public. The applicant, the governments, and the persons interested are entitled to present evidence and arguments. It is also permissible for persons in the audience to ask questions of the applicant or even of the scientific and technical experts, who are always conspicuously present at the hearings.[6]

Hearings may be conducted, testimony received, and arguments thereon heard by the whole commission or by one or more commissioners from each section 'designated for that purpose by the respective sections or by the Chairman thereof.' Opinions and orders, however, may be rendered under article VIII only with the concurrence of at least four commissioners.[7] If an opinion is by a majority vote, that vote is final, no appeal being allowed either governments or individuals on questions of law or of fact. If there is a dissent from the majority decision, both the majority and the minority opinions must be transmitted to both governments. In the event of an even division, separate reports are made by the commissioners on each side to their respective governments. It is then the responsibility of the two governments to attempt to agree on an adjustment of the question or matter of difference.

Significantly, the IJC is empowered to make its approval of an application conditional upon 'the construction ... of remedial or protective works to compensate so far as possible for the particular use or diversion proposed.' It may also 'require that suitable and adequate provision, approved by the commission, be made for the protection and indemnity against injury of any interests on either side of the boundary.' With respect to uses and diversions, the exercise of this authority is discretionary; with respect to cases where the water level is likely to be raised on the other side of the boundary as a result of proposed 'obstructions in the boundary waters or in waters flowing therefrom or in waters below the boundary in rivers flowing across the boundary,' the exercise of the authority is mandatory.

These provisions raise a number of basic questions. First of all, what constitutes 'suitable and adequate' compensation? In some cases the construction of remedial works would be adequate. In other cases it might not be, as, for example, where land was being flooded by the construction of a dam or a farmer was cut off from access to his land by impounded waters. A second, important and timely, question: if compensation is to be paid, how is this to be carried out in practice? Thus if the IJC, in its efforts to prevent downstream flooding, should decide to require, as a permanent arrangement, higher levels for Lake Superior, it might seem equitable for the downstream interests to compensate any Lake Superior interests that were injured by the new regulations. But how could that be done? The cost could be astronomical.[8]

A third question: does the IJC have the authority to attempt to determine the extent of damages from implementing an IJC Order of Approval and to order the benefiting interests to make compensation? The treaty of 1909 is not clear on that point. On numerous occasions the IJC has ordered an applicant to pay compensation, but, as a general rule, it has left to the two governments the difficult task of fixing the compensation to be paid. One noteworthy occasion when it deviated from that sensible policy was in 1942 when it delegated to Seattle and British Columbia the authority to determine what compensation the Seattle Light and Power Company would pay the province as compensation for the proposed flooding of some 5500 acres of provincial lands when, and if, the Ross Dam on the Skagit River, a trans-boundary stream, is raised by 122.5 feet. And that deviation has been cited as grounds for challenging the legality of the commission's action in approving the flooding of the Skagit Valley.[9]

In arriving at its decisions the commission takes note of Canadian and American statutes but has never considered that it is bound by them. Neither has it ever felt under any necessity to adhere to the doctrine of stare decisis (of standing by decided cases). Instead, it has chosen to adjudicate each case on its own merits. It has also preferred 'to formulate decisions in a pragmatic fashion apparently from the practical consideration that if a difficulty can be settled without pronouncements on the law, "prudence may dictate that such a pronouncement should not be made."'[10]

There have, however, been exceptions. The most significant is that the commission has not hesitated to make authoritative rulings relative to its own jurisdiction. In so doing it has enunciated a number of significant principles. Here, in summary, are representative examples. Mutual authorization of an obstruction by the two federal governments constitutes a 'special agreement by the High Contracting Parties,' in the sense of articles III and VIII of the treaty, and thereby automatically places a matter outside the jurisdiction of the commission.[11] Although the IJC has no jurisdiction over uses 'heretofore permitted' or 'hereafter' to be permitted by 'special agreements,' it does have jurisdiction over alterations, reconstructions, or repairs in such existing waters.[12] 'The Commission has jurisdiction over uses and diversions from waters flowing from boundary waters if such uses or diversions are in effect diversions from boundary waters.'[13] Unless again approved by the commission, a permitted unequal diversion ceases to be operative if the purpose of the diversion is modified.[14] Before an applicant can use the approval which he obtains from the commission he must, if the necessity of the case arises, 'treat and settle with those whose property right he encroaches upon.'[15]

The decisions of the IJC are always arrived at in an executive session. If it approves the application, it often constitutes a board of control to exercise, on behalf of the commission, continuing supervision over the implementation of the project. Although it has been criticized for its inflexibility, the commission normally permits changes of its orders only for very special reasons, as, for example, when it permitted, in February 1973, a change in the water level of Lake Superior to alleviate very serious flooding conditions in the lower lakes.[16]

The commissioners, it is generally agreed, have handled applications with a commendable measure of neutrality and impartiality – justifying the remark of former commissioner Kyte that, when serving as a court the IJC 'recognizes neither national, geographical, nor political divisions.'[17] With only a few exceptions, its decisions have won acclaim and approval. Nor have any of its orders ever been deliberately disobeyed, even though it has no legal powers of enforcement. Further, all but two of its orders have received unanimous approval and in one of these instances the application was dismissed for lack of jurisdiction on a four-to-two vote.[18]

The picture, however, has not been one of unvarying sunshine and brightness. There have also been dark patches. Most disinterested persons would agree that the IJC erred when it approved the flooding of the Skagit Valley. They probably would also agree that it made a mistake when, ignoring important environmental factors, it issued an Order of Approval in 1937 allowing construction by Canada of remedial works in the Richelieu River.[19] But these were honest mistakes, made at a time when hardly anyone was giving much thought to environmental matters.

Less defensible were the positions and actions of various persons involved in the controversial St Lawrence River Power Company application of August 1918. The company, a subsidiary of the Aluminum Company of America, applied to the IJC for permission to construct a submerged weir in the south channel of the St Lawrence River near Massena, New York, in order to increase the flow of water to the company's Massena plant, which was engaged in generating power used in the production of aluminum for war purposes.[20] Canadian spokesmen immediately challenged the competence of the IJC to pass upon the company's application. Article VII of the Webster-Ashburton Treaty of 1842, they pointed out, specifically states that 'the channels on both sides of the Long Sault Islands ... shall be equally free and open to ships, vessels and other boats of both parties.' Since the proposed construction would completely block navigation south of Long Sault Island, it was improper for the commission even to discuss the proposal. In any event, the Canadian spokesmen asked, would it not be better if the application were withdrawn and the two federal governments entered into direct negotiations? That procedure would, no doubt, obtain speedier results and, at the same time, enable the two governments to draft a plan for the comprehensive development of the entire Great Lakes–St Lawrence River system.[21]

The American authorities rejected both the Canadian arguments and the alternative proposal. The navigation clauses of the Webster-Ashburton Treaty, they asserted, had been superseded by the treaty of 1909, which placed all such questions within the jurisdiction of the IJC. There had never been navigation up the south channel, and for ten years the only downbound navigation had been that of small pleasure boats. Implementation of the Canadian plan called for a treaty, which would entail excessive delay. The only satisfactory procedure was prompt commission approval of the application.[22]

To the intense annoyance of Prime Minister Borden and his cabinet colleagues, the commissioners of the Canadian Section joined the members of the American Section on 14 September 1918 in approving the construction and maintenance of the weir for five years.[23] Whether they were influenced primarily by pressures exerted by representatives of the company and of the War and State departments or acted largely on the basis of their own independent conclusions that the war effort demanded the speedy approval of the application, it probably would be impossible to determine. In any event, despite the prompt issue of a Canadian Order-in-Council asserting that the IJC Order could not be regarded 'as binding upon this Dominion,'[24] the works were built and were continued in use until the construction of the St Lawrence Seaway in the 1950s. But the episode cost the IJC much support in governmental quarters in Ottawa and, undoubtedly, raised questions in Canadian minds as to whether the commissioners were not too responsive to American pressures and arguments.

Another spot on the commission's escutcheon was its inability to arrive at an agreement in the 1950s with respect to the approval or disapproval of an American request for permission to construct a dam at Libby on the Kootenay River. This was because it was divided on the issue, the American commissioners favouring and the Canadian members opposing the proposal.[25]

Despite these minor debit items, the IJC, operating under its quasi-judicial authority, has most assuredly earned the complimentary appellation of 'North America's International Court of Justice.'

The arbitral function assigned the IJC by the Boundary Waters Treaty, is set forth in article X, which states: 'Any questions or matters of difference arising between the High Contracting Parties involving the rights, obligations, or interests of the United States or of the Dominion of Canada, either in relation to each other or to their respective inhabitants, may be referred for decision to the International Joint Commission by the consent of the two Parties.'

This grant of arbitral power was most unusual for that day and age in that it makes no exceptions as to the types of subject matter that may be submitted for decision. However, unlike article IX, references under article X may be made only with the consent of both parties. For the United States that entails obtaining the advice and consent of the Senate, and for Canada the consent of the governor general in council. Once the two governments have agreed to make a submission, obtaining the consent of the governor general in council, would, of course, be purely a routine matter. By contrast, securing the consent of the Senate could mean either a radical change in the proposed terms of reference, the *compromis d'arbitage*, or even an outright rejection of the *compromis*.[26]

When sitting as an arbitral tribunal – as when conducting an investigation under article IX – the IJC is authorized 'to examine into and report upon the facts and circumstances of the particular questions any matters referred to it, together with such conclusions and recommendations as may be appropriate, subject ... to any restrictions or exceptions which may be imposed with respect thereto by the terms of the reference.' But, unlike its procedure under article IX, a majority of the IJC have 'the power to render a decision or finding upon any of the questions or matters so referred.' If the commission is evenly divided, it is authorized to make a joint report to both governments, or separate reports to their respective governments, showing the different conclusions arrived at with regard to the matters or questions so referred. The two governments are then required to refer the matters upon which the IJC failed to reach a decision to an umpire chosen in accordance with article XLV of The Hague Convention of 1907 for the Pacific Settlement of International Disputes. The umpire has the power 'to render a final decision.'

Numerous writers have praised the good judgment and mutual trust that motivated the framers of the treaty of 1909 to include article X in their handiwork, and article X does indeed confer exceptional power upon a unique organization. But, surprisingly, thus far no reference has been made under that particular article. The reasons are not altogether clear. During the first decade of the IJC's existence the usual explanation was that Canadian–American relations had been so cordial that no need had arisen for an appeal to the treaty's arbitral provisions. Perhaps so, but one wonders about the Chicago Water Diversion issue. Was it not important enough to merit the attention of the IJC? As for the period since the early 1920s, there have been a number of occasions when the commission's arbitral powers might have been invoked. Instead, the issues have either been settled by diplomacy or else were referred – as were the *I'm Alone*, the Trail Smelter, and the Gut Dam issues, each in turn – to specially created arbitral tribunals.

One reason for the failure of the two governments to utilize the IJC's arbitral powers has, no doubt, been 'the efficiency of the Commission when acting under its other powers,'[27] making unnecessary a resort to article X. A second reason, we suspect, has been a feeling on the part of the authorities of both countries that it would be unwise for the IJC to get deeply involved in acrimonious controversies, since such involvement might either divide it along national lines or arouse bitter animosity towards it, the result in either event being a serious lessening of the agency's effectiveness in the discharge of its other important functions.[28] During the 1930s American authorities refused to refer the Trail Smelter controversy to the commission for arbitration because they had no confidence in the members then constituting the commission.[29] From 1942 through 1962 the authorities of both governments probably doubted whether the commissioners were sufficiently versed in the law to perform satisfactorily arbitral functions.[30] Significantly, at no time during the years 1942–62 were there more than two lawyers on the commission at the same time; during one four-year period

(1951–4) the only lawyer was the chairman of the American Section, A.O. Stanley, then over eighty-five years of age.

Since 1965 three of the six IJC members have usually had legal training. Thus there now would be less reason to question the competence of the commission to serve as an arbitral tribunal. And, in truth, a sentence inserted in the Columbia River Treaty of 1961 suggests that the two governments recognize that the IJC is competent to exercise an arbitral function. 'Differences arising under the Treaty which the two countries are unable to resolve,' the accord asserts, 'may be referred by *either*' to the IJC 'for decision.'[31] This, of course, makes arbitration more likely than under the general arbitral power of the treaty of 1909. Since, however, the commission's non-arbitral functions grow progressively heavier, the governments may still consider it inadvisable to assign to the IJC the difficult, time-consuming burdens of arbitrating disputes. The power, however, is available to be used should the need and circumstances so dictate. Questions may arise which the IJC cannot effectively deal with acting under its other powers. In such events, it could be asked to exercise its arbitral function.[32] Thus article x may very appropriately be viewed as a 'safety-valve.'[33]

4

The IJC: the investigative function

The investigative powers of the IJC are set forth in article IX of the Boundary Waters Treaty of 1909, which asserts:

The High Contracting Parties further agree that any other questions or matters of difference arising between them involving rights, obligations, or interests of either in relation to the other or to the inhabitants of the other, along the common frontier between the United States and the Dominion of Canada, shall be referred from time to time to the International Joint Commission for examination and report, whenever either the Government of the United States or the Government of the Dominion of Canada shall request that such questions or matters of difference be so referred.

The extensive nature of this jurisdiction is obvious. Unlike the quasi-judicial power of article VIII, the investigative function is not restricted to questions involving the use, obstruction, or diversion of waters but extends to any questions or matters of difference arising 'along the common frontier' between the two governments or between their inhabitants. Furthermore, as long as the matter relates to the 'common frontier,' there are no limitations on the commission's power to examine questions of law or fact involved in any dispute or problem. Article IX, in short, provides Canada and the United States with investigative and conciliatory machinery of the type that the Bryan Treaties of 1914 attempted, with only modest success, to set up between the United States and a large number of other countries.[1]

In the original rules, the only specific reference to the procedure the IJC was to follow in the discharge of its investigative function was that, 'as far as applicable,' its rules governing quasi-judicial proceedings were also to apply to proceedings submitted under article IX, as well as under article X. Over the years, however, other rules relating to the conduct of investigations were developed, which in 1964 were incorporated into the new rules of procedure.

Significantly, it is more difficult to involve the commission's investigative jurisdiction than its quasi-judicial. As we have already observed, private individuals, corporations, and subordinate governments can, with a minimum of cooperation from one of the national governments, get an application before the IJC. By contrast, only the national governments have the power to initiate an investigation. Of course, private and public groups may, and often do, initiate the agitation that leads to action, as, for example, in dealing with specific water pollution problems, but the actual investigations are undertaken only on instructions from the national governments.

Until recently it was not clear from the commission's rules of procedure whether a request for an investigation could be made directly to the IJC by one government without the prior concurrence of the other government. The general view three or four decades ago was that this was not possible.[2] The new rules of 1964, however, specifically state that 'one of the Governments, on its own initiative,' may 'present a reference to the Commission at the permanent office in its country.' This, however, is not a very meaningful rule. An investigation on the authorization of only one of the two countries would arouse bitter feelings on the part of the non-cooperating state; at the same time, it would raise difficult financial questions since article XII of the treaty of 1909 provides that 'all reasonable and necessary' expenses of the IJC 'shall be paid in equal moities by the High Contracting Parties.' More important still, the IJC would be so greatly handicapped in the conduct of its investigations as to lead inevitably to an incomplete, if not one-sided, report.

Although the Canadian government appears never to have replied to an American query of 1914 as to whether it would permit the IJC to investigate and report on the best procedure for developing the waters of the Great Lakes–St Lawrence Basin,[3] in recent years it has become an accepted principle that, unless a government has exceptionally cogent reasons for not wanting a matter referred to the IJC, neither country will reject a request by the other for an investigation. Thus Canada – with a noticeable lack of enthusiasm – at American insistence, agreed in 1956 to a second investigation of the proposed Passamaquoddy tidal power project.[4] Similarly, in the early 1940s the United States, with an equal lack of enthusiasm, agreed – upon Canadian insistence – to IJC investigations with respect to the regulation of the use and flow of the Souris River and its tributaries.[5] In practice, all references are either joint or complementary ones, each government presenting to the IJC at the permanent office in its country in similar or identical terms the question or matter to be examined and any restrictions or exceptions that are to be imposed.

As soon as practicable after the receipt of the reference, the secretaries place notices of the forthcoming investigation in the *Canada Gazette* and the U.S. *Federal Register* and send out press releases to the local newspapers and organized groups. Also a preliminary hearing may be held to help with the publicity and to obtain useful information. Then follows the selection of the board of experts to conduct the required technical investigation, which generally lasts several months or years.

Prior to the signing of the Great Lakes Water Quality Agreement of 1972 the boards were expected to carry on their activities in a most inconspicuous manner. 'The Commission itself was the only body permitted to hold public hearings, and/or public meetings, or release information to the public,' the justification being that the boards and reference groups should be permitted to do their work 'free of public pressure.'[6] Beginning in 1973, as part of a comprehensive, carefully orchestrated campaign to promote public understanding of boundary problems and increase support for the IJC, the commission gave the boards permission to send out their own press releases and, if they chose to do so, to open their meetings to the news media. In 1974 provision was made for the boards (after obtaining IJC permission) 'to hold public meetings (but not public hearings), take public opinion surveys, conduct programs to disseminate information or any such activities "as might be appropriate."'[7] In 1977 PLUARG (the Pollution from Land Use Activities Group) advanced the participation process an additional step by bringing the public into the process of formulating the recommendations which it incorporated into its final report to the IJC.

Despite these changes, the boards still avoid undue publicity. Thus they attempt to respect competitive secrets of companies investigated and to avoid using the powers of subpoena and cross-examination, believing these policies aid in obtaining detailed information. For the same reason, the contents of interim board reports generally are not publicized, although the rules specify that copies of, or a digest of, a board's final report should 'ordinarily' be made available for examination by the governments and interested persons prior to the holding of final hearings on the reference.

Public hearings are held whenever the IJC thinks that they may be helpful. But, 'subject to any restrictions or exceptions which may be imposed by the terms of the reference,' the rules decree, 'a final hearing or hearings shall be held before the Commission reports to Governments.'

And in truth the hearings have come to have a well established place in the IJC Proceedings. They are held in the locale affected by the problem under study and are primarily for the purpose of affording interested persons or groups an opportunity to comment on the report or reports of the board.

Sceptical-minded persons have questioned whether the hearings actually serve at all well their avowed objectives. They note that most of the witnesses at the hearings represent government agencies or business concerns and that the people who represent local organizations seldom give any evidence that they have 'really identified the attitudes of the group as a whole.' They further note that the hearings do not and 'cannot guarantee that all proper evidence will be heard, or ... that what evidence is presented will be systematically appraised.'[8] Despite their obvious deficiences, the hearings do supply the IJC with information and opinions and, equally significantly, help to build up public support for proposed commission decisions.

Following the hearings, the commissioners report to the two governments. As is the case with decisions under article VIII, reports may be unanimous or by a majority, or there may be an equal division. When the IJC is unanimous, a joint report is made to both governments; when there is a disagreement, both governments receive majority and minority reports; when there is an equal division along national lines, each section makes a separate report to its own government. Interestingly enough, the commissioners have submitted separate reports only once: in 1955, when they were unable to agree on the use and apportionment of the waters of the Waterton and Belly rivers which rise in Montana and flow into Alberta.[9]

The commission's reports, unlike its orders under article VIII, are only advisory. They may or may not be accepted by the two governments. In practice, however, over the years most of the organization's recommendations have been accepted and implemented in whole or in part. But, significantly, the IJC is authorized by the treaty to include in its reports not only 'the facts and circumstances of the particular questions and matters referred' but 'such conclusions and recommendations as may be appropriate, subject, however, to any restrictions or exceptions which may be imposed with respect thereto by the terms of the reference.' More significantly still, the Great Lakes Water Quality Agreement of 1972 gives the IJC the authority, on its own discretion, to make at any time 'special' reports not only to the national, state, and provincial governments but to the 'public' concerning any problem of water quality in the Great Lakes. Whether this new power will appreciably increase the usefulness of the IJC remains to be seen, but there can be no doubt that factual information effectively presented can bring powerful leverage to bear on all levels of government.

How the IJC has discharged its investigative responsibilities, and the difficulties it has encountered, may be illustrated by considering the references it has handled relating to Great Lakes water pollution.

Interestingly enough, the first draft of what became the Boundary Waters Treaty of 1909 included provisions prohibiting the pollution of boundary waters and giving the IJC the authority to enforce such a prohibition. The provisions, however, evoked strong objections from the American Secretary of State, who indicated that 'the most that he would accept was an anti-pollution clause covering boundary and trans-boundary waters over which the joint agency would have no jurisdiction.' Consequently, the only reference to water quality incorporated into the final treaty draft is that of article IV: '... boundary waters and waters flowing across the boundary shall not be polluted on either side to the injury of health or property on the other.' And even this declaratory statement was criticized in the American Senate on the grounds that it proposed to give an international agency police power over national water resources, although in the end the senators withdrew their objections after Canada gave assurances that the rule would be enforced only in 'more serious cases.'[10]

It was this important, though legally ineffective, article IV statement that provided the basis for one of the very first references to the IJC. This was in 1912 when, following severe epidemics of typhoid fever in several Great Lakes cities, it was asked to determine whether boundary waters were being polluted in violation of article IV and, if so, what could be done to remedy or prevent such pollution.[11] After months of intensive investigations, conducted by experts drawn from various levels of government, supplemented by extensive public hearings, the commission in 1918 reported that, although the open lakes were essentially pure, the waters of the St Clair, Detroit, and Niagara rivers were grossly polluted. Consequently, it recommended that it be given the authority not only to adopt regulations restricting pollution of boundary and trans-boundary waters but to enforce those regulations in both countries.[12] The reaction of the two governments was to request the commission to prepare specific proposals for effecting its recommendations.[13] Accordingly, in 1920 it submitted a draft agreement to empower the commission, at the request of either government or on its own initiative, to determine whether the waters were being polluted in breach of the treaty, to hold hearings, and to report results.[14] Significantly, the draft did not recommend that the IJC itself engage in enforcement measures but rather that the two governments accept that responsibility.

Surprisingly, the commission's modest recommendations were not accepted and implemented. The reasons appear to have included the opposition of industrial concerns and municipalities to governmental surveillance, the advent of chlorination of municipal water supplies, the inability of the two governments to agree upon a completed draft agreement, and most important of all – once the typhoid threat subsided – general public apathy about the pollution problem.

By the mid-forties, however, the picture had significantly changed. With the tremendous growth of population, and of industry and shipping in the Great Lakes region, and a corresponding increase in the volume of pollutants being dumped into the lakes and connecting channels, the apathy of earlier years gave way to concern and vigorous demands for government action. In response to complaints from Detroit that its domestic water supply was being contaminated by pollutants discharged into the St Clair River, the two governments in April 1946 directed the IJC to investigate and report on the waters of the St Clair River, Lake St Clair, and the Detroit River. In October the reference was extended to the waters of the St Marys River; and in April 1948 it was further extended to include Niagara River.[15] Basing its findings largely on the studies of its technical boards and on data drawn from a series of public meetings, the IJC found that the waters were indeed being polluted – largely from inadequately treated domestic sewage and from industrial wastes. It recommended that the governments adopt the 'Objectives for Boundary Waters Quality Control' incorporated into its report, and that the IJC be given the authority to undertake 'a continuing supervision over boundary waters pollution through boards of control appointed by the Commission.'[16]

The IJC 'Objectives' – the first of their kind on an international basis – along with the other recommendations were accepted by the two governments in 1951 and subsequently were adopted, in whole or in part, in the pollution abatement programs of enforcement agencies in both countries. The IJC, operating through its joint boards of control, began to maintain close surveillance over the connecting channels, notifying those responsible for any objectionable pollution and, in the absence of corrective measures 'within a reasonable time,' making recommendations to the appropriate government authorities as to further action.

Despite these significant developments, progress towards attaining the IJC water quality objectives was painfully slow for a time. Neither industry nor the municipalities seemed fully aware of the seriousness of the pollution problem or inclined to exert themselves unduly to implement a code of federally sponsored water quality standards. Nor did the national, state, and provincial governments demonstrate much leadership or concern, especially with respect to obtaining the funds needed to carry forward an effective control program. Eventually, however, through a carefully conducted public relations campaign, the IJC and its boards of control were able to win a greater measure of cooperation. Industry spent millions of dollars on new pollution control processes and a number of the municipalities took steps to eliminate the discharge of raw sewage into the rivers. Most important of all, by the late sixties the interested legislatures began appropriating larger grants for control measures and setting forth more meaningful guidelines.

These achievements, however, still left much to be desired. Thus public meetings convened by the IJC in 1969 revealed that several industrial concerns on the St Marys, the St Clair, and the Detroit rivers were not meeting state and provincial water quality standards and that untreated municipal sewage was still being discharged into the rivers.[17] In the meantime, the pollution of Lakes Erie and Ontario and the international section of the St Lawrence River was causing increasing public concern. In the late 1950s Governors Averill Harriman and Nelson A. Rockefeller each, in turn, recommended an IJC investigation. Although the Department of State took up the matter with the government in Ottawa,[18] for a time the Canadian authorities did not seem inclined to join in a cooperative attack on the problem. Since the bulk of the pollutants originated south of the boundary, they may have felt that a first step should be for the American neighbours to initiate a clean-up program in their own jurisdictional waters. Again, they may have hoped that the riparian states and Ontario could be depended upon to undertake the needed remedial work.

The situation, of course, rapidly worsened. By the early 1960s Lake Erie was reported to be turning into a 'dead lake.' Dozens of bathing beaches had been closed, fish were rejected at a Toronto market, and a pollution expert warned that if Great Lakes pollution was not soon halted industry would move to clean water in other states and provinces.[19]

Finally, recognizing that Ontario and the states could not, through their uncoordinated efforts, deal with the mammoth problem, the two national governments, on 7 October 1964, requested an investigation and report from the IJC on the waters of Lake Erie, Lake Ontario, and the international section of the St Lawrence River.[20]

The submission of the reference marked the launching of the most extensive water pollution investigation ever undertaken anywhere. It was spearheaded by two advisory boards – the International Lake Erie Water

Pollution Board and the International Lake Ontario–St. Lawrence River Water Pollution Board – but it also had the cooperation of twelve agencies from the two national governments 'and five other jurisdictions' and enlisted the services of several hundred scientific, engineering, and technical experts. Data gathered by the United States Federal Water Pollution Control Administration and by state and Ontario agencies were made available to the boards, while additional information was collected by other participating agencies and by the IJC members themselves, acting both individually and through public hearings.

Between December 1965 and August 1970 the boards submitted ten annual and two interim reports to the IJC and the IJC itself presented three interim reports to the governments before submitting its final report in December 1970. Not surprisingly, the final report found that the reference waters were being seriously polluted and that contaminants originating in one country were moving across the boundary, degrading the quality of the water in the other country. Lake Erie was 'in an advanced state of eutrophication,' while acclerated eutrophication was also occurring in Lake Ontario, the eutrophication being mainly due to the nutriments, particularly phosphorus, found in municipal sewage and to a lesser degree in agricultural runoff and some industrial wastes.[21]

Remedial action, the IJC noted, had been made difficult by the existing jurisdictional and legal problems. With seven jurisdictions having laws relating to the prevention or control of pollution of these waters, it was understandable that 'the policies and goals and the vigour with which they are pursued in the several jurisdictions are not uniform; and there is considerable variation in the actual laws, their administration and enforcement.'

As a remedial program the IJC listed twenty-two recommendations, including: (1) the two national governments, Ontario, and the riparian states adopt and enforce the water quality objectives set forth in chapter xv of the report; (2) the two governments agree on an integrated program of phosphorus control; (3) the federal, provincial, and state governments support fully the commission's water quality surveillance and monitoring programs for the waters; and (4) the IJC be given the authority and means (through the creation of a water quality board and other joint machinery) for the coordination of control programs, for surveillance of water quality, for monitoring compliance with proposed Canadian–American agreements on water quality standards, for reporting to the governments, and for making such recommendations as it might consider appropriate.[22]

To discuss the findings, a joint working group, consisting of top-level officials from the two national governments and observers from the interested provincial and state governments, was established. But for a time agreement on an action program was threatened by jurisdictional issues. Thus Premier John Robarts of Ontario unequivocally asserted that water pollution control in Canada was a provincial responsibility, while the representatives of the concerned states firmly insisted that their interests would have to be safeguarded. It was only after spokesmen of the two national governments had indicated a willingness to give Ontario and the riparian states 'full-fledged and active representation' on the proposed Water Quality Board that the threatened impasse was ended[23] and the way was opened for the approval of a slightly revised version of the IJC recommendations. A few weeks later the IJC and the working group reports were considered at a Canada–United States ministerial meeting, which approved the basic IJC recommendations for inclusion in an agreement covering all the boundary waters of the Great Lakes System. Finally, climaxing the years of investigations and discussions, came the signing of the Great Lakes Water Quality Agreement by President Nixon and Prime Minister Trudeau in Ottawa, 15 April 1972.[24]

Article II of the agreement sets out some general water quality objectives for the boundary waters; article III refers to specific water quality objectives, set forth in an annex, representing 'the minimum desired levels of water quality'; article V provides that programs and other measures directed towards the achievement of the water quality objectives are to be developed and implemented 'as soon as practicable in accordance with legislation in the two countries' – with 31 December 1975 specified as the date when such programs and measures should either be completed or in the process of implementation. Article VI itemizes the responsibilities that the IJC is to exercise in assisting in the implementation of the agreement. Significantly, these include not only surveillance of water quality, monitoring compliance with Canadian–American agreements, and making recommendations for corrective measures – which it has long exercised with respect to some of the Great Lake connecting channels, as well as the St Croix, Rainy, and Red rivers – but also tendering advice to the interested governments; assisting in the coordination of joint activities envisaged by the agreement and of Great Lakes water quality research; submission of progress reports at least annually; making, on its own initiative, special reports concerning any problem of water quality in the Great Lakes System; publication, at its discretion, of any report, statements, or documents prepared by it in the discharge of its functions under the agreement; and carrying out independent verification of the data and other information submitted by the various governments. Article VII outlines the joint institutions, described above, that were to assist in the Great Lakes water control program and empowers the IJC to submit an annual budget to cover the anticipated expenses of that program.

Although critics were quick to point out various deficiencies in the agreement – particularly its vagueness as to the commitment of funds, its failure to fix hard deadlines for the completion of essential cleanup tasks, and its failure to specify that phosphates in detergents were to be reduced – most commentators were convinced that the new accord would be extremely helpful. Thus C.B. Bourne suggested that it should 'breathe life into Article IV' of the Boundary Waters Treaty of 1909;[25] C.R. Ross thought that it would assist the IJC by providing the needed framework for tackling urgent pollution control problems;[26] and still other commentators stressed the increased leverage that the agreement would give the IJC. And, in truth, its enhanced powers are impressive – particularly its coordinating duties, its power to prepare and publish reports on its own initiative, and its authority to carry out independent verification of data submitted by the various governments.

In the final analysis, however, the value of the agreement will largely depend upon the political will and determination of the government leaders. Have they such will and determination? The dominion government, Ontario, and most of the concerned states have demonstrated a willingness to appropriate funds and to take other actions called for by the agreed upon arrangements. But to at least early 1974 there were grounds for wondering whether will and determination were not sadly lacking in Washington. First came President Nixon's veto of a $24.6 billion water pollution control bill that contained funds for the lakes cleanup program. Then, after Congress had overridden the veto, the president impounded approximately one-third of the voted funds. When the EPA administrator indicated that most of the available funds would be spent on the lakes rather than on downstream rivers, Congress rebelled and approved legislation to forbid the EPA to set such priorities. Premier Davis of Ontario and Governor Miliken of Michigan charged that the president's action jeopardized the pollution fight; while the IJC's *Second Annual Report: Great Lakes Water Quality*, released in the spring of 1974, expressed regret that full funding had not been available and indicated that in some areas water quality seemed to be getting worse rather than better.[27] Eventually the courts ruled that the impoundment had been illegal, and the funds were released. But the wrangle had left its impact. The IJC report noted that, whereas 84 per cent of the Canadian population living in the Great Lakes basin had adequate sewage-treatment facilities, in the United States only 35 per cent of the lakes' area population had such facilities.

Nor did the passage of time bring significant improvements. In fact, the

IJC's *Third Annual Report* on water quality, released in December 1975, while noting that progress had been made in reducing concentrations of phosphorus and chloride in Lake Erie, stated that for the first time Lake Ontario was showing signs of oxygen deficiency in the deeper waters and that sixty-nine individual geographic locations were 'problem areas.' The commission's *Annual Report 1975* observed that, whereas 94 per cent of the Ontario population was receiving adequate sewage treatment in 1975, only 60 per cent of the American population had adequate facilities. More disturbing still, completion of eleven major American projects, serving 6.3 million people, had been deferred beyond 1975. As for the control of industrial pollution, that effort was 'still to be undertaken, to say nothing of being actually achieved.'[28]

The IJC, the report noted, had expressed its concern to the governments about the concentration of polychlorinated biphenyls (PCBs) in the lakes and had urged the national governments to undertake national discussions on the hazard. The commission believed that early warning mechanisms for screening new chemical substances were required. It also felt that compatible vessel waste regulations, as called for by the 1972 agreement, should be installed without further delay. Moreover, since the only compliance date in the agreement had passed (31 December 1975), it was imperative that new target dates be adopted. There was danger that, 'because of the energy crisis, inflationary pressures and other factors,' the momentum that had been achieved would not be maintained.[29]

In a special report on an early draft of the proposed new Great Lakes Water Quality Agreement, the IJC expressed guarded optimism about the cleanup program. While the high hopes of 1972 for quick results had not been realized, much had been achieved. Both countries were committed to, and had major programs under way for municipal sewage treatment and phosphate removal facilities. The necessary programs, the commission was confident, could be implemented, 'without any substantial changes in the 1972 agreement.'[30]

A less optimistic outlook emerged from public hearings and discussions among scientists held in both countries in 1977–8. Increased studies had revealed that the lakes were plagued with hitherto unappreciated problems; they were being polluted, not only from salt, pesticides, fertilizers, and other land-use sources, but also from airborne toxicants such as PCBs, mercury, zinc, lead, and iron.

The agreement, signed 22 November 1978, presents in great detail specific abatement objectives that were dealt with more in generalities in 1972. It sets specific limits on emissions of toxic chemicals, phosphates, hazardous substances, and radioactivity. Significantly, it fixes specific goals for more than thirty new pollutants. Its most sensitive provision is one obliging the governments 'to seek the necessary appropriations of funds and the cooperation of state and provincial governments to carry out the agreement.' Reportedly, it was reluctance by the American Office of Management and Budget to accept this commitment that delayed by months the signing of the agreement.[31]

The new accord, it is important to note, extends anti-pollution efforts beyond the lakes themselves to their tributary drainage system. For a time Canada balked at this provision, but eventually it agreed to a compromise: that the control program be applied to a tributary only when pollution from it is directly affecting the lakes.[32]

The agreement leaves the government organizations and procedures pretty much as they are outlined in the 1972 accord. In 1977 IJC spokesmen noted with concern that the draft then being circulated called for a number of 'joint activities' but, in most instances, gave no indication as to what agencies were to carry out the activities. The IJC requested, and the negotiators agreed, 'that the Parties not establish any additional institutions related to the agreement that would operate in isolation from or outside the ambit of the ... Commission.'[33]

Another challenge to the commission's authority, however, still exists. This is a proposal to place the scientific and secretarial staff of the Windsor office under the operational control of the Great Lakes Water Quality Board rather than keeping it, as at present, directly under the IJC itself. Commissioner Keith Henry (who later was to leave the IJC) asserted that such a move would 'emasculate' the commission by removing its one independent watchdog agency. Other commissioners refused to express public views on the issue, but the United States cochairman of the board asserted that Henry's fears were unfounded since members of the board were 'loyal servants' of the IJC rather than of their respective governments.[34] The new agreement failed to resolve the issue. An annex merely states that, 'consistent with the responsibilities assigned to the Commission, and under the general supervision of the Water Quality Board,' the director of the Windsor Office is responsible for carrying out the office's functions. The governments, however, promise that the arrangement will be reviewed and possibly modified.

The revised agreement does not, of course, offer any definite assurances that the new program will achieve the desired results. The accord and the various reports of the IJC and its boards have detailed what needs to be done; but it is still up to the governments to decide which of the IJC recommendations are to be implemented and how that implementation is to be effected. Unfortunately, no well established procedure exists in either national government for dealing in an efficient manner with commission recommendations.[35] A few years ago a member of Parliament complained: 'Once studies and recommendations are made they seem to go into limbo somewhere.'[36] In earlier years that most certainly was true for many pollution control recommendations. That does not seem to be true today. Although fumblings and delays do occur, all levels of government generally get around to dealing with the IJC reports and recommendations.

Why not let the IJC implement and enforce its own recommendations? This move has, in fact, been proposed by various persons, including several members of the Canadian Parliament.[37] The proposal, superficially considered, looks most attractive, but is, in fact, totally unrealistic. For one thing, it is highly improbable that either the provinces and states or the national governments would be willing to relinquish their enforcement powers to an international agency. Furthermore, enforcement calls for a police force and a hierarchy of courts, neither of which the IJC now has or is likely to acquire in the predictable future.[38]

This is not to say that the joint agency is entirely lacking in means of influencing the enforcement process. When no action is taken, the IJC can ask for explanations. In general, it can be, and – as Commissioner Ross has argued – should be, more aggressive in following up its recommendations.[39]

The IJC's annual report for 1974 offers convincing evidence that vigorous pressures, properly applied, can achieve results. The report states that upon receiving information in 1971 from the Advisory Board on Pollution Control, St Croix River, that the Georgia-Pacific Company was not taking effective action to reduce its pollution of the river, the IJC requested the Environmental Protection Agency to take such steps within its authority as were 'appropriate and necessary to obtain compliance at the earliest possible date with existing water quality objectives and standards in the St. Croix River.' The EPA responded by seeking a permanent injunction against the company. A few months later the Justice Department brought legal action. Shortly afterwards Georgia-Pacific submitted plans and started construction of waste treatment facilities.

There are, however, procedural changes which, if adopted, might increase the IJC's effectiveness. A few of these will be considered in the following chapter. Here three or four may be mentioned. One would be to give the agency the authority 'to hold public hearings at which government agencies are required to answer questions put by the Commission concerning their programs for water quality control' and 'be enabled, by federal legislation in both countries, to appear before the enforcement agencies of Canada and the United States, to point out specific cases of non-compliance with the water quality objectives which have been adopted by international agreement.[40] Another would be to adopt water quality standards for all other Canadian–American boundary and trans-boundary waters and to assign to the IJC the responsibility for maintaining continuous surveillance over those waters.

5

The IJC: an appraisal

In May 1956, at the height of the controversy over conflicting Canadian and American plans for the development of the waters of the Columbia River, Prime Minister Louis St Laurent and President Dwight D. Eisenhower issued a press release announcing that the two governments had decided 'to examine together the subject of waters which flow across the international boundary' and the possible revision of the Boundary Waters Treaty of 1909.[1] A year later a Canadian delegation headed by Jean Lesage, minister of northern affairs and natural resources, travelled to Washington for discussions on these two topics. But the exchanges were ended by the defeat of the Liberal government in the Canadian election the following month.

Recently other concerned persons have suggested that the treaty should be thoroughly re-examined and completely revised. Even defenders of the document admit that it contains 'some shortcomings' because needs and perceptions have changed since 1909, but they warn that it would be 'far wiser to allow the Treaty to stand as it is ... than to open up a "Pandora's Box" in an effort to achieve an ideal instrument through amendment,' and that, in any event, the accord has proved to be quite broad and flexible.[2] In truth, the IJC has been kept in tune with the changing needs and circumstances of the day not only by the other agreements that have been negotiated over the years but also by expanded use of article IX and by new procedures and practices developed by the commission itself. In particular, in recent years it has been able to assist the two governments in dealing with a broad range of environmental problems, giving it, in fact, the commissioners aver, 'an environmental posture that now influences its own perceptiveness and, perhaps, also the perceptions of the two governments.'[3] Given this situation, the treaty need not be overhauled, but a number of changes could be made in the functions, procedures, and organization of the IJC, assuming that if the governments wish to see changes made they will find ways to effect them.

During its more than sixty-eight years of operation the commission has, in truth, achieved more than a modicum of success. Thus to 1979 it had dealt with fifty-nine applications and forty-six references and had supervised twenty-six boards and dozens of committees and working groups. On only four occasions did it divide along national lines or fail to reach an agreement.

It has been particularly praised for its fact-finding and 'for presenting to the two Governments agreed-on facts as a basis for action.'[4] It has also won commendation as 'a forum in which contentious issues can be debated and selfish interests subjected to the light of rational argument without directly involving those at the highest level of government.'[5] Quite recently it has likewise come to the fore as an expediter, as, for example, in initiating action looking towards the cleaning up of pollution both in the St Croix and the Rainy rivers and in increasing Lake Superior water levels to afford flood relief to the Lower Lakes.

Some of the matters dealt with by the IJC have, of course, been of limited importance. However, it has investigated and reported on questions, such as the St Lawrence Seaway and Power Project, the water levels of the Great Lakes, the comprehensive development of the waters of the Columbia River Basin, and the pollution of boundary waters – all involving property interests to the value of hundreds of millions of dollars. It has also successfully resolved such highly controversial issues as the Lake of the Woods water levels[6] and the apportionment of the waters of the Souris River,[7] which on other continents would have led to the sending of ultimatums and the marching of troops. Furthermore, by tackling many problems before antagonisms could arise or politicians could seize upon them for partisan purposes, the joint organization has, unquestionably, defused many potentially controversial issues. No less importantly, the very existence of the commission, the mere knowledge that it is available for use in case of need, has, no doubt, had a powerful salutary effect upon Canadian–American relations.

There have, however, been occasions – a number of them, no doubt – when one or both governments have been unwilling to submit controversial issues to the commission for investigation or decision. For example, during the governmental discussions that preceded the submission to the IJC in 1964 of a reference relative to the maintenance of stable Great Lakes water levels, Canada turned a deaf ear to an American suggestion that the study include a review of proposals for the southward diversion of Canadian waters.[8] Similarly, in 1972 the United States rejected a Canadian proposal that the IJC be asked to investigate and report on the environmental consequences of the movement of oil by tankers through the coastal waters of the two countries.[9] It is also interesting to note that the authorities in Washington refused to accept unconditionally the IJC's report of 1930 relative to damages caused by fumes from a smelter near Trail, British Columbia, although they did agree that the report should serve as the basis for the treaty signed in 1935.[10] More significantly still, the two governments have yet to refer an issue to the commission for arbitration and have asked it to investigate and report on only a very few disputes involving the interests of the inhabitants of one country in relation to those of the other country. Although there have, no doubt, been numerous reasons for this failure to utilize fully the IJC, on some occasions one factor has been a lack of confidence in the capability of some of its members.[11]

The IJC and its boards have occasionally taken an unreasonably long time to complete their investigations and to prepare their reports. For example, a board appointed to study Great Lakes water levels took nine years to report its findings. The IJC has also been criticized for failing to press vigorously for the implementation of its recommendations and for being reactive rather than initiatory.

Nor have the decisions and positions of the commissioners always been such as to inspire confidence. In a previous chapter, reference was made to serious errors of judgment made by the IJC with respect to the St Lawrence River Power Company application of 1918, the Richelieu River application of 1937, and the Skagit River Order of Approval of 1942. Even less to the credit of the joint agency was the bitter controversy that arose and continued for months between General McNaughton, chairman of the Canadian Section, and Len Jordan, chairman of the American Section, over Columbia River engineering plans.[12]

On balance, however, the credit items certainly outweigh the debits of the balance sheet. The IJC has, unquestionably, served well the interests of both countries and the cause of Canadian–American relations in general. One reason for its success, most certainly, has been the large measure of support accorded it by the interested governments. This is not to say that they have always provided as much financial assistance as would have been desirable, or that they have consistently shown proper appreciation for the services it has rendered. Nevertheless, appropriations have regularly been made – in recent years in increasing amounts[13] – and all levels of government have made available from their specialized services the engineers, scientists, and other experts requested by the IJC.

A second reason for the commission's success has been the great measure of independence that it has been permitted to enjoy. It is true that its autonomy has been somewhat less than the drafters of the Boundary Waters Treaty had visualized; they had assumed that IJC members would have guaranteed tenure and that each national section would enjoy independence relative to salary and financial operations. In practice, of course, neither of these expectations has been realized.[14] Nevertheless, with respect to virtually all other matters, the IJC has been free of governmental direction or control. Thus the concerned governments have usually refrained from attempting to influence the IJC in its deliberations and have never attempted to nullify any of its decisions. The commissioners, in turn, have generally abstained from soliciting the views of the governmental authorities regarding matters before the commission and have not attempted to influence the work or decisions of the legislative and executive organs of the two countries.[15]

Also important is the fact that the IJC was set up as a permanent, as opposed to an ad hoc, agency. This has enabled the commissioners to develop a technique in procedure, a knowledge of the subject matter, a degree of continuity and consistency, and an *esprit de corps* among its members which no temporary tribunal constituted to deal with particular questions could possibly develop. When members have served together for years they acquire a confidence in one another's detachment of mind, enabling the commission to approach its problems, not as 'ex parte' advocates 'striving for national advantage under instruction from their respective governments, but as members of a single body seeking solutions to common problems, in the common interest.'[16] It is only when they lose confidence in their colleagues and begin acting like diplomats under governmental instructions – as happened during the Columbia River discussions – that the IJC loses some of its effectiveness and falls short of the ideals of its creators.

Another element of strength has been the absence of an umpire. Prior to 1909 most international tribunals consisted of one or more representatives of the countries directly concerned and a chairman drawn from an impartial third country. During the drafting of the Boundary Waters Treaty, George Clinton, the principal American negotiator, urged that the treaty provide for a neutral umpire to avoid the possibility of deadlocks within the IJC; but his Canadian counterpart, George Gibbons, had a strong feeling that an umpire would defeat the whole object of a commission. 'There would,' he argued, 'be great difficulty in agreeing and the Commission would be much more likely to get along where they had to try and agree upon conclusions than if a standing umpire were in existence.'[17] Of course, Gibbons' view prevailed and, although the commission has never been called upon to exercise its arbitral function, its creditable record when operating under articles VIII and IX suggests that his argument was sound. With no umpire to appeal to or to influence, and acutely aware of the unfortunate consequences likely to result from a failure to agree, members have laboured strenuously to find mutually acceptable North American solutions to all questions and have usually succeeded.

A related factor has been the principle of legal equality written into the treaty and incorporated into the commission's rules of procedure. In spite of the fact that the population, national income, and military strength of the United States are many times those of its northern neighbour, the two countries not only have the same representation on the commission and on its technical boards and study groups, but, so far as the IJC organization and procedure are concerned, are equal in every other way that treaty or practice can establish. This, combined with the fact that the American appointees have never attempted to capitalize on the greater political and economic strength of their own country to obtain for it special concessions or influence, has contributed to the growth among the Canadian people of a considerable measure of confidence in the IJC – a confidence demonstrated in a negative sort of way, for example, in 1956, when Canadian commentators expressed concern over the announced intention of the two governments to shift the Columbia River negotiations out of the hands of the IJC into those of the diplomats.[18] This Canadian feeling has, of course, contributed to the development of a stronger, more effective commission.

Of major importance in the success of the IJC, all observers agree, has been the skill, competence, and dedication of the experts who perform the basic chores of assembling technical information, answering questions at public hearings, writing reports, and serving on the investigative, the regulatory, and the monitoring boards. Being drawn as they are from among the best informed specialists of the two countries, and being dedicated to finding the 'proper and correct solution' to the problems at hand, they produce reports that not only command respect but enable the IJC to speak with authority.[19]

Another factor in the IJC's success has been its efficient, pragmatic procedures, procedures 'that would be difficult to duplicate in the traditional institutions of diplomatic intercourse.'[20] Particularly important has been its custom of going to the people instead of requiring them to come to it; its affording all persons an opportunity to be heard; its avoidance of red tape and circumlocution; its practice of dealing with each problem on its own merits rather than on strictly legal grounds; and its ignoring of precedents and the basing of its decisions largely upon facts and political considerations. For these and other reasons, at an early date the commission acquired a reputation for impartiality and efficiency that disposed the people on both sides of the border to accept its decisions and recommendations.[21]

Also not to be overlooked are the principles of law set forth in the Boundary Waters Treaty, as well as in other boundary waters agreements negotiated by the two countries since 1909. True, as is suggested below, a few of the principles are outmoded and need modification. But in general they have proved sensible and workable, based as they are on considerations of equity and common sense. Certainly they have provided the IJC with the essential guidelines for operating under either article VIII, IX, or X.

Still another factor in the IJC's success has been the good judgment it has shown in its orders and recommendations in taking into account local and regional requirements. Thus its approach to the multiple-purpose development of the Saint John River Basin, where there are relatively few competing interests on both sides of the boundary and where the streams are partly boundary waters, has been different from its approach to the development of the Columbia River, a trans-boundary stream, where there are many competing interests. Similarly, in dealing with the St Lawrence River it has recognized the paramount importance of navigation and power development; whereas in dealing with references relating to rivers of the Western Plains the needs of irrigation have been given priority.[22]

There has also, no doubt, been more than a modicum of luck in the IJC's success. Thus the IJC was created, and its rules and procedures established, well before water resource issues had become crucial to the two countries and before the emergence on both sides of the boundary of vigorous national sentiment. Another fortunate circumstance is that only two countries are involved; thus St Lawrence boundary water problems do not raise as many national issues as do those of the Rhine, the Danube, or the Jordan. A related factor is that, aside from the Columbia River issue, the disputes that the IJC has been asked to deal with have not assumed the character of Canadian–American confrontations but rather of conflicts among such functional interests as power, navigation, and riparian landowners, the interests within each country restraining each national section from assuming an extreme position. A case in point was the Trail Smelter controversy of the 1930s, when the economic and social pressures demanding a speedy end to the air pollution problem were counterbalanced by the pressures of persons and groups who argued that overly stringent controls would lead to the closing of the smelting plant.[23]

Finally, and undoubtedly most important of all, the IJC has been successful because it was established and has been maintained by two nations of peace-loving peoples who hold compatible ideals, harbour similar ambitions, and, aside from the French Canadians, speak the same language. They also have a common background of law, a 'long experience in the pacific settlement of disputes,' and a 'common interest in the preservation and use of boundary waters.'[24] In short, the North American environment has been especially favourable for the successful operation of the joint agency.

In view of the considerable success achieved by the commission, it is not surprising that IJC enthusiasts have long advocated an expansion of its powers. Thus in the 1920s Loring C. Christie expressed the belief that some method might be found to adapt the IJC 'to the business of regulating the ... rum-running problem ... or even to the immigration problem.'[25] In the thirties President Roosevelt talked about referring the 'tariff matter' and 'a lot' of other things to the joint agency;[26] in 1963 Judge Norris recommended that during the period of the proposed trusteeship for Canadian maritime transportation unions 'the matter of the harassment of Canadian vessels in U.S. ports' be referred to the IJC for study and report.[27] In the mid-sixties the Merchant-Heeney Report, drafted at the request of President Lyndon Johnson and Prime Minister Lester B. Pearson, suggested that the two governments 'examine jointly the wisdom and feasibility of extending the Commission's functions';[28] while the 'Tupper Report,' prepared by ten Republican 'moderates' in the House of Representatives, recommended that the IJC be asked to add 'facilities for the joint study of technical aspects of foreign policy issues between the two countries' and be requested 'to make recommendations for a continental program of water sharing and hydroelectric power development.'[29] More recently still, a study-discussion group, the Canada–United States University Seminar, has recommended that the commission's functions be expanded to encompass certain responsibilities relative to policy formulation, planning, and management of the water and associated land resources of the Great Lakes Basin; or, alternatively, for the Great Lakes Basin, that the IJC be replaced by a new agency with such powers.[30]

If such a proposal were politically feasible, the author would heartily applaud the first alternative of the university seminar. Certainly comprehensive, long-range planning for the benefit of all uses within the Great

Lakes is urgently needed. In particular, land use cannot be ignored since 'it is the various land-based activities in both countries which are generating most of the problems showing up in the waters.'[31] But, given the concern of all levels of government, particularly the Canadian, to preserve intact their governmental powers, obtaining approval for either alternative is not a possibility for the predictable future.

As for the other cited proposals for expanding the powers of the IJC, these, in the opinion of the author, are of doubtful wisdom. Thus he questions the advisability of requesting investigations and reports of the IJC with respect to matters where it has had no experience and has demonstrated no special expertise. Since commissioners are usually either lawyers or engineers by training, it is no reflection on their competence to question whether they would be fully qualified to conduct hearings and prepare reports on such matters as the tariff, science, and technology, or 'the technical aspects of foreign policy between the two countries.' Furthermore, an important factor in the IJC's success, it is generally agreed, has been the limiting of its jurisdiction mainly to boundary water questions.[32] If it begins to deal with a great variety of new and technical questions, it may be less successful. More than that, it may impair its credibility and effectiveness. In that connection, one wonders whether the governments were not ill-advised when they asked the IJC to recommend a solution to the difficult problems of Point Roberts, a tiny enclave in the State of Washington separated from the American mainland by water. An IJC board recommendation that the enclave and certain adjacent lands be developed into an international conservation and recreation area met with vigorous opposition from American residents. The commission abandoned that proposed solution but it has not yet been able to find a satisfactory alternative plan.[33]

There are also matters of time, staff, and finances that cannot be overlooked. During the years 1973 and 1974 the commission sat in formal session for 106 and 97 days respectively, exclusive of travel. In addition, numerous other meetings held during the year required the attendance of one or more commissioners from each section and staff.[34] During 1975 the IJC spent 64 days in executive session with its boards or the public.[35] At present each section, aside from the Windsor office, has only a relatively small number of professional staff members. Additional duties would of necessity entail the hiring of more personnel. That, in turn, would mean larger appropriations. It is already difficult to obtain from Congress the minimum of funds required by the American Section. It is likewise becoming increasingly difficult for the individual departments to find the money needed to participate in IJC-sponsored investigations. Very soon one may expect them to start insisting that the IJC pay all the costs.[36] In short, unless the governments are prepared to increase significantly IJC appropriations, the joint organization will not be in a position to take on many additional responsibilities.

If both increased funds and personnel can be obtained, the IJC could, unquestionably, usefully take on a few new duties. One of these might very well include the responsibility mentioned in the preceding chapter, the maintaining of continuous surveillance over all boundary and trans-boundary waters to see that approved standards are met. A second would be to give the IJC, in the approving words of the Canadian Senate Committee on Foreign Affairs, 'the authority on its own initiative to make preliminary examinations or assessments of potential pollution problems along the boundary, to point out potential sources of trouble and dispute and to suggest to the two governments that a reference should be made. This would, in effect, constitute a watching brief on environmental problems all along the border.'[37]

At present the IJC must await a reference from one or both governments before making an investigation into such problems. Had the commission had this watch-dog type of responsibility it might have headed off the Garrison Diversion problem (a North Dakota irrigation project that, as originally projected, posed serious adverse effects on Canadian portions of the Souris, Assiniboine, and Red rivers). Since it did not have such a responsibility, the irritant was allowed to develop much too far before it was finally referred to the IJC in October 1975, resulting in a modification of the project to overcome most of the Canadian objections. Since the joint agency already has a watching brief with respect to air pollution along the border, this would seem a logical additional duty for it to assume.

Another function which the IJC is already discharging on a limited basis but which might well be accorded additional attention is that of gathering and disseminating information relating to land use planning, economic development, environmental problems, and other matters along the border. This would not only enable the commission to discharge more effectively the public information program that it is now promoting, but would also afford it an opportunity to play an important role in binational planning.[38]

If the staff and technical information can be obtained, it might likewise be a sensible move to give the IJC the responsibility for maintaining continuous surveillance over the levels of Great Lakes waters and possibly other boundary waters. Certainly no boundary problem in recent years has caused greater public concern and agitation than the fluctuating water levels.[39]

In the opinion of the author a number of procedural changes might profitably be made. One would be for the governments (in order to guarantee that when they submit references the essential funds will be available) to establish some consistent system in joint funding procedures. Another would be for them to make their references to the IJC more specific and capable of being handled in a relatively short period of time.[40] The IJC, in turn, should make more interim recommendations, thereby giving the governments opportunities to act more frequently. The governments should establish regularized machinery within which IJC recommendations can be dealt with more efficiently and within a shorter period of time.

Certain procedures could be instituted that might provide the Canadian and American peoples with more information regarding IJC recommendations and activities and, at the same time, enlist their support. This is an area in which the joint agency in recent years has already made noteworthy advances. In the late 1960s it sponsored several public meetings in order to bring into the open the non-compliance of industries and municipalities with the water quality standards that the governments had established for the connecting channels of the Great Lakes.[41] Beginning about 1972 the IJC – partly in response to heightened public concern over water and air pollution problems – abandoned its earlier 'low profile' posture and launched a dual-purpose program of informing the public and of obtaining a larger citizen input to the commission's activities. This has included the preparation of guidelines for the IJC boards in their dealings with the public and the appointment of an information officer for each national office and for the regional office in Windsor.[42] Another helpful innovation would be to place non-governmental people on some or all of the commission's investigative boards. This should guarantee that the public has access to information and could 'serve as a safety valve and assure that issues are not overlooked.'[43] Still another potentially useful innovation would be to give the IJC the authority to publicize all of its recommendations. As a Canadian Senate report has observed, 'Commission recommendations can only be effective when they are adopted and carried out by governments. In the past there have been important instances where no government action was forthcoming.' Thus it seems essential that the IJC's freedom of publicity extend to publicizing 'the shortcomings of governments in all areas' and asking for explanations, after the elapse of a suitable period of time, 'as to why no action has been taken.'[44]

To aid the commission in the performance of its quasi-judicial function under article VIII of the Boundary Waters Treaty, it would be helpful if the governments would give the joint agency guidelines to be applied when apportioning benefits and damages between upstream and downstream interests. Even more helpful would be an informal agreement that the order of precedence for water uses set forth in that particular article be modified as the circumstances might seem to require. In 1909 there were, no doubt, adequate reasons for always giving navigation priority over power and irrigation, but that most certainly is not true today. In fact, 'setting priorities which apply to the entire boundary does not make sense.'[45] Situations vary, and any satisfactory order of use should take into consideration both the economic and the social needs of the people of a given basin. For example, navigation should perhaps be given a high priority in the use of the waters of the Great Lakes–St Lawrence Basin, while power development might properly be placed ahead of navigation in the valleys of the Saint John and the St Croix Rivers, and irrigation ahead of both navigation and power in the arid regions of the West. Nor should one overlook the interests of industry, fisheries, shore property, and recreation. Under certain circumstances, each of these has claims that might place it near the top of any priority list.

When and if the treaty is formally revised it might be desirable to substitute for article II of the 1909 treaty a clause to the effect that each country 'is entitled within its territory, to a reasonable and equitable share in the beneficial uses' of all boundary and trans-boundary waters, determined in the light of the relevant factors in each particular case.[46] If such a revision is unacceptable to one or both governments, a second-best arrangement might be to amend the treaty to provide that if one country makes a change in the existing regimen of boundary or trans-boundary waters which in the opinion of the IJC deprives the other country of its 'reasonable and equitable share' in the use and benefits of that system, it is the obligation of the government of the country making the change to guarantee the aggrieved party or parties access to legal remedies.

Another change worthy of serious consideration is that the treaty's definition of 'boundary' waters be extended to include Lake Michigan. The original Gibbons–Clinton treaty draft listed that lake as a 'boundary' water.[47] But, at the insistence of Secretary Root, it was omitted from the final draft.[48] The argument advanced by Gibbons, however, in support of its inclusion – that the Great Lakes constitute a single interdependent system – has even greater validity today given their acute pollution and water level problems.

Either by legislation or treaty amendment, the two governments should include air pollution as another form of trans-boundary pollution not permitted when it presents a threat to the health and property on the other side. Even though only a declaration, such a statement would most certainly exert powerful pressures in support of cleaner air.

Still another treaty provision meriting attention is article x, which sets forth the commission's thus far unused arbitral function. With, no doubt, the thought of encouraging the two governments to utilize this potentially important function, various suggestions have been brought forward from time to time. One has been that article x be revised to give the commission automatic jurisdiction over, 'any questions or matters of difference' that either government may care to refer to it;[49] a second has been that arbitration references be permitted without the consent of the Senate, the president acting for the United States as the governor general in council is currently authorized to act for Canada;[50] and a third has been that Canada and the United States negotiate a new treaty of two short articles, one obligating 'each party, on application from the other, to submit all disputes to judicial settlement,' and the other designating 'some existing body to adjudicate' or providing for 'a new standing tribunal to deal with all cases not clearly covered by one or another of our present arrangements.'[51]

In the opinion of the author, the third suggestion is the best of the three. However, because the IJC has somewhat of a technical, engineering orientation, a new tribunal, staffed by personnel well versed in Canadian, American, and international law, might be preferable to utilizing 'some existing body.' In any event, the character of the organization is less significant than the inclination, or lack of inclination, on the part of the peoples and governments to resort to arbitration.

To focus briefly now on the commissioners. As one way of helping to increase the IJC's prestige, it might be desirable to give the chairman of each section the diplomatic rank of minister. It would also be helpful if a provision were incorporated into the Boundary Waters Treaty providing for the appointment of another person to act in the place of a commissioner who is unable to perform his duties because of death, absence, or incapacity.[52] With the possible exception of the wranglings over the Columbia River project, nothing has ever done more to discredit the IJC or to reduce its effectiveness than the long periods when it has had only four or five active members.

Still another helpful change, one suspects, would be legislation guaranteeing the chairman of each section permanence of tenure, but imposing compulsory retirement at seventy-five or even an earlier age. It goes without saying that the American Section must never again be permitted to become what a Department of State official once called 'a dumping ground for outworn political talent.'[53] As a contribution to that end (and as one means of increasing the political independence of the American commissioners), it might be desirable to require that the appointment of the American members be subject to Senate confirmation.

Although the types of problems that the IJC will be dealing with in the years ahead cannot, of course, be forecast with any degree of accuracy, it is safe to predict that an increasingly large segment of its activities will relate to water and air pollution control and the environment in general. The number of references, as compared with applications, is likely to increase, as well as its surveillance and monitoring assignments.

It would, however, be rash to assume that the volume and variety of the commission's activities will significantly increase. As will be shown later, increasingly in recent years many procedures and channels of communication not involving the joint institutions have been developed to deal with common problems. If the trend continues, the IJC hereafter may be assigned fewer additional responsibilities than have been given it recently. But such a development should not be a cause for concern to friends of the joint organization. The commissioners have more than enough business to occupy their time and thoughts. What they need most urgently is more money and personnel to enable them to deal expeditiously with the assignments they have already been given.

6

Fisheries: agreements and arrangements

Although fishing represents only a small fraction of the gross national product in both Canada and the United States (1 per cent in the former and one-half of 1 per cent in the latter), in both countries the fishing interest exerts a considerable influence in government affairs. This is due in part to the concentration of its voting strength in several coastal regions, in part to increasing recognition of the importance of fish as a food rich in proteins, and in part to the traditionally close link of fishing with the naval and commercial life of the nation.

Despite the fact that the inland and tidal fisheries of North America have been exploited since the earliest years of exploration, it was not until late in the nineteenth century that Canada and the United States made any serious attempts to formulate principles and procedures for dealing with fishery conservation on a cooperative basis, and it was not until well along in the present century that they began establishing joint commissions to preserve and develop the jointly shared fisheries. One reason for the delay was the early widespread acceptance of the highly erroneous assumption that the resources of the sea were inexhaustible and therefore required no conservation; a second was the great number of governments involved, entailing the reconciling of widely divergent laws and regulations, as well as conflicting views and interests.

At the time of Confederation legislative jurisdiction in Canada with respect to both coastal and inland fisheries was vested in the federal Parliament. No less important, in 1898 the Judicial Committee of the Privy Council ruled that the enactment of fishery regulations is within the exclusive competence of the national legislature.[1] At the same time, however, the committee held that the grant to the federal government did not include any transfer of proprietary fishing rights, which remain with the provinces unless specifically transferred to the government at Ottawa. For example, the provinces can legislate with respect to such matters as prescribing the manner in which a private fishery is to be conveyed or leased, and the provinces, as well as the federal government, may impose licence duties on fishing for purposes of taxation. Moreover, shortly after the committee's decision was rendered, several of the provinces, by agreement with Ottawa, took over the active administration of fisheries within their boundaries.[2] Thus under Canadian federalism both the national government and the provinces have important responsibilities with respect to fisheries, but the dominant position is that of the government at Ottawa.

By contrast, under the American division of powers, control over fisheries is the primary responsibility of the individual riparian states. In fact, prior to 1898 many constitutional lawyers questioned whether there was any legal basis for regulation of fisheries by the government at Washington. But in that year, in a noteworthy opinion, Attorney General John W. Griggs asserted that the federal government had 'the power to enter into treaty stipulations with Great Britain for the regulation of the fisheries in the waters ... along the international boundary,' even though the treaty might supersede state laws.[3] Twenty-two years later, Griggs' opinion was given official judicial sanction when the Supreme Court, in its historic Missouri v. Holland decision, affirmed the authority of the federal government, under its treaty-making power, to enact legislation for the protection of migratory wildlife.[4] Thereafter the power of the government in Washington to regulate fisheries in boundary waters was quite generally acknowledged. The power, however, everyone recognized, was one that should be exercised only with the greatest of discretion and always with full regard for the rights of the states, whose ownership of the fish and control over all fishing activities were still unchallenged.

The establishment of jurisdictional guidelines was, of course, only a first step towards the formulation of workable Canadian–American arrangements for the regulation and conservation of the boundary-water fisheries. Much more onerous was the problem of getting the interested states and provinces to cooperate with one another and with the federal governments in the drafting and enforcement of conservation measures. Here the difficulties were mainly American, rather than Canadian, in origin. From Confederation onward Canada enforced certain uniform conservation measures in all the contiguous waters on its side of the boundary. These included the utilization of a closed season and the prohibition of certain types of fishing gear. By contrast, there was no uniformity on the American side. There the individual states enforced strict regulations, lax regulations, or no regulations as policy, pressures, or expediency dictated.[5] The logical result was a rapid depletion of the fisheries resources in all the boundary waters, especially in the Great Lakes.

To save the threatened fisheries, interested persons and organizations first attempted to obtain the adoption and enforcement of uniform regulations by the states and provinces. When, largely because of the refusal of all of the states to cooperate, these attempts failed, attention shifted to the establishment of a permanent joint commission to prepare and administer a common system of regulations. Both a commission of legal experts in 1896 and the British–American Joint High Commission of 1898–9 recommended the creation of such an organization.[6] Neither of these recommendations, however, was acceptable to all of the involved governments. But in 1908, following two years of diplomatic negotiations,[7] a Convention was signed, on 11 April, providing for the appointment of a two-man commission with responsibility for drafting 'a system of uniform and Common International Regulations' for the protection and conservation of the various fisheries in the agreed-upon contiguous waters, covering such matters as open seasons, the size and use of nets, and the propagation of the fisheries.[8] Each government was to put into operation and enforce by legislative and executive action the regulations, restrictions, and provisions with appropriate penalties for violations. Each was to exercise jurisdiction over offenders found within its territorial waters regardless of nationality, as well as over its own citizens or subjects found within its jurisdiction who had violated the regulations within the waters of the other party.

The authorized commission was promptly organized and early in 1909 presented a joint report recommending the immediate adoption by concurrent legislative action by the two national governments of sixty-six conservation regulations, including such matters as closed seasons, the size and types of gear that might be used, and the introduction on both sides of the border of a uniform system of licensing boats engaged in the sockeye salmon fisheries.[9]

With a minimum of debate, the regulations were adopted in their entirety by the Canadian Parliament in 1910.[10] In February of the same year they were submitted to Congress by President Taft with a strong recommendation that they be speedily approved,[11] and a bill to implement them was introduced, eventually finding its way to the Senate Committee on Foreign Relations. There they encountered the bitter hostility of American fishing and canning interests, who wanted no restrictions on their own freedom of action.[12] Early in 1911 Canada proceeded to promulgate the regulations, at the same time holding that the United States was legally bound to do likewise.[13] Legal experts in the Department of State did not agree, and an attempt was made to persuade Congress to approve the regulations with amendments.[14] This the Senate eventually did, but the House of Representatives failed to take any affirmative action.[15] Not surprisingly, in October 1914 the British Ambassador in Washington advised the Department of State that the Canadian government proposed to resume its liberty of action with respect to fishery regulations.[16] Immediately thereafter the Fisheries Commission was dissolved and the several governments continued their half-hearted, separate attempts to regulate an industry that could not be effectively regulated through parallel action.

But the drastic decline in the catch of halibut and other valuable fisheries in contiguous waters made some action imperative; accordingly, when the Canadian government, in February 1917, suggested that a Canadian–American conference be convened for the purpose of taking 'up the whole subject of fisheries on a continental basis' President Wilson readily agreed.[17] Each country thereupon designated three representatives who, following a series of public hearings and investigations, in the autumn of 1918 presented a joint report, which included among its recommendations the following: (1) the enactment of reciprocal legislation on the subject of a 'closed time' on halibut fishing in the North Pacific; (2) the negotiation of a treaty and regulations for the protection of sockeye salmon of the Fraser River system; (3) the adoption by New York, Pennsylvania, and Ohio of legislation similar to the existing Canadian regulation with respect to a four-year prohibition of sturgeon fishing in Lake Erie.[18]

The conference recommendation relative to the halibut fisheries was greeted with general acclaim on both sides of the border. Nor is that surprising. Except for the salmon fisheries, the halibut fisheries, although currently employing only about 1000 fishermen, are the most important of the Pacific area and the reserves of that area are the greatest in the world. But in 1918 they were in a serious condition. Because of overfishing, the catching of many undersized halibut, and the failure of the two countries to provide protection to the fish's spawning grounds, they were imminently threatened with extinction. Thus the annual catch, which had totalled 66,542,000 pounds in 1913, by 1918 had dropped to a mere 39,213,000 pounds.[19]

In keeping with the recommendations of the conference, on 24 October 1919, the two governments signed a convention agreeing to establish and enforce a closed halibut season and to cooperate in carrying out scientific investigations of that industry.[20] They also, most unwisely as it turned out, included in the convention provisions calling for reciprocal port privileges for Canadian and American fishermen, supervision of the lobster and salmon fisheries, and reciprocal free trade in fresh and fresh-frozen fish. These provisions aroused so much opposition in the United States that the president did not even bother to submit the convention to the American Senate.

The urgency of the problem of conserving the halibut fisheries could not, however, long be ignored. In an attempt at self-help, during the winter of 1921–2 American halibut interests concluded an agreement for a voluntary closed season, but this was not observed.[21] In August 1922 the Canadian government, after noting with regret that there appeared to be little likelihood that the government of the United States would be able to obtain ratification of the draft agreement of 1919, went on to recommend that the two countries enter into an agreement which would deal with the Pacific halibut fishery only.[22] American authorities accepted the recommendation,[23] the final outcome being a new convention signed 2 March 1923[24] and, after some delay, ratified by both governments.

The Halibut Convention is unique not only because it was the first treaty to be completed by a dominion without the signature of a British diplomat,[25] but also because it was the first one concluded anywhere for the conservation of a threatened deep sea fishery.[26] It provided for an entire cessation of halibut fishing in the territorial waters and in the high seas off the western coasts of Canada and the United States from 16 November to 15 February, both days inclusive. It also provided for an International Fisheries Commission of four members, two appointed by each country, the duties of which were to make 'a thorough investigation into the life history of the Pacific halibut' and to make recommendations as to the regulation of the fishery which might be deemed 'desirable for its preservation and development.'

Unfortunately, the closed season as set forth in the convention failed to cure the ills of the fishery. In its first report, submitted in 1928, the commission noted that, in spite of the fact that the amount of gear then in use was about two and one-half times the quantity formerly used, the catch was only about forty per cent of the former yield. Moreover, six units of gear were required in 1926 to catch as many fish as one unit caught in 1906. What was needed, the commission concluded, was more extensive and selective regulation of the fishery.

The commission's report led to the drafting of a second halibut convention, signed 9 May 1930.[27] It differed from that of 1923 most significantly in that it converted the commission from an investigatory to a true regulatory agency. More precisely, the commission was now authorized to change or suspend the closed season specified in the convention, to establish closed zones, to fix the type of gear to be used, to limit the catch in the areas into which it divided the fishing grounds, and to regulate the licensing and departure of vessels for purposes designated in the convention. Enforcement of the commission's regulations was left to the appropriate agencies of the individual governments.

A convention signed 29 January 1937 broadened slightly the commission's regulatory power by giving it the authority to control the taking of halibut caught incidentally in fishing for other species in areas closed to halibut fishing and to prohibit the departure of vessels for any area for halibut fishing when those which had already departed would suffice to take the area's catch limit.[28] On 2 March 1953 this convention of 1937 was replaced by still another,[29] which introduced four important modifications. First, in recognition of the fact that there now were a number of international fishery commissions, it changed the title of the halibut commission from 'International Fisheries Commission' to 'International Pacific Halibut Commission.' Second, at the request of American authorities – who wanted to give Alaska as well as the state of Washington and the federal government representation – it increased the size of the commission from two to three members for each country. Third, it gave the commission regulatory authority with respect to halibut caught incidentally in fishing for other species of fish during the open season, as well as during the closed season provided for by the convention of 1937. Finally, and most important of all, it granted the commission the authority, if it saw fit, to establish more than one open season during the year.

The diplomats who drafted the successive halibut conventions were concerned with a resource found largely on the high seas and therefore outside the jurisdiction of the individual states and provinces. Not so the unhappy men who laboured for decades before finally formulating an acceptable plan for the conservation of the sockeye salmon of the Fraser River run. They were dealing with a species of fish which, while spending much of its adult life on the high seas, usually passes through the territorial waters of both the state of Washington and the province of British Columbia in leaving and returning to its natural spawning grounds on the upper Fraser and its tributaries. With respect to its conservation and exploitation, both the state and the province have special interests that they have never been backward in asserting or in safeguarding. Nor is this surprising for salmon comprises the most important group of fish species of the North Pacific; the sockeye is the most valuable of the five species found on the Pacific Coast; and the Fraser is 'the best sockeye river in the world.'[31]

The sockeyes spend the first one or two years of their lives in the lake or river nursery where they are born. Afterwards, they swim out to sea, where they remain through two and a half or three and a half seasons. Then they return in summer and early fall to spawn and die in their native waters in British Columbia, moving in from the continental shelf to enter Juan de Fuca Strait and then Puget Sound before heading for the Fraser River. During the early years it was on this homing migration that hundreds of thousands of them were caught with purse-seine and gill-net on the high seas and in Canadian and in American territorial waters.

For years all attempts to formulate a coordinated Canadian–American plan for dealing with the threat to the sockeye fishery had been aborted by vigorous states' rights sentiment in the state of Washington and the reluctance of the fishing interests of that state to submit to effective regulation. By 1918, however, influential voices were being raised on both sides of the border in favour of cooperative action by the two federal governments. These voices found powerful reinforcement not only from a drastic decline in the volume of catch resulting from wartime increased intensity of fishing, but also from a disaster which befell the sockeye fishery in 1913–14, when rock slides at Hell's Gate in the Fraser River canyon created a severe impediment to the upstream passage of the salmon. The extent of this disaster was not to make itself fully apparent until some years later, but a drop of nearly 80 per cent in the sockeye yield of 1917, over that of the last 'big year' of 1913,[32] called pointed attention to the critical condition of the fishery and provided a major impetus to the convening of the Fisheries Conference of 1918.

The conference not only recommended the negotiation of a Canadian–American convention to promote the regulation of the fishery, but drafted an agreement and a set of regulations elaborating the general principles embodied in the agreement.[33] The agreement proposed to establish an international fisheries commission for the study of the life history and needs of the Fraser River sockeye salmon and to empower it to make appropriate recommendations concerning any changes in the regulations considered desirable. The draft proposals also included closed season dates, net regulations, limits on the area for use of purse-seines, limits on the number of gill-nets allowed in British Columbia, limits on the number of fishing licences granted in the state of Washington, and provisions for enforcement of the regulations by the two federal governments.

The agreement was signed at Washington 2 September 1919, and, along with the regulations, was promptly approved by Canada. But, because the proposed regulations would have greatly affected the purse-seine interests of Washington, opposition arose, not only from the purse-seiners themselves but from the Puget Sound canners, who relied on the purse-seiners for their supply of salmon. Moreover, Secretary of State Robert Lansing and several senators objected to article 2 of the convention, which was so worded, they argued, that a man might be tried and condemned for an offence in one country, and then, if he came to the other country, be tried and convicted there for the same offence.[34] The Senate refused to give its consent to ratification and the agreement was withdrawn from that body.

In 1920 an amended treaty was submitted to the Senate. When it also encountered uncompromising opposition from vested interests in the state of Washington, it too was withdrawn. For two or three years thereafter an attempt was made to regulate the fishery through coordinated Canadian–state action. When the attempt failed and the annual salmon catch continued its downward trend, diplomatic negotiations were renewed, the outcome being a new convention, signed in 1929. After wining the approval of a special committee of the Canadian House of Commons by a single vote, the agreement was shelved by the American Senate, 'pending fuller inquiry.' In the end, it was never ratified by either government but was used as the basis for still another agreement, signed 26 May 1930.[35]

The new accord called for the appointment of a joint commission with research and regulatory responsibilities not only in the American and Canadian waters frequented by the salmon but also in the extraterritorial waters between the 48th and the 49th parallels of north latitude lying west of the American and Canadian coasts and the entrance into the Juan de Fuca Strait. The joint agency was to make a thorough investigation into the life history of the Fraser sockeye salmon, hatchery methods, spawning ground conditions, existing obstructions to migration of the salmon, and other related matters. It was to conduct sockeye-salmon fish-culture work in the waters covered by the convention and was to take all necessary measures connected therewith. It was 'to limit or prohibit taking sockeye salmon in respect of all or any of the waters' covered by the accord. In order to secure proper escapement of the salmon during the spring fishing season, it might prescribe the size of the meshes in all fishing gear and appliances that might be operated during that season in both Canadian and American territorial waters. It might also prescribe the size of the meshes in all salmon gear and appliances in all seasons operated in the fishery on the high seas. It was to exercise its regulatory powers throughout the year; and it had the very special responsibility of adjusting the catch so as to give each country an equal share.

The joint regulations were to be promulgated by orders of the chief executives of the two countries and were to have the force of law. They were to be enforced by regular law-enforcement officers of the respective countries, each having jurisdiction over, and responsibility for, prosecution of offenders of that country.

The Canadian House of Commons approved the convention on 29 May 1930, but, as on previous occasions, bitter opposition to American ratification made its appearance in the state of Washington, where both of the state's national senators and its governor vigorously supported the negative position of the fishermen. The governor, Ronald H. Hartley, dogmatically asserted that there was no justification for substituting international for state and provincial control over the sockeye fishery.[36] Because of the opposition, the Senate Foreign Relations Committee was not disposed to report the convention favourably but implied that it should be returned to the Department of State for redrafting.[37] The Canadian authorities, however, let it be known that they were not interested in participating in the drafting of still another sockeye agreement. Quite the contrary, if the American government did not care to ratify the convention of 1930, the government at Ottawa would likely accede to the demands of many British Columbia fishermen that all restrictions be removed on the catching of Fraser River salmon and that Fraser sockeye eggs be transported to Canada's northern rivers, thereby opening the way to the development of new fisheries in exclusively Canadian waters on the ruins of the old.[38] Since the American Senate had so little regard for Canadian interests or opinions, Canada, a Canadian Cabinet member asserted, would simply have to 'devise ... measures solely in the interest of Canadian fishermen.'[39]

Although officials of the Department of State were fully aware that the Senate's procrastination was placing a serious strain on Canadian–American relations, they were so afraid that Washington spokesmen would demand the convention's withdrawal from the Senate that for months they did not dare to press for its ratification.[40] The passage of time, however, brought changes favourable to ratification. In 1933 Hartley was succeeded as governor by Clarence D. Martin, who soon indicated a more open-minded attitude regarding a salmon agreement. The following year the Washington state legislature outlawed all use of salmon traps within the state's boundaries, thereby reducing opposition to the convention for two reasons: first, by leaving the seine fishermen in an uncontested position, it made them more amenable to international regulation of the fisheries; and, second, because the prohibition of traps reduced the American share in the Fraser River sockeye fishery to about 40 per cent, the 50–50 sharing of the catch authorized by the convention was now favourable to the fishermen of Washington.

After an extensive study carried out in 1934–5 of the sockeye fishery and the positions of the various segments of the industry, influential persons in Washington state, working mainly through the state's Planning Council, came to the conclusion that, if Canada would accept certain conditions, the United States should ratify the convention of 1930. These conditions, as finally and officially presented, were: (1) that the International Pacific Salmon Fisheries Commission have no power to authorize any type of fishing gear contrary to the laws of the state of Washington or the Dominion of Canada; (2) that the commission not promulgate or enforce regulations until the scientific investigations provided for in the convention had been made covering two cycles of sockeye salmon runs, or eight years; and (3) that the commission set up an advisory committee composed of five persons from each country who would be representatives of the various branches of the industry (purse-seine, gill-net, troll, sports fishing, and one other), which committee would be invited to all non-executive meetings of the commission and be given full opportunity to examine and to be heard on all proposed orders, regulations, or recommendations.

Although having serious misgivings regarding condition number two, the Canadian government – to avoid further costly delays – agreed to the three conditions, which accordingly were incorporated into the Protocol of Exchange; whereupon the convention and protocol were approved by the American Senate and ratifications were exchanged 28 July 1937. Although effective regulations could not start until 1945, the International Pacific Salmon Fisheries Commission – the second of the bilaterial commissions that Canada and the United States had established – immediately assumed its other duties. Thus ended, as Henry Reiff has noted, 'a record of astonishingly myopic self-destructive acquisitiveness in favor of one of the most forward-looking enterprises ever undertaken jointly by two governments in relation to a common resource of the sea.'[41]

Significantly, the success achieved by the Salmon Commission led to an important expansion of its jurisdiction. When the Sockeye Convention was drafted in 1930 it was generally agreed that of the five important species of salmon found in West Coast waters – the sockeye, the pink, the chinook, the coho, and the chum – only the sockeye needed the attention of an international commission. Of the other four species, the chinook, the coho, and the chum could easily be regulated through the individual efforts of the states and of Canada, while the propagation of the pink had been so adversely affected by the rock slides in the Hell's Gate Canyon of the Fraser in 1913–14 that this species had been reduced to economic unimportance.[42] With, however, the commission's construction in 1944–5 of fishways around the Hell's Gate barrier, the pinks began appearing in increasing numbers on their former spawning grounds on the upper reaches of the Fraser River. By the early 1950s they had become so numerous and so much in demand as an item of food as to stimulate intense competition between the fishermen of Washington and those of British Columbia. Because the salmon passed through American waters before entering the Fraser River in Canadian territory, the American fishermen regularly obtained some 80 per cent of the total catch.

From time to time, Canadian spokesmen urged the negotiation of a pink salmon treaty comparable to that covering the sockeye salmon, but the American interests were reluctant to relinquish their special advantage. Then, at the special urging of the Department of Fisheries in Ottawa, Canadian fishermen stepped up their operations, with the result that by 1955 they were getting almost 40 per cent of the pink salmon catch.[43] The predictable outcome ensued. Realizing that the cutthroat competition was threatening the continued existence of the fishery and that they had more to lose than to gain from its continued non-regulation, spokesmen of the American interests came out strongly in favour of the treaty. The final result was a protocol, signed 28 December 1956, revising the salmon convention of 1930 to place the pink salmon fishery under regulation by the International Pacific Salmon Fisheries Commission.[44]

The protocol, which went into effect 3 July 1957, provides for a coordinated investigation by research agencies of the two governments and for the conservation of pink salmon stocks which enter the waters described in the convention. It makes more explicit the scope of the commission's regulatory powers over both the pink and the sockeye fisheries by the addition of the following clause: 'All regulations made by the Commission shall be subject to approval of the two Governments with the exception of orders for the adjustment of, closing, or opening of fishing periods and areas in any fishing season and of emergency orders required to carry out the provisions of the Convention.' It deletes from the convention the provision that if any Canadian waters are closed all American waters must be closed and vice versa. It provides for a division of the pink salmon catch, as well as the sockeye, as nearly as practicable, equally between the Canadian and the American fishermen. And it expanded the commission's advisory committee from five to six from each country.

The fisheries of the Great Lakes also came in for much attention from Canada and the United States during the 1920s and 1930s, and properly so for they are the greatest freshwater fisheries in the world and have long been of special importance to the peoples of North America. In spite of a serious decline in recent years of the annual catch of the more highly prized fishes, the lakes are still an important source of supply of numerous species, such as ciscoes, whitefish, lake trout, lake herring, yellow perch, chubs, alewives, and (quite recently) coho salmon. In 1973 the total catch added up to 111.4 million pounds and was valued at $17.7 million. The fisheries afford full-time employment to approximately 3700 commercial fishermen and part-time employment to an additional 1900.[45] They also regularly provide excitement and pleasure to tens of thousands of sports enthusiasts seeking the thrills of freshwater fishing.

Indeed, the ready access of the Great Lakes to both commercial and sports fishermen, the constant demand of North American consumers for freshwater fish, and the failure of the riparian states and Ontario to enforce conservation measures for many years posed a major threat to the continuation of the fishery. Thus at the height of the sturgeon fishery over 7,000,000 pounds were taken from the lakes in one year. In 1934 the total catch was down to less than 100,000 pounds. By 1940 the species was virtually extinct. For many years the catch of freshwater herring was about 10,000,000 pounds annually. With the invention and widespread use of the bull-net, the catch by 1924 had climbed to 25,000,000 pounds. Then the decline set in, the catch dwindling to a mere 200,000 pounds in 1934. And so also with the whitefish. From an early annual catch of 3,500,000 pounds the production of this commercially important fish took a nose dive to only 500,000 pounds in the mid-thirties.[46] On both sides of the boundary concerned persons demanded that steps be taken to halt the downward trend of production. But what could be done? What remedial actions would be acceptable to the interested governments, fishermen, and canners?

One cautious, though promising, move was the creation in 1932 of a permanent Lake Erie Advisory Committee, composed of one representative from each of the four states fronting on Lake Erie, one from Ontario, and one from the United States Bureau of Fisheries. Several meetings of this committee produced a list of fishing regulations for the lake which, upon being formally approved on 28 February 1933 by the conservation director of Ontario and the various interested states, came to be known as the 'Toronto Agreement.' But the cooperative arrangement soon was in difficulties. Largely because of political pressure, New York, in the fall of 1933, found it impossible to enforce the agreed-upon regulation on the closed season. Whereupon the other signatories used New York's failure as justification for their own violation of that particular regulation. In 1934

Ohio, by officially sanctioning the use of gill-net mesh less than three inches in length, violated one of the assumptions on which the agreement was based. When Ohio refused to withdraw the approval of the use of such nets, New York permitted the resumption of the use of the bull-net and once again extended the fishing season beyond the date fixed in the agreement. These violations eventually culminated in the complete abrogation of the Toronto Agreement and the dissolution of the Lake Erie Advisory Committee.[47]

Following the collapse of the Toronto Agreement, some sentiment developed in favour of the formation of an interstate compact to promote the conservation of the Great Lakes fisheries, and early in 1938 a resolution of consent to the formation of such a compact was approved by Congress and signed by the president.[48] But the resolution was not implemented, possibly because most fishery specialists and students of government came to the conclusion that the conservation of the Great Lakes fisheries could not actually be accomplished through the device of an interstate compact. They pointed out that no compact could be effective which did not include Ontario as well as the eight lakeside American states; that the authorities in Washington would undoubtedly object to the negotiation of an agreement between the Great Lakes states and Ontario or the Dominion government;[49] and that, 'under any circumstances,' the compact device 'would not be a very effective one' for dealing with the fishery conservation problem.

Other approaches that received some consideration were: (1) the ceding of control over the Great Lakes fisheries by the states to the government at Washington, and (2) the enactment by the states of legislation granting discretionary control over the fisheries to the state conservation departments. The first of these approaches, however, was rejected as involving the granting of more power than the state legislatures seemed likely to relinquish and the second as entailing too many formidable obstacles. Gradually opinion shifted around to the view that the most satisfactory arrangement would be the negotiation of a formal agreement between the two federal governments. And that was the plan eventually adopted. After extensive public hearings and exhaustive investigations by a joint board of inquiry created in 1940, a comprehensive convention was signed, 2 April 1946, covering all of the fisheries of the Great Lakes.[50]

The convention provided for the establishment of an International Fisheries Commission for the Great Lakes with the authority to formulate and recommend to the interested governments specific fishery research programs and studies. It was also to plan for the effective management of fishery resources of the lakes. Most important of all, it was to prepare regulations with respect to open and closed seasons, open and closed waters, the size limits for each species of fish, the time, methods, and intensity of fishing, the extent and nature of stocking operations, and the type and specifications of fishing gear. The regulations were to be approved by the president and the governor-in-council and were to be enforced by the lakeside states and Ontario. If, however, there were complaints that the regulations were not being effectively enforced, the federal government concerned was to take appropriate measures to ensure proper enforcement.

The convention, as it turned out, was never to be approved, or even made the subject of a hearing, by the American Senate. The principal reason, apparently, was the vehement objections raised by vested American interests – particularly by spokesmen of the Ohio commercial fishermen. Thus a resolution approved by the Senate of that state asserted that the convention would deprive Ohio and other states of their proper 're-sponsibility and valuable interests' and would delegate forever to an international governmental agency 'the sovereign rights' of the United States and the state of Ohio over the American portion of Lake Erie.[51]

After waiting for three years in the hope that opposition to the convention would subside, the Canadian and the American authorities concluded that a new accord would have to be drafted and, accordingly, started once more their wide-ranging, time-consuming conversations with interested governments, persons, and groups.[52] But for months the discussions made little headway. The American fishermen wanted no regulation that might even temporarily reduce their catch and earnings. Nor did they want to be placed in a position of dependence upon a geographically remote international agency to deal with problems that traditionally had been handled by their individual state governments. By the early 1950s, however, most of the Great Lakes fishermen came to realize that they had problems that were much too large and too complicated to be handled by Canada and the individual states, each working more or less independently of the others. In addition to over-fishing and water pollution, they now were increasingly plagued by the parasitic sea lamprey, a vicious predator which, after having long infested the waters of Lake Ontario, in the early forties began grievous depredations upon the fisheries of Lake Erie and the Upper Lakes.

The lamprey, which attaches itself to the fish by the suction-like cup of its mouth and drains off the blood and body fluids of its host, attacked first such soft-scaled species as the trout and the whitefish. As these became progressively scarcer it began to feed upon pike and perch, in fact upon almost anything that moved. The fishermen appealed to their respective governments for relief, and dozens of conservation and research agencies were set to work to try to find some poison or contrivance that would kill or catch the lamprey without harming valuable fish. The search, however, proved to be both frustrating and expensive. Furthermore, as the study and experimentation continued it became increasingly clear that the fight against the lamprey demanded a 'joint and unified effort on the Great Lakes by the United States and Canada, with the full co-operation of their respective political subdivisions.'[53] Late in 1952 American officials held preliminary treaty negotiations with their Canadian counterparts. Through 1953 and on into 1954 the discussions were continued, the final outcome being the signing, 10 September 1954, of a second Great Lakes Fishery Convention, modifying and replacing the draft of 1946.[54]

Following the pattern of the unperfected convention of 1946, the new agreement created the Great Lakes Fishery Commission with three principal duties: (1) to formulate and coordinate research programs designed to determine what, if any, measures may be required 'to make possible the maximum sustained productivity' of any stock of fish in the convention area which is of common concern to the United States and Canada; (2) on the basis of such research, to recommend appropriate measures to the two governments; and (3) to formulate and implement a comprehensive program to eradicate or minimize the sea lamprey populations in the Great Lakes.

The commission, it will be noted, was made responsible for implementing, as well as for formulating, the lamprey control program. But, significantly, unlike the proposed convention of 1946, and unlike the halibut and salmon commissions, it was not given the authority to regulate fishery operations. With respect to fisheries in general its only responsibilities were to formulate research programs, to recommend such programs to the federal governments, and to coordinate research made pursuant to such programs. It was for the individual governments to determine whether the programs were to be implemented and how they were to be implemented. Indeed the convention specifically affirmed that it was not to be construed as restricting in any way the rights of the riparian states or of Canada or Ontario to make or enforce fishing laws or regulations within their respective jurisdictions 'so far as such laws or regulations do not preclude the carrying out of the Commission's duties.'

The convention area embraced all five of the Great Lakes, their connecting waters, and the St Lawrence River from Lake Ontario to the 45th parallel of latitude. It also included the tributaries of each of these waters to the extent necessary to achieve the objectives of the accord.

Because the new convention omitted the provisions of the earlier one calling for the regulation of the commercial fisheries by an international commission, it did not provoke the violent objections that had been directed at its predecessor. At Senate hearings Ohio spokesmen took the position that, if the other riparian states and Canada desired to establish the international commission, Ohio would not oppose it.[55] Since the other states and Canada did desire the establishment of the proposed commission, the convention speedily obtained the required ratification and entered into force 11 October 1955.

When it is recalled that the first serious efforts to establish permanent Canadian–American fishery commissions were made in 1898 one can only feel amazement that so much time and effort were required to bring to fruition the three binational commissions. Of course the jurisdictional and technical difficulties were enormous, and the concern of the fishermen regarding the possible impact of substituting international for local regulation of the fisheries is understandable. Yet, even when allowances are made for these and other considerations, it can hardly be denied that the record, as summarized above, reflects little credit on either the American fishermen or their governmental representatives. Quite the contrary, revealing astounding short-sightedness and selfishness, they demonstrated an amazing determination to go their own way and derive the greatest possible immediate benefits from the exploitation of the fisheries regardless of the consequences. The most that can be said in mitigation is that, when they finally became convinced that Canadian–American cooperation was essential for dealing with the fishery problems, they abandoned their earlier myopic stance and joined their Canadian counterparts in the establishment of the joint organizations based upon the principle of equal Canadian and American representation and control.

7

Fishery commissions: organizations and procedures

During the prolonged debates over the draft salmon convention of 1930 the fishermen of the state of Washington insisted that the Senate's approval should be conditioned on Canada's acceptance of an amendment to the effect that two of the three American members were to be citizens of Washington, appointed on the recommendation of the governor.[1] It was only after Secretary of State Hull had pointed out that the acceptance of such a reservation would seriously restrict the appointive power of the president[2] that they finally withdrew their demand and allowed the convention to be ratified. They had, however, made their point. When the time came for the president to choose the three American commissioners, two of the three appointments went to residents of the state of Washington (B.M. Brennan, a member of the Washington State Commission of Fisheries, and Edward W. Allen, a prominent attorney of Seattle and long-time member of the International Fisheries Commission) and the third to Charles E. Jackson, the deputy commissioner of fisheries of the Department of the Interior – thereby setting a precedent that has continued to the present.

British Columbia has also regularly had two of its residents on the Salmon Commission. Thus in 1937 one Canadian appointment went to Thomas Reid, a member of the House of Commons from British Columbia, a second to A.L. Hager, of the Canadian Fishing Company of Vancouver, and the third to W.A. Found, deputy minister of fisheries, at Ottawa.

This concept of area and interest representation received a substantial boost from an American statute of 1956 which specified that one of the members of the American Section of the Great Lakes Fishery Commission should be a federal official and the other two should be residents of the Great Lakes states 'duly qualified by reason of knowledge of the fisheries of the Great Lakes,' of whom one should be an official of a Great Lakes state.[3]

When the total number of commissioners was increased in 1965 from six to eight the understanding was that both the Upper Lakes region and the Lower Lakes region should be represented. Although the authorities in Ottawa are not restricted by law in filling Canada's positions on the commission, in practice they have always found it expedient to appoint, along with one or two senior officials from the Department of Fisheries (now the Department of Fisheries and Oceans), at least one specially qualified person from Ontario, the province directly concerned.[4]

This same general pattern prevails in appointments to the International Pacific Halibut Commission. Thus in 1957 that agency's membership consisted of the following: for the United States, an official of the Fish and Wildlife Service (of the Department of the Interior), a representative from the Seattle halibut fleet, and a resident of Alaska; for Canada, an official of the federal Department of Fisheries, a member of the British Columbia fishing industry, and an active halibut fisherman.[5]

Obviously, there are dangers involved in filling appointments on the basis of the representation of geographical, economic, and social interests. Viewing himself as the special representative of the seine fishermen, or of the canners, or of the government of British Columbia, a commissioner may lose sight of the fact that there are national, as well as international, interests to be served and become little more than a special pleader for narrow economic or geographical interests. There is the additional danger that excluded interests will demand representation and will feel highly aggrieved when and if their demands are refused. However, if a commission is to perform satisfactorily its duties, it is essential that it have the confidence and support of the commerical fishermen, the canners, and the general public in the areas most directly concerned.[6] One way to obtain such confidence and support is through the representation device. As for the interests not represented on a commission, the more important of these, as explained below, can, and do, obtain representation on the advisory committees utilized by all of the commissions.

Both the Halibut Convention of 1930 and the Salmon Convention of 1937 specifically state that the commissioners 'shall hold office during the pleasure of the High Contracting Party by which they were appointed.' Although the Great Lakes Fishery Convention makes no reference to tenure, one may assume that the Greak Lakes Fishery commissioners also hold office at the pleasure of the appointing authorities, viz., the president for the United States and the governor-general-in-council for Canada. All of this suggests that members of the commissions may be ousted for political reasons as well as for incompetence or misconduct. And in truth there have been charges, some with a ring of authenticity, that political ousters have actually occurred. For example, in August 1937 the Canadian press reported that the resignation of George L. Alexander from the International Fisheries Commission was at the request of Premier T.D. Pattullo of British Columbia, who wanted the post for one of his political supporters.[7] However, there is at least one instance on record of a commissioner refusing to resign when requested to do so and retaining his position.[8] The fact of the matter seems to be that the fishery commissionerships generally are not viewed as political 'plums.' This, no doubt, is partly because they carry no salaries but only travel allowances; partly because it is quite generally understood that only persons with special technical knowledge or administrative experience can adequately perform a commissioner's duties; and partly because the tradition of giving representation on each commission to the two federal civil services and to the specially concerned fishing interests of each country leaves little leeway for political appointments or removals. For a Canadian appointee an additional safeguard against an arbitrary political dismissal is the two-year term that he is granted at the time of his appointment. If his performance is satisfactory, he is given two-year extensions, through orders-in-council, more or less as a routine matter.[9]

A characteristic common to the three commissions is their use of advisory committees. Although not required by either treaty or legislative enactment, since 1931 an advisory committee, consisting of representatives of the halibut fishermen and boat-owners, has been utilized by the Pacific Halibut Commission. Called the Conference Board, and originated for the specific purpose of winning the confidence and support of the fishing industry for the commission's regulations, it first consisted of three members from Canada and three from the United States appointed by the commission as a whole.[10] Later it came to include a dozen or more members elected by the fishermen's and vessel owner's organizations in the principal halibut ports of Seattle, Vancouver, Prince Rupert, Ketchikan, Petersburg, and Juneau.[11] It meets annually with the commission to discuss regulations and problems of the industry.

The Protocol of Exchange of the Salmon Convention of 1930 authorized the commission to set up a joint advisory committee of five persons from each country to represent the various branches of the industry. In practice, the three American commissioners choose the American advisers and the three Canadian commissioners choose the Canadian advisers, giving representation in each country to the following fishing interests: the purse seine fishermen, the gill-net fishermen, the troll fishermen, the sports fishermen, the reef-net fishermen, and the salmon processors.[12]

Even more elaborate is the committee system that has been developed for the Great Lakes fisheries. In origin it derives from the Convention of 1954, which states that 'Each Contracting Party may establish for its Section an advisory committee for each of the Great Lakes' and decrees that all the members of these committees may attend all commission sessions except those held in camera. In implementation of the convention, an American law permits each riparian state to have a maximum of four committee members. In making its selection from a list proposed by the governor of each such state, the American section of the commission is required to give 'due consideration to the interests of state agencies having jurisdiction over fisheries, commercial fishing industry of the lake, the sports fishing of the lake and the public at large.'[13] In recent years the commission as a whole has utilized a Scientific Advisory Committee, a Management and Research Committee, a Sea Lamprey Control and Research Committee, a Finance and Administration Committee, and from time to time ad hoc committees to study specific problems.[14]

Since a major reason for the utilization of the advisory committees is to give the concerned states, provinces, fishermen, and canners an opportunity to keep an eye on the commissioners and to look after their own individual interests, it would not be surprising if the commissioners viewed the committees with less than enthusiastic approval. The truth of the matter, however, is that they have invariably welcomed the creation of the committees.[15] They understand full well that commercial fisheries are different from transportation, public utilities, and other industries clearly 'affected with a public interest.' They recall that it was with extreme reluctance that the states and the fishing interests gave their approval to the establishment of the international commissions. And they are acutely aware that they will be able to perform effectively their own duties only with the goodwill and active assistance of the concerned interests.

In actual operations the committees have amply demonstrated their worth. As Herrington notes: 'They serve a two-way function. They provide detailed and practical advice to the commission, particularly with respect to the relation between the problems and proposals considered by the commission and the practical operations of the fishery and the state governments. They also serve an invaluable function in informing the various segments of the interested public of the work of the commission and the justification for the various acts which it may perform. In the present commissions they are proving extremely helpful in maintaining public support.'[16]

Staff arrangements set up by the dozen or so commissions currently dealing with the fishery problems of the Atlantic and Pacific oceans have generally been of either one of two distinctive types. One utilizes an international administrative and research staff (under the general supervisory control of the commission) to plan and carry out a research program and to determine what conservation measures are needed. The Halibut, the Salmon, and the Inter-American Tropical Tuna commissions are of this type. The second type consists of a small administrative and research staff which, in cooperation with the scientific advisers provided by the parties to the convention, prepares, plans, and coordinates the fishery research programs, while leaving the actual research to be financed and carried out by the individual governments. Examples of this type include the North Pacific, the Whaling, and the Fur Seal commissions. A third arrangement is a cross between these two basic types. It is represented at the present time solely by the Great Lakes Commission, whose staff has both research and operational responsibilities with respect to the sea lamprey but has only advisory and coordinating duties relative to fisheries in general.

That for both the halibut and the Fraser River salmon programs Canada and the United States chose in each instance to set up a separate research organization was probably largely due to the lack at the time of the creation of each commission of a sufficiently large staff of specialists in governmental service to discharge the research functions authorized successively in the halibut and the salmon conventions. There was also, undoubtedly, a feeling in each instance that the efforts of the two countries to rehabilitate the fisheries could be more effectively coordinated under a single staff than under two separate national staffs.[17] That significantly different arrangements were made in 1954, when the Great Lakes Fishery Convention was signed, appears to have been primarily due to: (1) the insistence of the states in the Great Lakes area that the role of the international commission be sharply restricted, (2) the existence at that time on the state and provincial levels of staff and facilities adequate for all the research requirements of the Great Lakes fisheries except for the fight against the sea lamprey, and (3) the desire to obtain for the lamprey control program the financial and research resources and the coordinated control that could best be provided by an international agency financed and supported by the two federal governments.[18]

Because it utilizes, whenever feasible, the research agencies of the interested governments, the Great Lakes Fishery Commission is able to get along with a total staff of six – an executive secretary and five other office workers. Operational and most research duties relating to the Great Lakes fisheries in general are handled by the riparian states, Ontario, and the federal governments, while the bulk of the commission's research and operational tasks relating to the sea lamprey are farmed out on a contract basis to the Bureau of Sport Fisheries and Wildlife in the Department of the Interior for work in the United States and to the Department of Fisheries and Oceans for work in Canada. By contrast, the Salmon and the Halibut commissions, each handling operations directly, have in recent years maintained staffs of fifty-three and twenty-three employees respectively.[19] For both the Halibut and the Salmon commissions the director of investigations is appointed by the commissioners, while the other staff members are recruited in accoradance with well-established merit regulations.

Since the employees of the three commissions are paid from funds appropriated by the national legislatures, it is not surprising that the executive authorities of both governments have occasionally attempted to subject them to national civil service regulations. These attempts, however, have invariably been stoutly – although not always successfully – resisted by commission spokesmen. Thus a letter from President Hoover's office in 1931 stating that employees of the International Fisheries Commission were to be given no pay increases during the fiscal year 1932 evoked from the commission's chairman, John P. Babcock, the tart reply that it should not be forgotten that the commission was international in character: 'It was surely not the intention of the treaty establishing the Commission to ask the Canadian members ... to conform to regulations adopted by the United States Government. Moreover, the employees of this Commission are employed jointly by the United States and Canada, and if the employees of the Commission are subject to the regulations of the United States, they must also be subject to the regulations adopted by the Dominion of Canada. This of course would be an impossible condition.' Under an opinion rendered by the attorney general in 1929, Babcock added, 'Commission employees have ... been denied the privileges of Federal employees of the United States, as they are also those of Canada, and it would be unfair to burden them with the disabilities of employees of either or both countries.' The commission would grant no salary increases during the fiscal year 1932, but, lest an unwise precedent be established, it hoped that the president would consider fully its position.[20]

The following year it was from Ottawa that a challenge came, when the Canadian government, acting as paymaster for both member countries, sent pay checks to IFC staff members for the month of July 1932 for smaller amounts than those approved by the commission's director of investigations and its chairman. Babcock immediately wrote to W.A. Found, the Canadian deputy minister of fisheries and a fellow commissioner, asserting that employees of the commission 'are not civil servants of either Canada or the United States, and, consequently, cannot be subject to the Civil Service regulations of either country.'[21]

Babcock's protest did not result in the restoration of the funds deducted from the paychecks. Nor did it end all challenges to the commission's autonomy. Quite the contrary, in 1935 it was asked to submit to the Department of Fisheries detailed information regarding its anticipated financial needs. This time, however, Babcock's strong protests received the vigorous backing of one of his American colleagues, E.W. Allen, who appealed for support to William Phillips, the American under secretary of state.[22] Phillips promised to inquire into the administrative procedures utilized by other international commissions and then determine whether it would be appropriate to request the Canadian authorities to modify the practices objected to by a majority of the commissioners.[23] Apparently solutions soon were found both for the immediate issue of the preparation of budget requests and for the broader question of the IFC's autonomy. In any event, the record of written complaints ends in 1935.

Prior to 1957 staff employees of none of the six international fishery commissions on which both Canada and the United States have membership were afforded an opportunity to belong to group pension plans. Those who wanted insurance and pension benefits had to make their own arrangements with private insurance companies. Each was also obliged to rely upon his own bargaining power, and such influence as the director of investigations and the individual commissioners could exert, to obtain for himself pay increases, annual leaves, and various 'fringe benefits.' Given this weak bargaining position, the employees fared reasonably well. At the same time, they were annoyed at having to pay more for their insurance and pension plans than federal employees paid in either Canada or the United States.

A major step towards remedying this situation was taken 29 July 1957, when a corporation, the International Fisheries Commissions Pension Society, was set up in Canada for the purpose of obtaining pension benefits for the employees of the international fishery commissions. The society, with headquarters in Ottawa, its own board of six directors, three from Canada and three from the United States, immediately initiated negotiations with both Canadian and American insurance companies. By June 1958 a group annuity contract had been signed between the society, acting on behalf of those employees working for three commissions with headquarters in Canada and three with headquarters in the United States, and the Sun Life Assurance Company of Canada.[24]

Although each commission has a separate annuity contract, the same general plan applies to all of the employees working for commissions with headquarters in Canada and in the United States. In each country the pension scheme is a contributory one, financed in part by payroll deductions from the employees' paycheck and in part from funds made available by the individual commissions. The plan provides an income to the employee from the date of his retirement to the time of his death, with retirement at sixty-five (or earlier, with a reduced benefit, if he has completed five years of service). If he leaves the service before the age of retirement, he gets back the total of his contributions, plus interest, or, if he has at least five years of service and so elects, a deferred pension beginning at the age of sixty-five. If he dies before pension payments commence, his beneficiary receives the total of his contributions with compound interest. Participation in the plan is optional, although the experience is that all new employees join. In addition, the employees are covered by the respective social insurance programs of Canada and the United States and are afforded an opportunity to obtain, at modest cost, both group insurance and a group long-term disability coverage.

In large part, because so few persons are included in the pension plan, its benefits are not comparable to those enjoyed by employees of either of the two federal governments. Nor are the available life insurance policies and medical insurance schemes as generous. Despite these facts, morale among the workers of the commissions has always been high and the turnover surprisingly low.[25]

The usual procedure in the preparation of a budget by an individual commission is for the executive secretary, after consultation with the chairman, to draft preliminary estimates of income and expenses. The estimates are then discussed at a meeting of the commission, after which the two federal governments are asked to provide the necessary appropriations, each supplying funds in proportion to the benefits it is expected to receive.

Any budget approved by one of the commissions is usually accepted with a minimum of discussion by the Canadian cabinet and Parliament. In the United States, of course, such is never the case. Generally the Department of State – which handles the budgetary requests of all the fishery commissions to which the United States belongs – will submit to the Office of Management and Budget the financial requests as presented by the commission. But both that agency and the congressional appropriations committees usually revise – almost always downward – the original estimates. In fact, for years one of the most onerous responsibilities of William

C. Herrington, special assistant for fisheries and wildlife to the under secretary of state, was to defend the State Department's proposed appropriations for the fishery commissions. He not only had to listen to jibes, such as that of Senator McClellan, 'We have more commissions than we have kinds of fish, I believe,' but had also to explain why the lamprey control program was slow in achieving results, why the Russians and the Japanese were permitted to enter traditional North American fishing grounds, and, most frequently of all, why the appropriations request was higher than it had been the preceding year.[26] Herrington's usual strategy was to remind the legislators of the adverse effects that budgetary cuts would have on the work of the commissions. On one occasion he also warned that there was a very real danger that Canada might 'look increasingly to unilateral action designed to be of benefit solely to Canadian fishermen.'[27]

Sometimes Mr Herrington and his Senate champions obtained the full amount of their requested appropriations; sometimes they did not. When they failed, the commissions were obliged to postpone staff pay increases or to cut back on some proposed activity. Nevertheless, everything considered, the commissions have been reasonably successful in obtaining funds. Thus appropriations by the two governments to the Halibut Commission grew from $20,000 in 1925 to $762,000 for the fiscal year 1975–6; to the Salmon Commission from $30,000 in 1937 to $1,440,000 for 1977–8; and to the Great Lakes Commission from $809,155 in 1957 to $4,450,300 in 1978.[28] Of course, the scope and variety of activities engaged in by the individual commissions underwent comparable increases.

Each of the commissions has always held at least one meeting a year. All of them have also held special meetings. The Halibut Commission alternates between sites in Canada and the United States. The Salmon Commission usually meets at its headquarters office, in New Westminster, British Columbia. The third commission, the Great Lakes Fishery, while holding most of its meetings at its headquarters in Ann Arbor, Michigan, moves about a great deal, meeting whenever it is convenient to do so in a town or city near the lake or portion of a lake currently under intensive study or the focus of lamprey control operations.

For all of the commissions the regular annual meeting is an occasion for reviewing with their respective staffs and advisory committees and the representatives of the fishing industry the problems, achievements, and prospects of the fishery and for discussing and – generally after revisions – for adopting the regulations which, upon being approved by the two governments, become the operating guidelines for the forthcoming fishing season. The special meetings usually are convened to deal with problems that cannot conveniently be left for the regular meetings.

An interesting question arises with respect to the individual commissioners: are they free to speak and vote as they see fit, or do they have the status of instructed delegates? So far as the members of the Great Lakes Commission are concerned, it is clearly apparent that a commissioner is expected to uphold the position of the government that appointed him – assuming that such a position has been determined. Article II of the originating convention of 1954 specifies that the authorized commission is to be composed of 'two national sections, a Canadian Section and a United States Section,' each section with one vote and all decisions and recommendations to be made 'only with the approval of both Sections.' By contrast, neither the Salmon Convention of 1930 nor the successive Halibut Conventions makes any mention of national sections. They do, however, refer to each country's 'representation on the Commission' and both provide that each country shall pay the salaries and expenses of 'its own' members. The salmon agreement specifies that 'no action taken by the Commission ... shall be effective unless it is affirmatively voted for by at least two of the Commissioners of each High Contracting Party.' The earlier Halibut Conventions provided no rules of voting, but the revised convention of 1953 requires a concurring vote of at least two of the commissioners of each party for all commission 'decisions.' Thus, like their fellow countrymen on the Great Lakes Fishery Commission, members of both the Halibut and the Salmon Commission, it would seem, are expected to represent the views and interests of the individual countries that appointed them and pay their expenses. And in actual practice a commissioner is always fully cognizant of the national viewpoint on all important issues.[29]

Despite what is stated above, members of the Halibut and Salmon commissions have usually been able to conduct discussions and arrive at decisions with very little national bias in evidence. For example, in 1955 Senator Thomas Reid, member of the Salmon Commission from 1937 through 1967, noted that 'from the very beginning operations of the Commission were completely unbiased by national interests.'[30] In a similar vein, Edward W. Allen has observed:

Generally speaking, the relations between American and Canadian Commissioners have been exceedingly friendly and there has been cordial cooperation. Once in a while, unfortunately, there has been a commissioner on one side or the other who has been ultra nationalistic, but I have frequently commented on the fact that in the twenty-three years in which I was on the halibut commission, we did not sit on two sides of the table, but the four or six sat as one body. Every action was unanimous. The same situation prevailed almost entirely throughout the fourteen years I was on the salmon commission. But, on the North Pacific Commission, the commissioners sit as three distinct groups. (U.S., Canadian, and Japanese) and, although the commissioners are all friendly personally, the same harmony does not exist as in the case of the halibut and salmon commissions.[31]

Largely, it would seem, because the Great Lakes Commission does not have its own research staff but must depend on the services provided by the interested governments, it has never been able to develop the 'family-type of relationship' among its members that has so characterized the other two commissions, especially the halibut during the earlier years of its existence. The contracting out of research and operational duties and the attempt to coordinate the research programs of the various governments have led to some national conflicts.[32] Nevertheless, its members have also been able to harmonize differences and to discharge their duties in an efficient manner.

8

Fishery commissions: activities and appraisal

Professor Crutchfield and other economists have long charged that, by concentrating on achieving the 'maximum sustained productivity,' the Halibut Commission has largely ignored such economic considerations as increased efficiency in the use of labour and capital.[1] Recently similar charges have also been directed at the Salmon Commission. Note, for example, the comment of a Canadian official of the United Fishermen and Allied Workers Union: 'Consider the sheer economic waste of 10,000 men frantically competing one or two days per week, as regulated by the government, for a limited volume of salmon and then sitting idle for the balance of what used to be a normal five-day operation.'[2]

But other commentators have contended that it is better that the commissions not become involved in the economic aspects of fishery regulation. To do so, they insist, would make their tasks more complicated and difficult, would involve them in political controversies, and, in any event, would be unnecessary since the fishing industry itself is quite capable of dealing with marketing and other economic questions.[3]

Another indictment sometimes brought against the fishery commissioners is that in their efforts to promote the interests of their particular species of fish they overlook the needs of persons and groups interested in other resources or in multiple resource development in general. This, for example, was one of the charges that General McNaughton and his supporters brought against Senator Thomas Reid and his colleagues for opposing the diversion of water out of the Columbia River into the Fraser.[4] There is, no doubt, some validity to this indictment. There have been occasions when the salmon commissioners have appeared to be interested in nothing but the salmon stock of the Pacific Coast. But perhaps they should not be too harshly criticized for opposing the development of power on the Fraser and other salmon streams. It is generally agreed that the construction of high dams and the changing of the level and temperature of salmon streams have adverse – often disastrous – effects upon most species of salmon.[5]

In any event, the individuals who have been critical of the commissions have been very much in the minority. The demonstrated ability of the commissioners to discharge their duties in an efficient, harmonious manner has not only won for them wide praise, but has given them great prestige among fishery experts, academicians, and the general public on both sides of the boundary. Moreover, any regulation proposed by a commission, or any new undertaking suggested, is usually promptly and fully accepted by the two federal governments. In fact, the Halibut and the Salmon commissions have been permitted to enjoy such a high degree of autonomy 'that the tasks of the two governments have been less to be advised by the commissions than to confirm their decisions.'[6]

Do the commissions merit the high prestige and confidence that they enjoy? Considering the magnitude of their responsibilities and the difficulties that they have encountered, their achievements have indeed been impressive. The Halibut Commission, for example, was given the task of studying, and after 1930 of regulating, a fishery which covers a coastline approximately 2000 miles in length which can be studied only at sea and under the most difficult of conditions. It must obtain not only extensive data regarding the physical characteristics and growth of the different 'races' of halibut but also as full a statistical record as possible of the catch of the individual fishing vessels.[7] And it has to establish regulations acceptable both to the interested governments and to the industry being regulated. Even more extensive are the responsibilities of the Salmon Commission. In addition to having the power, like the Halibut Commission, to establish closed seasons, to issue licences, and to regulate the type of gear to be used, it has responsibilities not assigned the other commission: (1) the construction and maintenance of hatcheries and other facilities and (2) the adjusting of the catch to give each country an equal share of the sockeye and pink salmons. As for the Great Lakes Commission, while it was given no power to draft fishing regulations, it was delegated some other formidable duties. One of these was to formulate and implement a comprehensive lamprey control program. For more than a decade Ontario and the Great Lakes States, with some assistance from the two federal governments had been searching in vain for a solution to the lamprey problem. In 1955 the principal responsibility was shifted onto the shoulders of the joint commission with its office staff of only four (later increased to five) people. Equally burdensome was the job assigned the commission of formulating a general research program for all of the fishes of the Great Lakes and of coordinating the research undertaken. When it is recalled that in 1955 there were eight states, one province, and two federal governments with general research programs already well established, and that state and provincial rights are deeply embedded in the thinking of the peoples of the Great Lakes region, the difficulty and delicate nature of the commission's tasks may be appreciated.

For all three commissions a potential source of difficulty has always been the rugged individualism of the North American fishermen, their impatience with governmental restraints or controls, and their reluctance to share with others any fisheries that they view as primarily their own. Nor have the commissioners been able to ignore a certain Canadian mistrust of the United States and a suspicion that Canada invariably comes out the loser in any important enterprise that she undertakes either jointly or cooperatively with her powerful neighbour.[8] And there has always been the difficulty of convincing sceptical American legislators that the benefits to be derived from the restoration and conservation of the fisheries are commensurate with the sizeable sums of money that Congress has been asked to appropriate each year to pay the American share of the expenses of the commissions.

The lamprey control program, in particular, has evoked on a number of occasions highly critical comments from members of the House of Representatives. For example, at successive hearings before the Subcommittee of the House Committee on Appropriations, the subcommittee chairman, John J. Rooney of Brooklyn, demanded to know how much money had been spent on the program and how many lampreys had been killed. When told that it figured out at $7.50 per lamprey, he concluded: 'that's a lot of money to kill some eels.'[9]

On occasions the fishery commissions have even had difficulties with other international commissions. For example, the proposal pushed by General McNaughton and other Canadian members of the International Joint Commission in the 1950s to divert some of the waters of the Columbia into the Fraser and to erect certain power works on the latter river was most disturbing to all members of the Salmon Commission. In fact, one of the Canadian commissioners, Senator Reid, was so concerned that late in 1955, in collaboration with his colleagues, he prepared and transmitted to General McNaughton and to the two federal governments a report setting forth in vigorous language the fatal consequences that, in their opinion, the consummation of McNaughton's project would have upon the salmon of the Fraser River.[10] Some fifteen months later the director of the Salmon

Commission warned a House of Commons committee that there could be 'no such thing as dams and salmon on the main Fraser river.' It could be one or the other but not both.[11] There are grounds for believing that the eventual abandonment of the McNaughton diversion proposal was at least partially due to the active opposition of the Salmon Commission.[12]

Despite the difficulties, each of the commissions has important achievements to its credit. The Halibut Commission, for example, quickly established effective working relationships with all branches of the halibut industry and acquired from the vessel captains the records of the individual catches, from which the yield per unit of fishing effort for each section of the coast is obtained. From the statistical data it collected, the commission discovered that the different stocks of halibut were in different stages of depletion. Accordingly, it divided the fishery into four areas and set up appropriate regulations for each: area 1, south of Willapa Harbor, and area 4, in the Bering Sea, were left unrestricted; annual quotas were established for areas 2 and 3; and fishing was altogether forbidden in the so-called 'nurseries.' Later, quotas were also established for areas 1 and 4. In 1938 certain fishing gear was forbidden. The effectiveness of the regulations was soon apparent. In 1931, the year before the start of the regulation of the industry, the total Pacific coast halibut catch was only 44,000,000 pounds; by 1962 it had reached 75,119,000 pounds.[13] Since 1964 a number of developments have contributed to a very serious decline of the halibut stocks. Of these, the most important has been the catching of increasingly large quantities of fish by fishermen not covered by the Canadian–American halibut agreements, i.e., by operators of small setline American and Canadian vessels and salmon trawlers, by Canadian and American sportsmen, and, most important of all, prior to 1974–6, by fishermen on Japanese and Soviet trawlers.[14] Even though the joint agency can be faulted for not sounding the alarm earlier and more insistently relative to the dangers of overfishing, the assertion can still validly be made that the commission has provided 'a model of international adjustment and orderly regulation' and that its activities represent cooperative efforts of worldwide significance.[15]

In its efforts to preserve and extend the sockeye and pink salmon stocks the Salmon Commission has used a three-pronged attack: (1) it has attempted to prevent overfishing by establishing closed seasons, by regulating the types of gear the fishermen are permitted to use, and by providing emergency measures to allow the escape of adequate stocks for spawning purposes; (2) it has urged the two governments to remove obstructions to salmon migrations and to construct fish ladders at Hell's Gate Canyon and at other places; and (3) it has attempted to assist and protect propagation by improving the conditions of the spawning grounds, by lessening the mortality of salmon eggs and salmon young, and by artificial propagation. For a time these efforts promised to be spectacularly successful. Between 1949 and 1957 the Fraser River sockeye runs registered a significant improvement.[16] Thereafter for a decade the number of young sockeyes emigrating from the Fraser River continued to increase, but, for some undetermined reason or reasons, the returning adult runs did not. The same was true of the Fraser River pink salmon migrations.[17] But good productions of both species have been achieved since 1968, with exceptionally large productions in 1974, 1976, and 1977.[18] In fact, the commission noted in its report of 1968 (p. 6) that the 'current annual value of the Fraser River sockeye and pink salmon fishery has increased by $9,298,000 to fishermen and $17,737,000 in the wholesale value since the years immediately following the Hell's Gate obstruction.' That, most certainly, is an achievement. The commission also merits high praise for providing additional proof that joint agencies can operate harmoniously in behalf of the mutual interests of two independent nations.[19]

The record of the Great Lakes Fishery Commission is one of moderate success. For months following the commission's creation, the lamprey control program attempted to eradicate the pests through the use of electrical barriers placed in the tributary streams of the Great Lakes used by the lampreys as spawning grounds. This method, however, not only proved extremely expensive but was not outstandingly successful. In 1959 the United States Fish and Wildlife Service announced that it had developed 'selective poisons' that were 'unconditionally successful' in killing lamprey larvae while causing no harm to other fish. Immediately thereafter the commission launched an extensive chemical treatment program in the infested Lake Superior streams. In 1960 the program was extended to Lakes Michigan and Huron. Lake Ontario was added in 1971. By 1971 initial treatment of tributary streams had been completed and many streams had received one or more additional treatments. As for results, the effectiveness of the control program in Lake Superior was soon plainly evident. Annual counts taken at assessment barriers indicated that by 1962 the adult lamprey population had been reduced by 80 per cent and by 1966 to 90 per cent. Although counting has not been done on the other lakes, indirect checks show that considerable progress has been made on those lakes also.[20]

As the lampreys were brought under control the riparian states and Ontario launched, and have continued to carry forward, mammoth programs of planting stocks of lake and rainbow trout, coho and chinook salmon, and kokanee in all of the lakes. These plantings, along with the lamprey control program, have given rise to the development of a very successful sport fishery in lake trout and other salmonids. At the same time, profitable commercial fisheries based on herring, chubs, whitefish, smelt, alewives, perch, and carp, and other less desirable species, have been built up in all of the lakes. Although the commission's objective of self-maintenance of the trout and salmon populations through natural reproduction has not yet been achieved, the prospects are quite promising.[21]

The fight against the lamprey is, of course, far from over. Quite the contrary, the lampreys appear to be reacting to the control program through faster growth and a higher percentage of females in the spawning run. What is most urgently needed is increased financial appropriations on a regular basis to make possible an intensification of the surveillance and stream treatment programs and the development of new control methods. Although the Canadian government has consistently met the commission's budgetary requests, Congress has again and again refused to grant increases – thereby seriously impeding the commission's activities. In fact, its financial situation became so precarious in 1969 as to cause its chairman of that year, Lester Voight, to criticize publicly the government in Washington, stating that a lack of financial support might force a temporary abandonment of the control program in Lake Huron. As it turned out, the continuation of the program was made possible only by supplemental funds provided by Michigan, the Upper Great Lakes Regional Commission, and the Department of Fisheries and Forestry of Canada, and by reducing lamprey research and surveys on Lakes Superior and Michigan.[22] In 1970 and 1971 also the commission was obliged to abandon several scheduled projects because of the failure of Congress to appropriate sufficient funds to cover the American share of the cost. Despite its problems and frustrations, the commission is justified in viewing with pride its achievements in dealing with the lampreys. In the not too distant future it should be able to give more attention to the other side of its work: the formulation and coordination of general research programs looking towards the maximum production of the fisheries.

What factors have most contributed to the success of the commissions? One, most certainly, has been the high calibre of the commissioners – men such as John Babcock, A.J. Whitmore, Edward W. Allen, William M. Sprules, and Thomas Reid, who have worked energetically, competently, and cooperatively for years in the advancement of scientific conservation and exploitation of the individual fisheries. A second factor, all commentators agree, has been the well-trained, efficient staff, free of partisanship, headed by a capable director, that each organization has been able to recruit and retain – despite mediocre pay scales and non-existent fringe benefits during the earlier years. Also important have been the advice and support that all of the commissions have received from their respective advisory committees. The Great Lakes Fishery Commission, in particular, has relied very heavily on its committees, and one writer has gone so far as to assert that the success of the Halibut Commission has been 'due in large part to its willingness to consider at all times the wishes and interests of the halibut industry, expressed through the Conference Board.'[23] That, unquestionably, is an exaggeration, but there can be no doubt that in both advisory and liaison capacities, the committees have greatly facilitated the work of the individual commissions. Another factor has been the great amount of time and effort that each commission has devoted to the collection of scientific data. This has provided a fund of information of great value with respect to the biology of each species of fish under its jurisdiction (including population estimates, migration patterns, and size and age composition of the stocks), as well as hatchery methods, spawning grounds, and other matters. No less importantly, the joint agencies have been able to present problems and opportunities for their amelioration in terms that have been 'understandable, familiar and acceptable to the two countries' policymakers.'[24] Also not to be overlooked have been other factors such as the following: the Halibut Commission has been dealing with only one species of fish, the Salmon Commission with only two, and the Great Lakes Commission has focused its attention largely on a single problem, the eradication of the sea lamprey; for a number of years only the two signatory powers were exploiting the halibut and salmon fisheries covered by the conventions; the convention area of each commission has been clearly defined; the regulations have been consistently applied; recently the pressure of Japanese and Soviet fishing fleets has made the two North American peoples acutely aware of the similarities of their interests; and, finally and most important of all, the participating countries have a similarity in taste and technology and a long tradition of goodwill and mutual trust.

Despite the achievements of the commissions, difficult days, most observers believe, lie ahead. Of the many problems confronting the halibut and salmon fisheries one of the most vexing – aside from obtaining funds from Congress – is the increasing vigorous competition among the fishermen for a limited supply of fish. This poses for the commissions, as well as for the fishermen themselves and the interested governments, certain challenging questions. One of these is: are unlimited numbers of fishermen to be permitted to join the uneconomic scramble for catches? If not, will the two governments adopt some form of licence limitation or restricted entry?[25]

A second and related problem is the entry of the fishermen of third countries into the halibut fisheries of the Pacific. Unless they have agreed to renounce or to limit their rights, third countries are not bound by rules of international law to restrict the fishing activities of their subjects as long as such fishing is conducted on the high seas. Unfortunately for Canada and the United States, the halibut of the Pacific Coast are regularly caught on the high seas. In 1937 it was only because of a vigorous Canadian–American protest that a British fishing vessel was dissuaded from participating in the halibut fisheries.[26] In recent years Japanese fishermen have taken a special interest in those fisheries. In 1952, by the provisions of the International Convention for the High Seas Fisheries of the North Pacific Ocean, Japan, in effect, agreed to refrain from exploiting the halibut, salmon, and herring stocks that had been built up by the United States and Canada in the North Pacific provided these two countries fully utilized them.[27] But in 1962 – after the tripartite International North Pacific Fisheries Commission had unanimously concluded that the halibut of the eastern Bering Sea no longer met the rigid qualifications for abstention – the member governments agreed that this stock should be removed from the abstention requirement and in 1963 Japan was permitted to begin fishing for halibut in that particular area. Understandably, that meant vigorous competition for Canadian and American halibut fishermen. No less significantly, Japanese fishermen have taken large quantities of halibut incidentally while fishing for other bottomfish. In 1973 Japan agreed to establish trawl closures in the eastern Bering Sea for 1974 and later agreed to their continuation through 1975.[28] But for years the Soviet Union adamantly refused to accept the abstention principle. Even though North American fishery experts were uncertain as to whether the mammoth Soviet vessels fishing 25 to 50 miles off the North American coast were actively fishing for halibut and salmon, there could be no doubt that the catch of halibut incidentally to groundfish operations in the Eastern Bering Sea had a considerable effect on the recruitment to Canada–United States halibut stocks.[29] In 1975 the Soviet authorities agreed to prohibit trawling in the Bering Sea and Gulf of Alaska areas. It will, however, be several years before these closures are reflected in increased halibut catches.

A potentially serious threat to the salmon industry is the increasing demand of the people of the Pacific Northwest for electrical energy. Both population and industry in the area are rapidly expanding. The available power development sites on non-salmon-spawning streams are rapidly being used up. When all of the good ones are exhausted, vigorous pressure for the construction of dams on salmon-spawning streams is certain to be exerted. If it comes to a 'knock-down-drag-out' fight between the salmon industry and the proponents of hydroelectric energy, the power interests are likely to win. But perhaps it will not come to that. Certainly common sense dictates that the salmon be safeguarded. As Roderick Haig-Brown has so eloquently remarked: 'The Pacific salmon are almost the last of the North American continent's mighty manifestations of abundance. They are an abundance that man, by taking thought, can live with, maintain, use and enjoy.'[30]

A matter of special concern to Canada is the winning of American acceptance of modifications of the Salmon Convention of 1930 that would enable Canadian fishermen to obtain a larger share of the Fraser River salmon catch. The basic Canadian position, repeatedly affirmed since 1970, is that, as a general principle, each country should harvest the salmon originating in its own rivers. Since, however, the fish in the Puget Sound and offshore areas are intermingled, and interceptions by fishermen of one country of salmon bound for the other country cannot be entirely eliminated, Canada has advocated, as an interim arrangement, a reduction in the American share of the salmon passing through international waters to the Fraser River from the 50 per cent allowed under the convention of 1930 to not more than 25 per cent. In return, Canada would reduce its interceptions of salmon bound for American waters and, at the same time, bear the total cost of constructing new spawning channels in the Fraser River.[31]

The American position is that the United States has 'special interests in the Fraser River salmon runs by virtue not only of the investment it has made in the joint programs, but also through factors of history and geography.' These interests, it insists, must be given proper consideration in any modifications of the convention of 1930.[32]

At discussions conducted 8 May 1973 between Canadian and American fishery experts, various solutions to the problems of interception were considered. When no solution acceptable to both countries could be found, a spokesman for the Canadian delegation announced that the persistence of the existing unsatisfactory state of affairs would lead Canada to take unilateral action 'aimed primarily at harvesting our own Fraser River stocks.' The reply of the American spokesman was that such 'retrogressive' Canadian moves would force his government to 'take such actions as may be necessary to protect the interests of United States fisheries.'[33]

Fortunately, a Canadian–American fishery war was averted, at least temporarily, by a decision of the two Governments to renew, with certain modifications, a 1970 agreement on reciprocal fishing privileges. The agreement, signed in 1973 and since then renewed annually, extended the accord from 15 June 1973 to 24 April 1974, and provided, among other things, for a reduction of Canadian fishing privileges off the state of Washington to an area between Carroll Island and Cape Flattery and a reduction of American fishing privileges to a small area near the entrance to the Strait of Juan de Fuca.[34] But the governments still have the problem of formulating a mutually acceptable permanent solution of this extremely difficult issue.

Until such a solution is found, a project strongly urged upon the two governments by the Salmon Commission since 1972 has little chance of being approved and implemented – that is, the construction of spawning channels on the Fraser River system, at an estimated cost of $14 million. Both governments recognize the desirability of the project, but the authorities in Ottawa have taken the position that they do not want further American contribution to facilities on the all-Canadian Fraser system. This has made it impossible for the commission to move ahead on a program which, it says, could triple catches of sockeye and double pink salmon catches and, at the same time, have beneficial effects on other salmon and trout fisheries.[35]

The operations of both the Salmon and the Halibut commissions are certain to be affected by the establishment of 200-mile fishery zones by Canada and the United States. Exactly what that effect will be is still uncertain. It should be largely beneficial. Whether that proves to be true or not, the changed jurisdictional situation makes imperative a thorough review of the role of these and other international fishery commissions. In fact, the director of the Halibut Commission has urged such a review of his organization – especially with respect to the limitations of the 1953 halibut convention, different national goals, problems of enforcement, and administrative deficiencies.[36] The Salmon Commission would also, no doubt, benefit from a sweeping re-examination.

As for the work of the Great Lakes Commission, after the lamprey problem is reduced to manageable proportions, the most serious threat to the fisheries of the Great Lakes will undoubtedly come from the pollution of the lakes by industrial and human wastes. Following the discovery in 1970 of dangerously high levels of mercury in the bodies of Great Lakes fish, fishing in Lakes St Clair and Erie was temporarily halted. The Great Lakes Commission, while acknowledging that it did not have direct responsibility for the maintenance of water quality, expressed its determination, through liaison with the International Joint Commission and other governmental agencies, 'to encourage the establishment of water quality standards that incorporate fisheries as well as other interests.'[37] More recently still, commission members have been given additional cause for concern by the discovery of polychlorinated biphenyl in the bodies of many coho, lake trout, pickerel, and pike of the lower lakes at levels greatly in excess of what is considered safe for human consumption. The commission, it is safe to predict, will watch with the keenest of interest the progress of the pollution cleanup program in all of the Great Lakes.

There is still another problem relating to the commissions that has long caused concern to students of international organization and administration. In fact, it was raised more than three decades ago by Professor Linden A. Mander of the University of Oregon, and that is whether the uncoordinated establishment of fishery commissions on the North American Continent is not likely to result 'in a vast repetition and overlapping of functions ... unwieldiness and decline in efficiency.' Mander noted that the Halibut and the Salmon commissions each has a separate statistical division and wondered 'whether under these circumstances overlapping does not occur, whether one outstanding person could not manage the statistical work of both commissions and achieve more effective correlation, and whether overhead costs would not be lessened through the reduction of office expenditure, postage, equipment, etc., and of the number of salaried officials.'[38] Since that time other students of government have raised the same question. For example, in 1953, in a favourable report on the revised halibut convention, the Senate Committee on Foreign Relations commented on the increasing number of fishery commissions that the United States was participating in and recommended that the Department of State give some thought to 'the feasibility of consolidating or combining some of the commissions with a view to greater efficiency and a reduced overall cost.'[39] The reply of the department spokesmen, given in April 1955, was that they were not at that time in a position to consider drafting a convention to cover all areas of the Atlantic or Pacific. It was quite possible that further experience would show that having one fishery commission not only would not provide any increased efficiency in the handling of fishery problems but would be more expensive to operate than the existing specialized commissions. With an over-all convention it would be more difficult to focus attention on specific problems and to maintain public interest and support. In any event, they added, thus far the necessary coordination of American participation in the various commissions, the avoidance of duplication, and the maintenance of a consistent United

States policy had been adequately accomplished through the activities of the office of the Department of State assigned to that function.[40]

A somewhat different reply was given by the Canadian minister of fisheries, James Sinclair, when approximately the same question was asked by a member of Parliament in the spring of 1955. The establishment of a single joint fisheries commission, the minister agreed, would probably be a desirable goal, 'but since we have had a fair amount of difficulty even negotiating the treaties on these major species I think we would have to have a lot more experience and a lot more acceptance before we could negotiate one treaty to cover all fisheries of concern to the two nations.'[41]

Thus all indications point towards the continuation of the three Canadian–American fishery commissions as well as the other fishery commissions the membership of which Canada and the United States share with other countries. But the placing of the pink salmon under the jurisdiction of the International Pacific Salmon Fisheries Commission in 1956 suggests that when and if the decision is taken to extend joint regulation to other species of fish of common concern to the two countries, this is likely to be done by giving the responsibility to one of the existing commissions rather than by the creation of a new one. But, despite the splendid records of the individual commissions, there will still be grounds, in the opinion of the author, for asking whether the various fishery conservation programs could not be more efficiently and economically operated if they were subjected to more centralized planning and coordinated operations.[42]

9

The Permanent Joint Board
on Defence: origin

In no field has Canadian–American cooperation of the past four decades been closer or more consistently maintained than in the broad area of continental defence. This has been true in spite of the fact that defence cooperation started much later than did cooperation in such fields as fisheries, transportation, and hydroelectric power development and has aroused no small amount of concern and controversy in Canada.

Significantly, the first official proposal that Canada and the United States cooperate in matters of mutual defence came from President Franklin D. Roosevelt. Increasingly concerned over the aggressive policies and actions of Germany, Italy, and Japan, in March 1937 the president suggested that Canadian and American staff officers hold conversations about problems of continental defence. Not surprisingly, the president's suggestion evoked no great amount of enthusiasm from the super-cautious Canadian prime minister, William Lyon Mackenzie King. King, like many other North Americans, had long been imbued with the idea that the broad oceans isolated the Western Hemisphere from the danger spots of Europe and Asia. Even though he eventually became apprehensive over the spread of international violence and lawlessness, he was reluctant to face up to the fact that North America was rapidly losing its invulnerability to foreign attacks. No less importantly, the prime minister was acutely aware that any moves he might make that could conceivably be viewed as weakening Canada's traditionally close defence ties with Britain could have disastrous political consequences for himself and his government. Despite these considerations, he eventually agreed to the staff conversations.[1] More significantly still, when Roosevelt, in his Kingston, Ontario, address of 18 August 1938, assured his Canadian audience 'that the people of the United States will not stand idly by if domination of Canadian soil is threatened by any other empire,' the prime minister promptly responded with his own affirmation: 'We, too, have our own obligations as a good neighbour, and one of these is to see that, at our own instance, our country is made as immune from attack or possible invasion as we can reasonably be expected to make it, and that, should the occasion ever arise, enemy forces should not be able to pursue their way either by land, sea or air, to the United States across Canadian territory.'

This exchange of assurances marked a highly significant milestone in the slowly evolving Canadian–American defensive alliance. For the first time the two countries had publicly recognized 'their reciprocity in defence.'[2] More than that, they had enunciated principles that in the years ahead would govern – as they still do – their defence relationships.[3]

The outbreak of hostilities in September 1939, however, imposed a temporary halt to the rapidly developing North American 'front.' Canada entered the war at Britain's side, while the United States attempted for months the difficult feat of maintaining at least technical neutrality while giving all practical aid to the Allies. Liaison between Roosevelt and King was not completely terminated, but the staff conferences were discontinued, and for a time the neighbouring countries again went their separate ways. Then came the German blitzkrieg, the forced surrender of the armed forces of Belgium, the Netherlands, Luxembourg, and France and the massing of the German armed forces on the English Channel as though poised for an invasion. The peoples of North America felt shock, fear, and horror. North America's security, as well as Western civilization, they were convinced, now hung in the balance. Without delay, both Canada and the United States collected and dispatched to the British fighting men all the arms and ammunition that could possibly be spared from their own meagre reserves and each country greatly speeded up its preparedness program. Numerous Canadians, however, were not satisfied but called for the immediate establishment of a comprehensive Canadian–American defensive alliance. The possibility could not be overlooked, they affirmed, that the German assault on Britain would succeed, that the British government and fleet might seek refuge in Canada, and that Canada itself might be attacked. There was the further danger, some of them averred, that if Canada were attacked and the Canadian armed forces proved incapable of countering such attacks, the United States might insist on sending in its own armed forces. Thus the Dominion's best chance of maintaining its national existence would be to admit frankly that its defence 'must be worked out in cooperation with the United States on the basis of a single continental defence policy.'[4]

King was very much in a quandary. The unhappy course of the war had dispelled his earlier misgivings regarding the wisdom of entering into military arrangements with the United States. Both the security of Canada and the survival of Britain, he came to believe, demanded close military, political, and economic cooperation between Canada and her southern neighbour. The Canadian chiefs of staff were clamouring not only for the renewal of staff conversations but also for American planes, tanks, arms, and ammunition and a commitment of armed forces for the defence of Canada and Newfoundland. However, American military men were reluctant to deplete their meagre supply of arms or to commit troops for the defence of Canada and Newfoundland (believing a German assault more likely to be directed against Latin America and the Panama Canal).[5] Isolationist sentiment was still strong in the States, a presidential election was in the offing, and the American people were badly divided over the question as to whether fifty over-age American destroyers should or should not be turned over to Britain.[6]

It was the proposed transfer of the destroyers that provided the Canadian leader with the opening he was seeking. After learning that Roosevelt was attempting to persuade Churchill to grant the United States ninety-nine-year leases of bases in British possessions in the Western Hemisphere in exchange for the destroyers, King instructed Loring Christie, the Canadian minister to the United States, to obtain an interview with the president and to advise him that, while the prime minister was delighted with the proposed destroyer transfer, he hoped that during the discussions over that transaction an opportunity might be found for considering the question of the strengthening of naval forces on the North American side of the Atlantic.[7]

Roosevelt talked with Christie on 15 August. The following day the Department of State sent the president a letter from J. Pierrepont Moffat, the American minister in Ottawa, reporting a public demand in Canada for 'some form of defense understanding with the United States.'[8] Recognizing that a defence arrangement with Canada would facilitate the defence efforts of the two American countries, possibly open the way to the acquisition by the United States of naval and air bases in Nova Scotia, and, not least of all, help to win congressional approval of the bases-for-destroyers transaction, the president, in keeping with his impulsive nature, immediately phoned King, advised him that on the following day he would be attending military manoeuvres near Ogdensburg, New York, and invited him to come down for talks 'about the destroyers and ... about defense matters between

Canada and the U.S.'[9] The prime minister accepted the invitation and, apparently without bothering to consult his cabinet colleagues or the chiefs of staff, left the afternoon of the next day for Ogdensburg accompanied only by Moffat.

From the ensuing conversations – held in a railway car and participated in only by King, Roosevelt, and Secretary of War Henry L. Stimson – Roosevelt obtained King's blessing to exchange the American destroyers for British bases in the West Indies (but not for any bases in Nova Scotia), and King received assurances that some military equipment, desperately needed by Canada, would be made available. Most important of all, the two leaders, on the initiative of the president, agreed to set up 'a Permanent Joint Board on Defense' to 'consider in the broad sense the defense of the north half of the Western Hemisphere.' It was to consist of 'four or five members from each country' and was to 'meet shortly' to 'commence ... studies relating to sea, land and air problems including personnel and material.'

Interestingly enough, the agreement to establish the board (drafted by Roosevelt but verbally modified in accordance with suggestions of King and Stimson) was written originally on the dining car's tablecloth and almost got carried away to the laundry![10] The statement was released to the press but was never specifically ratified by Congress or by the Canadian Parliament. Eventually it was approved by the Canadian Privy Council but received no further sanction by the American government other than publication in the *Department of State Bulletin* and in the Department's *Treaties in Force* publication.[11] Thus there are good grounds for the assessment that 'no international arrangement of comparable importance has ever been concluded more informally.'[12]

Despite the hasty, informal manner of the agreement's drafting, there can be no doubt that its words and phrases were chosen with care and due deliberation. Consider, for example, the use of the word 'Permanent' in the title of the proposed new organization. When questioned by the prime minister as to the significance of the inclusion of that particular word in his original draft, the president replied that in his opinion the board should not be designed 'to meet alone this particular situation but to secure the continent for the future.' To which proposal King did not respond as he normally did when called upon to make commitments with far-reaching implications: that this was a matter for parliamentary decision. Quite the contrary, he gave the proposal his prompt and enthusiastic approval.[13] By so doing he, of course, helped to move Canada away from its traditional

British alignment into a permanent alliance arrangement with its powerful American neighbour, with, as suggested below, far-reaching consequences for his country.

The use of the word 'Joint' was, no doubt, intended to emphasize the reciprocity of the defence interests and obligations that had been avowed and accepted by the two leaders. What was being established, they wanted to affirm, was not a selfish, one-sided arrangement, but rather a mutually advantageous, cooperative enterprise, freely entered into by true partners striving towards common objectives. Although the population of the United States was approximately ten times that of Canada, each country was to have the same number of representatives, and the board was to operate on the democratic principle of the legal equality of the participating countries. That, of course, was in keeping with the precedent that had already been established by the International Joint Commission, the International Boundary Commission, and the bilateral fishery commissions.

The Roosevelt draft spoke of a 'Commission.' King raised the question as to whether 'Board' or 'Committee' might not be preferable. Recalling, no doubt, the difficulties that he and some of his predecessors had encountered with respect to appointments to the IJC,[14] he 'pointed out that Commission suggested the necessity of formal appointments by Governments.' He further observed that 'Board' was the word that had been used the night before in their conversation. 'Mr. Stimson agreed that Board would perhaps be better and the President did also';[15] hence 'Board' it was called.

The insertion of the word 'Defense' into the title was intended, we may reasonably assume, as an assurance to isolationist-minded Americans that the two leaders were thinking purely in terms of the defence of the Western Hemisphere and that Roosevelt was not planning to use the new agency for any back-door entry into the European war. The same was true of the Ogdensburg statement in general. 'As if to reject completely any suggestion of aggressive intent, the word "defense" appeared five times in ... the statement, once in each sentence but the last.'[16]

The publicizing of the agreement (or declaration, as it is sometimes called) evoked varied reactions. Two prominent Canadians, Richard B. Hanson, leader of the Conservative party, and Arthur Meighen, former Conservative prime minister, saw it as merely 'another Liberal attempt to abandon the Empire in preference to the United States.'[17] But most Canadians praised the agreement, some of them seeing it as a major contribution towards the building of North American defences and others viewing it primarily as an important boost to the Commonwealth's war effort.[18]

Most Americans also praised the new accord. Their general reaction was that the defence interests of the two countries now were the same; that the advent of air power had made continents the natural units for defence purposes; and that, in any event, the United States, in its own safety, could not permit the Nazis or the Japanese to win a foothold on either coast of the Western Hemisphere.[19]

The agreement was, of course, unique in that Canada, for the first time in its history, had become a party to a defensive alliance outside the Commonwealth of Nations, and the United States, a neutral, had, in effect, entered into a military alliance with a belligerent. Furthermore, instead of each country formulating its own defence policies without regard to those of its neighbour, as had been done in the past, each now was expected to consider jointly the defence of North America as a single problem.

More significantly still, the agreement, in effect, amounted to a veritable 'revolution': the end of the British century and the beginning of the American.[20] The American century, as Frank Underhill predicted, was to prove to be 'a much tougher experience' for Canadians than the British century had been[21] – so tough, indeed, as to elicit repeatedly in the sixties and seventies the charge that Ogdensburg had ushered in branch-plant dependency for Canada, as well as the status of an American military satellite.[22] But the fact of the matter is that in 1940 most Canadians believed that they were dependent upon the United States for their security and therefore had 'no choice but to follow American leadership.'[33]

10

The Permanent Joint Board
on Defence: jurisdiction, organization,
procedures, and evaluation

Partly, no doubt, because of the vague wording of the Ogdensburg Declaration, the Permanent Joint Board on Defence, from the very beginning, has done a good deal of 'picking and choosing' in establishing its jurisdictional boundaries. Thus, despite the declaration's assertion that the joint organization would 'consider in the broad sense the defense of the north half of the Western Hemisphere,' the board has always chosen to ignore the lands between southern Florida and the Equator and to concentrate on Canada, Newfoundland, Alaska, and continental United States. Similarly, because it recognized that important political issues were involved, during the entire wartime period it carefully avoided all discussions of Greenland. Apparently for the same reason it discussed only briefly the political future of St Pierre and Miquelon, the French islands off Canada's eastern coast. Also in recent years it has ignored such controversial topics as the Amchitka nuclear tests and Canadian participation in an ABM system. However, on several occasions it has adopted recommendations that have had only an indirect bearing on North American defence, as, for example, when it suggested during the war that the two countries construct facilities to improve ferrying services between North America and Europe.[1]

During the first eleven years of the board's existence each of its two national sections consisted of a civilian chairman, a representative from the country's foreign affairs department (who served as section secretary), and three or four armed services representatives. In 1951 the civilian representation was increased with the addition of a second member by both the Department of State and the Department of External Affairs. In 1973 both sections added officers of general rank from the policy branches of their respective defence departments. Also, in recent years the joint agency has afforded other interested departments an opportunity to send observers to its meetings, an opportunity that the Canadian Departments of Industry, Trade, and Commerce and of Transport have regularly utilized. In addition, since the mid-1950s service members have had assistants. Thus, when one adds the experts who frequently are brought in to participate in the discussions or to brief members, as many as twenty-five persons may be in attendance at a meeting.

Not surprisingly, the dominant members of the PJBD have usually been the chairmen, who, with the noteworthy exceptions of General A.G.L. McNaughton (chairman of the Canadian Section from 1945 to 1959) and Major General G.V. Henry (American Section chairman from 1948 to 1954), have all been civilians, an arrangement favoured by Roosevelt and King as one way of limiting the military's influence. Being appointed, as they are, from outside the public service, they have a freedom of action not enjoyed by the other members and, perhaps for that reason, 'also a greater responsibility.' Their main function is to do what they can to ensure 'that a broad view is taken of defence problems'; but they also lead discussions, try to keep them relevant, and, when possible, reconcile conflicting views.[2]

Significantly, aside from the chairmen, most board members have usually held other appointments as well. For example, during the latter part of his more than four and a half years of service on the PJBD (April 1941 to November 1945), Major General M.A. Pope served as military staff officer to the prime minister and military secretary of the War Committee; from August 1940 to November 1945 John D. Hickerson simultaneously served as secretary of the American Section of the board and as assistant chief of the Division of European Affairs of the Department of State; while H.L. Keenleyside headed up the American and Far Eastern Division of the Department of External Affairs while serving as a member of the board. This dual-position arrangement, in addition to effecting savings on salary expenditures, has enabled the members to render an extremely effective liaison service between their respective departments and the joint agency.

The chairman of the American Section is appointed by the president, and the other members of that section receive their appointments from the secretaries of defence and state. All of the Canadian members normally are named by the prime minister of the day.[3] Both the American and the Canadian representatives serve at the pleasure of the appointing authorities. There are, however, no known instances of members having been removed from the board for either disciplinary or political reasons.

As has been implied, the board has no permanent staff. Most of its secretarial work has always been done by the officially designated secretaries from the Departments of State and External Affairs. It is they who have the primary responsibility for preparing the agenda for the board's meetings and a summary of its discussions and decisions, for seeing that the necessary documentation is prepared by the appropriate members of the board, and for maintaining in each capital a file of documents and correspondence. In the United States, however, the Joint Chiefs of Staff also provide a military secretariat to handle administrative matters for the American Section, and the office of the senior United States Army member has regularly been a major repository of board records. In Canada, likewise, each represented department maintains its own documents and files.[4]

Formal joint meetings provide the medium through which most of the board's functions are discharged. The agency itself determines the frequency, date, and place of the sessions. Significantly, the number of meetings has varied widely from year to year. After its first meeting in August 1940, it met on the average once a month during the remainder of that year; in 1941 it met only eight times; in 1942, following American entry into the war, the number of meetings increased to eleven; thereafter, as the war moved farther from the Western Hemisphere and the initial problems were solved, the annual total declined to seven in 1943 and five both in 1944 and 1945. Since 1945 the number has varied from three to four a year, four being the general pattern.

Customarily, the meetings are held alternately in the United States and Canada. During the war the usual meeting places were New York and Montreal, although, in order to enable the members to study defence problems close at hand, one or more sessions were held in each of ten other cities. It likewise held one session aboard the s.s. *Princess Norah*, en route to Alaska, and one on an airplane between Winnipeg and Ottawa. Since 1948 the meeting sites have usually rotated between the defence establishments of the two countries. During the Diefenbaker era, as an economy move, Defence Minister Pearkes suggested that the agency confine its meetings to Ottawa, Washington, Montreal, and New York, but General McNaughton vigorously protested that the proposal was not only an unwarranted interference in the affairs of the board, but would, if implemented, result in the loss of intimacy in knowledge and of effectiveness of the board.[5] The minister did not press his proposal and the board continued its wide-ranging travels.

The PJBD's practice of largely avoiding the two capital cities as meeting places has been a matter of deliberate policy. Members like to get away from ringing telephones and office interruptions. They also want to be free of any conceivable governmental pressures. Thus members of the Canadian Chiefs of Staff Committee and the United States Joint Chiefs of Staff have never attended the board meetings, and embassy military liaison officers have never been involved in the board's discussions. All of this is, of course, in keeping with the attempts that have been made to guarantee the organization's independent position.[6]

Occasionally the board has met without the benefit of a formal agenda, the discussion being allowed to 'evolve as the occasion suggested.'[7] Generally, however, a formal agenda is prepared. Some items will be suggested by the military services or the foreign offices; other topics may be proposed by a defence minister, the prime minister, or the president. Most frequently, however, the topics are initiated by board members themselves. Regardless of its origin, each topic must be approved by both sections of the organization. Once agreement is reached regarding the topics, the agenda, along with the necessary documentation, is circulated to all members.

Since the sixth meeting, in October 1940, an important part of the documentation has been reports by the service members on the progress made in the implementation of plans for North American defence – plans that had been formulated by the board and approved by the two governments. The reports not only serve as gauges of progress but provide members with background information against which to consider any new proposals that may be advanced. During the war they served the additional function of giving the civilian members 'an opportunity to check on the progress being made in the implementation of decisions which, in some cases, had been reached against service objections.'[8]

Significantly, suggested solutions to many issues not infrequently are worked out in advance of the board meetings by another joint agency: the Military Cooperation Committee. The MCC, set up in 1946 under the auspices of the PJBD, originally consisted of service department representatives, Department of State and Department of External Affairs officials, and the secretary of the Canadian Cabinet Committee. In 1949 it was separated from the board and organized as strictly a military planning body, each section consisting of a chairman, a secretary, and six members from the defence services. Despite its change in status, it has continued to supplement the board's work by conducting studies – particularly on technical and coordination questions – and by making recommendations relative to military policy and planning to the PJBD for amendments and approval.[9]

The board has never followed the practice of keeping a verbatim record of its proceedings. Instead, it merely records in its *Journal* a summary of the more important discussions, along with complete texts of all decisions reached. No attempt is made to include in the record all topics considered or to indicate the various positions taken or the pro and con arguments. Instead, it simply sets down the main considerations involved and the decisions reached. Thus it is not surprising that Pierrepont Moffat, after spending a morning perusing summaries of a number of meetings, observed: 'They were not particularly interesting as by common consent a great deal of what is under discussion is not recorded unless there is an approximate meeting of minds.'[10]

Initially the *Journal* was drafted at the end of a meeting and then amended through correspondence. This, however, was so time-consuming that the board started the practice, still adhered to, of drafting the *Journal* during the course of the meeting and agreeing on its text before adjournment. After each meeting copies, with appended progress reports, are circulated to selected offices of both governments. Since many matters discussed by the board are highly classified, the *Journal* is circulated only on a 'need to know' basis, with a minimum of publicity.

The 'minimum publicity' rule is, in fact, one that has always characterized the board's activities. It was opposed at first by Fiorella H. La Guardia, flamboyant chairman of the American Section from 1940 to 1947, but was insisted upon by the notoriously cautious Mackenzie King.[11] By 1942 the mayor himself had become an ardent convert. This is strikingly revealed in the following excerpt from a letter written, in the mayor's inimitable style, to Archibald MacLeish, director of the newly created Office of Facts and Figures:

Please be assured that no extra labor will be placed on the shoulders of the Office of Facts and Figures by the Permanent Joint Board on Defense. This Board is composed of men who work and do not talk. They tend to business and do not go to cocktail parties. They are experienced officials and do not take advice from columnists. They are concerned in the successful prosecution of the war and not in newspaper publicity. Newfoundland, Puget Bay, Sault Sainte Marie, chain of airports to Alaska, exchange of information, radio code, transshipment of armed forces over each other's territory, command, military highway to Alaska – these are all some of the small incidents actually planned, studied, prepared, consummated and put into operation by the modest members of the Board without the benefit of publicity.

With kind personal regards, for more work and less talk, I am, with patience and fortitude ...[12]

Another principle that the board has consistently adhered to has been to conduct its meetings with a maximum of informality and with a free exchange of views. Unlike the International Joint Commission, the PJBD has no written 'Rules of Procedure.' In fact, the details of its own procedures have never been of any great concern to the board. Instead its emphasis has always been to establish within its membership a sentiment of mutual respect and confidence, in short, a climate favourable to a frank and thorough probing of common defence problems.

Theoretically, members are free agents, able to take whatever position they wish on a particular question. In reality, they are basically spokesmen for their respective governments. Almost always they will have discussed with their departmental colleagues – at least in general terms – all important matters likely to be brought up at a meeting. The briefs and documents that members present normally will have been read and approved by their section's top civil and military personnel. Thus, members generally have a reasonably good knowledge as to what will and what will not be acceptable to their respective governments and normally stay strictly within the limits of what they believe to be government policy.[13]

The agency's procedure is by way of discussion and agreement, never by vote. When differences arise, the members simply 'talk things out' or, if that proves impossible, carry the item over to the next meeting.[14] With one exception, all of its wartime conclusions were unanimous.[15] This is not to say that each member has always been satisfied with every board decision; rather it has meant that everyone has agreed that no other decision would be generally acceptable. For example, when the matter of the construction of a highway across Canada to Alaska was first considered by the board in November 1940, some of the Canadian members doubted that the prospective value of the road would justify the expenditure of the time, labour, money, and materials involved; consequently, the matter was temporarily shelved. When, however, the question was brought up again in 1942, and their American colleagues insisted that the road was urgently needed to move men and military supplies to Alaska, the Canadian members, 'for reasons of general policy,' lent their support to the endeavour.[16]

The more important wartime decisions of the board were embodied in its two basic defence plans and in thirty-three formal 'recommendations' to the two governments.[17] The recommendations covered, among other things: the exchange of information between the two sections of the board; the allocation and flow of material resources; a strengthening of the defences of Newfoundland and the Maritime provinces; the preparation of a detailed plan for the joint defence of Canada and the United States; the completion of both Canadian and American sections of the airway to Alaska; the construction of a highway to Alaska; the carrying out of cooperative measures for strengthening the defences of the Sault Ste Marie canals and locks; and the construction and maintenance of essential highways in Newfoundland. The board also submitted one formal report, in November 1940, containing detailed recommendations for improving the defences on both the Atlantic and the Pacific coasts. Since 1947 the formal recommendation procedure, always somewhat ponderous, has been less frequently used. If the governments want something done, the usual procedure is to refer the matter to the board; the board submits a brief, informal report; on the basis of the report, the governments take appropriate actions.[18]

Not surprisingly, oftentimes the board takes no definite position on the matters it discusses. The two sections explain their points of view and go over possible ways of meeting the difficulties. Later, back in their respective capitals, the members 'may then influence thinking and bring forward the point of view held by the members of the other Section.'[19]

The Canadian cabinet system seems to have lent itself to a more systematic processing of the board's wartime recommendations than did the American system. The Canadian Section reported to the Cabinet War Committee, presided over by the prime minister. After the advice of the Canadian chiefs of staff had been obtained, the committee would take appropriate actions. The American Section generally reported directly to the president. Usually La Guardia first obtained the concurrence of the interested executive departments and then submitted the board's recommendations to President Roosevelt for approval. For a time, however, he sent them directly to the president, who might, if he were so inclined, obtain the views of the appropriate department heads. In the postwar period the usual practice in both countries, has been for the recommendations or conclusions of the board to go directly to the interested departments.

The board, of course, merely recommends courses of action. It is for the two governments to decide whether to accept its recommendations. Usually they have chosen to do so. In fact, of the board's thirty-three wartime recommendations, all but one was accepted and implemented by the two governments.[20] During the period 1945–51 its record was equally good, but from early 1958 to early 1963 – the period covered by the nuclear weapons issue and the deterioration of Canadian–American relations – the board submitted a number of recommendations and suggestions which were either ignored or rejected by the Diefenbaker government.[21] With, however, the formation of the Pearson government, the agency's recommendations again regularly received prompt, favourable attention.

Not surprisingly, among students of Canadian–American affairs many widely divergent viewpoints may be found with respect to both the manner in which the board conducts its proceedings and its actual achievements. For example, one view is that over the years the joint agency has been little more than a 'briefing club for the enlightment and persuasion of Canadian generals and diplomats' – a place 'where Canadians meet Americans so the Americans can tell us what they intend to do and we can say Yessir.'[22] Another, radically different, viewpoint is that the national representatives meet on a basis of complete equality, with 'full, frank and free' discussions and equal regard for the views and interests of both countries.

The facts of the matter are that the amount of influence that each country exerts in the PJBD meetings depends in part upon the political and technological circumstances of the day and the qualities of mind and will of the individual members. Thus during the late fifties and early sixties, when the United States felt a special need for radar screens and interceptor bases in the Canadian North, Canadian views undoubtedly carried much weight. By contrast, in the late sixties and the seventies, as the usefulness of such installations declined with the gradual replacement of bombers by intercontinental missiles, Canadian views probably carried appreciably less weight. Similarly, during the fourteen years that General McNaughton served as chairman of the Canadian Section, the Canadian input probably was greater than it has been in any other period of the board's history. Because of his wide knowledge and experience, his strongly held opinions, and the high esteem in which he was quite generally held, McNaughton, we are assured, exerted 'tremendous influence' not only over 'the American military members on the Board, but also on American military thinking in Washington,'[23] For example, it was under his leadership that the Canadian Section was able to play a significant role in obtaining a modification favoured by Canada of the Anglo-American bases agreement of 1941 relating to Newfoundland, and it was largely through his efforts that the St Lawrence Seaway and Power Project was debated and approved by the board.[24]

Oftentimes, however, the principal role of the Canadian representatives has been that of cautioning their American colleagues against hasty or ill-advised actions or of insisting on safeguards to protect Canadian sovereignty. This defensive Canadian position is partly the result of the wide disparities between the two countries, particularly the much greater resources of military intelligence, technology, and systems analysis that the Americans have at their command. During the years 1942–4 a second factor, undoubtedly, was the concern that many Canadians came to feel over the influx of thousands of American soldiers and civilians into the Canadian Northwest, causing King, Vincent Massey, and other influential persons to conclude that Canadians would need to be particularly alert or they would lose effective control over large areas of their country. This concern abated somewhat in the final months of the war but revived with the renewal of active defence cooperation in 1946–7.[25] A third factor is that the PJBD has sometimes been used simply as 'a channel for securing Canadian consent to projects which the Americans wanted to carry out on Canadian territory.'[26] Thus in the nature of things the discussions have at times tended to be largely American proposals followed by Canadian reactions. If the Canadian response is not immediately forthcoming or is non-committal, American members have been known to resort to pressure tactics. For example, in 1942, in a letter to President Roosevelt commenting on the 'Crimson' project then before the board (a scheme for ferrying aircraft to Britain from the United States through airfields to be built in the Canadian North), LaGuardia made the following revealing comments:

The plan ... challenges imagination. It is so gigantic and dramatic. It took our Canadian colleagues by surprise and frankly they have not yet recovered. We recessed until Monday and we must put it through on that day as every day now is precious.

We may encounter the usual difficulties because of pride and the little brother attitude with which you are familiar.

There is a remote chance that I may need your help Monday to get a phone call through to the Premier.[27]

The impasse feared by the mayor did not materialize, but his letter suggests that 'railroading' is not confined to the halls of Congress.

In contrast, the Canadian Working Committee on Post-Hostilities Problems, created in 1944, thought Canada should continue membership in the PJBD 'where the tradition of equality is established and where the Canadian case may be frankly stated.'[28] General Pope asserts that during the 1940s board discussions normally were conducted 'in an atmosphere of cordial understanding';[29] and John Swettenham states that, although General McNaughton at times spoke with such frankness and bluntness as to 'shock' the secretary of the Canadian Section, differences were always 'faced in a forthright manner and smoothed away.'[30] No less significantly,

Keenleyside has written that when divisions of opinion occurred during the war years they seldom were along strictly national lines. 'Thus, it was not unusual to find Canadian and United States army representatives united in argument with Canadian and United States naval officers. Or some or all of the service personnel from both sides might be found opposing the views of the civilian members.'[31]

The one, and apparently only, occasion of the wartime period when tempers flared and divisions were drawn along national lines was in the spring of 1941 when the American representatives on the board tried to persuade the Canadian members to accept a Canada–United States defence plan that, upon American entry into the war, would have vested in the chief of staff of the United States Army the 'strategic direction' of the land and air forces of the two countries. The Canadian members indicated that they would be prepared to accept such an arrangement if Britain were overrun or if the Royal Navy lost control of the North Atlantic. They refused, however, to recommend to their government such an arrangement under more favourable circumstances, that is, the entry of the United States into the war and no actual threat of an Axis attack upon North America. When the American spokesmen persisted in pushing for American strategic direction under both contingencies, a 'first class row' ensued.[32] By an exchange of correspondence, LaGuardia and Biggar attempted to clear the air but only succeeded in raising the temperature by several degrees. LaGuardia suggested that it would be 'far better to trust to the honor of the United States than to the mercy of the enemy.' Biggar replied: 'Canada is all out in the war: The United States is not – yet. The time is therefore a very unpropitious one for it to be suggested that Canada should surrender to the United States what she has consistently asserted vis-a-vis Great Britain.'[33] In the end, however, goodwill and common sense prevailed. The American members had to be content with a defence formula which affirmed: 'Coordination of the military effort of the United States and Canada shall be effected by mutal cooperation, and by assigning to the forces of each nation tasks for whose execution such forces shall be primarily responsible.'[34]

What of the board's record? Has it justified the hopes of its creators? Although some fairly serious indictments (which will be considered later) have been brought against it, the author's general conclusion is that the board has done, and continues to do, a very creditable job. This conclusion is based in part on the thirty-three wartime recommendations of the board discussed above and in part on other of its activities, some of which are summarized in the following pages.

It was, of course, the intention of the board's creators that it perform only advisory functions. It would not operate as a planning organ. It would in no sense serve as a combined staff or as a rival of the military attachés in Washington and in Ottawa. It would have no executive or operational responsibilities. It would merely study and make recommendations for the improvement of defence arrangements between the two countries.[35]

As has been indicated, the board has, in truth, performed numerous investigatory-advisory functions, but its activities have not ended there. For example, during the year and fourteen weeks that elapsed between the board's opening meeting on 26 August 1940 and the Japanese attack on Pearl Harbor of 7 December 1941, the board discharged an important planning function – concerning itself with the preparation of defence plans for North America and Newfoundland. Following American entry into the war, and the assumption by military bodies of most planning responsibilities, the organization's concern with plans came to be confined largely to the political and economic implications involved in their execution.[36]

During the pre-Pearl Harbor period, the board's work, we are assured, was also 'of great importance in coordinating the defence plans of the two countries, promoting "a harmony of sentiment throughout the New World" with respect to the common enemy, and in identifying the Canada–United States defence undertakings ... with the wider issues of the war.'[37] After 7 December 1941 – especially following the establishment in Washington, in July 1942, of the Canadian Joint Staff, representing the Canadian chiefs of staff – the joint agency's coordination role became less significant. But the fact that the service members were in close contact with the chiefs of staff of their respective countries, and that, after 5 June 1943, the chairman of the Canadian Section was allowed to appear at meetings of the War Committee of the Canadian Cabinet, gave the board continuing usefulness as a coordinating body. Thus it is perhaps no exaggeration to say that 'throughout ... the war, the Defence Board continued to operate as the chief instrument for the direct coordination of the defensive military policies of the two countries.'[38]

Another non-advisory function the board has discharged with skill and effectiveness has been that of pushing for the implementation of its recommendations and for the expediting of North American defence in other ways, the rationale being that 'the Board has the duty to constantly review the situation and if any of its suggestions have not been acted upon it can draw this situation to the attention of the President and the Prime Minister.'[39] Most board chairmen, be it noted, have never been backward in appealing directly to the chief executives when action has seemed imperative.

For example, during the war, whenever an American agency or individual failed to carry out a board recommendation, Mayor LaGuardia would fly down to Washington and, 'utilizing his personal friendship with President Roosevelt and supported by his political influence in a major State,' would invariably return to the board 'with the desired directive in his pocket.'[40]

Until 1958 the chairman of the Canadian Section enjoyed comparable easy access to the Canadian prime minister and other ministers. In fact in 1954 General G.G. Simonds complained that McNaughton had 'a more ready access to senior cabinet ministers' than had the chiefs of staff, which was probably true.[41] During the Diefenbaker era, the chairman's access to the prime minister became appreciably less easy, but other ministers continued to be readily accessible.[42] This relative freedom to meet and to converse with the top political leaders has given the chairman of both sections an exceptional opportunity to influence policy – an opportunity that the more dynamic and self-assured chairmen, such as LaGuardia and McNaughton, have taken full advantage of.

Much of the expediting, understandably enough, has been engaged in by individual members acting on their own initiative. For example, in 1942, feeling that RCAF measures to provide air reinforcements for Alaska were inadequate, Lt. Gen. Stanley D. Embick, the United States Army member of the board, telephoned Air Commodore F.V. Heakes, the RCAF member, and asked him to arrange for quicker action, which was promptly done.[43] Similarly, in the spring of 1941, when both Canada and the United States were developing their respective facilities in Newfoundland, Lt. Col. Clayton Bissell, the American Army Air Force member, telephoned from Washington to General Maurice Pope, Canadian Army member of the board, in Ottawa, and asked if Canada would lend the United States half a million feet of the lumber the Canadian armed forces had at St John's. Pope said he would make inquiry and ring back. He called the Canadian Army engineers, who, in effect, said 'can do,' after which Pope phoned Bissell: 'Clayton, the lumber is yours.' The entire transaction began and ended in not more than eight minutes.[44]

Between meetings members are, in fact, in continuous contact with their opposite numbers through an exchange of letters, phone calls, and visits. Because most of them also hold responsible positions in government agencies, they are ideally situated not only to determine the dominant viewpoint within their individual departments but also to perform negotiating, as well as expediting, functions. Not surprisingly, board members have had a hand in the negotiation of most of the scores of agreements relating to defence matters signed by the two governments during the past thirty years.

A rather special wartime service of the PJBD was in formulating recommendations setting forth principles governing the disposal of American-owned equipment and American-built installations on Canadian soil. One of these, its 28th Recommendation, provided that, within a year after hostilities ceased, immovable installations were to be relinquished to the Canadian government, while movable facilities were to be removed or sold. This became the basis for a formal exchange of notes on 23 and 27 June 1944,[45] which helped appreciably to ease Canadian concern that at the end of the war the Americans might refuse to relinquish the advantages that they had obtained from their wartime expenditures.[46]

But, undoubtedly, the board's most significant function has always been that of collecting and exchanging information and serving as a forum for the frank and detailed discussion of defence issues. Drawing upon the great reservoir of personal friendships and mutual confidences built up over the years, members have been able to explore, without bitterness or rancour, the most sensitive of issues, oftentimes bringing to light some point on which there had previously been a lack of understanding. Moreover, by studying potentially controversial questions before either government has determined its policy, the board has often been able to anticipate difficulties and frequently to point the way to satisfactory solutions. The agency has also proved useful for testing ideas and, if found impracticable, for quickly rejecting proposed solutions.[47]

Many factors, it is generally agreed, have contributed to the success of the joint agency. These include the prestige and experience that it has acquired over the years, the spirit of goodwill and confidence built up among its members through their long and intimate contacts, the flexibility and expeditiousness of its proceedings, and its demonstrated ability to alter its functions, composition, and procedures in accordance with the needs and circumstances of the day. Still another factor, Wilgress and other observers insist, has been the board's mixture of military and civilian membership, enabling it to 'reconcile the conflict between military necessity and political expediency.'[48] The service members provide the essential expertise, while the civilian members make sure that the political and economic aspects of military cooperation are not overlooked. This is, of course, of special importance to Canada, the smaller member of the North American alliance, determined as it is to preserve its national sovereignty.[49]

The most significant achievements of the board, it is generally admitted, were attained during the early years of the war when, according to one writer, it shaped 'all the more important decisions regarding Canadian–

United States defence policies.'[50] But its contributions to North American defence have by no means been confined to the wartime years. As is indicated in the following chapter, during the years 1945–7 it was very much involved with formulating a workable basis for Canadian–American postwar defence collaboration.[51] Immediately thereafter it devoted literally dozens of meetings to such matters as weapons testing; the standardization of arms and equipment; the interchange of military observers and technical information; the planning of joint land, air, and naval exercises; the construction of LORAN and weather forecasting installations; the building of radar screens across the northern part of the continent; the launching of the North American Air Defence Command (NORAD) and the Canadian–American Defence Production and Development Sharing programs.[52]

With the creation in 1949 and afterwards of other intergovernmental agencies with an interest in North American defence, the board's usefulness as an advisory-coordinating-expediting agency suffered a marked decline. Moreover, with the present emphasis on intercontinental missiles and air defence in general (matters handled largely by the national military staffs), it seems highly improbable that the PJBD will ever again occupy a key position in the defence of North America. Nevertheless, the agency continues to render numerous useful services, particularly 'in assuring that the medium- and long-range plans for the defence of North America of each of the two governments are formulated in full knowledge of, and in harmony with, the other's plans and thinking.' In addition, it 'is also frequently seized of bilateral defence problems that may have political implications and thus cannot be solved at the strictly military level by the Military Co-operation Committee.'[53] Unless similar alternative machinery is created, it is likely to continue to be needed as long as the two countries choose to cooperate closely in matters of common defence.

Despite its demonstrated usefulness, the board has always had its critics. For example, in March 1941 C.D. Howe complained that the board was exceeding its authority when it discussed the question of the entry of new air transport lines into Canada from the United States.[54] A couple of months later the acting under-secretary of state for external affairs indicated dissatisfaction with the manner in which the joint agency was dealing with 'the whole Newfoundland situation.' The 'weight of the Service members and their concentration on purely military problems,' he stated, might cause the board to lose sight of the political aspects.[55] Near the close of the war academic observers contended that the board's propensity for secrecy had contributed on some occasions to the spreading of rumours, based on flimsy information, and on other occasions to the growth of popular dissatisfaction with the agency's seeming inactivity.[56] In the 1950s a retired Canadian general charged that the board's existence added 'confusion' to the direction of Canadian military affairs since it 'acts as a barrier to closer liaison between the Canadian and U.S. Chiefs of Staff and is redundant insofar as its military activities are concerned.'[57] Recently Professors Creighton, Warnock, and other academic critics have denounced the board, along with NORAD and other Canadian–American military agencies, as contributing to the growth of 'continentalism' and Canada's position as a satellite of the United States.[58]

It would, no doubt, be difficult if not impossible to prove or disprove most of the above charges. There can, however, be no doubt that the Ogdensburg agreement and the board have contributed significantly to the creation of the new balance of power that numerous Canadians since 1940 have found disturbing. The old balance, built around Britain, cannot be restored; whether any new counterbalance can be found for the overwhelming weight of the United States remains to be determined.[59]

Shortly after NATO's establishment in 1949, a joint meeting of the Canadian and the American chiefs of staff discussed the feasibility of transferring to that organization all the planning measures discharged by the PJBD.[60] For reasons that will be indicated later, American spokesmen opposed such a move and the decision was taken to continue defence planning under the auspices of the board. Since that time other proposals for the board's abolition have been advanced from time to time. Most of these have come from persons who favour Canada's withdrawal from all Canadian–American defence arrangements. Occasionally, however, they have come from critics who, disturbed at the relative inactivity of the board and the lack of vigour and enterprise on the part of one or the other of the joint chairmen, have concluded that the board has outlived its usefulness and should therefore be speedily dispatched and given a decent burial.

In their report of 1965 Merchant and Heeney suggested that the joint defence organ 'could be more fully utilized to the mutual advantage' of both countries. Following the presentation of the report, and especially after Heeney's appointment as chairman of the Canadian Section, a determined attempt was made to implement this particular recommendation. At American initiative, the board was utilized in 1968 as a forum for an extensive discussion not only of NORAD's renewal but also of American plans for the construction of a limited anti-ballistic missile system. Recently it has discussed such diverse topics as the terms of reference for NORAD's commander-in-chief, a continued American presence at Goose

Bay after the withdrawal of the Strategic Air Command Wing, the renewal of the Nanoose Bay torpedo range agreement, and the designation of a single property manager for some surplus land at the United States Naval Station at Argentia, Newfoundland.

However, still more needs to be done to increase the board's usefulness. For one thing, more issues could be submitted to it for study and report. For example, a comprehensive joint study of all the implications of a North American ABM system should have been useful to both governments. In the second place, all issues falling within the competence of the board should be submitted before they become critical or charged with public controversy. In the third place, the relationship between the board and NATO – especially between the board and the Canada–United States Regional Planning Group – should be clarified. In the fourth place, the military services representatives should be permitted to retain their board positions for longer periods of time than has been the usual practice. This would enable them to acquire greater familiarity with continental defence problems and with their Canadian or American counterparts.[61] Finally, the two governments must not succumb, as they have on a few occasions in the past, to the temptation of retaining in ofice elderly gentlemen, sometimes in failing health, simply out of regard for their sensibilities and their earlier distinguished careers. Even though the chairmanship of a section is a part-time job, it can be effectively filled only by an individual who, in addition to commanding the confidence and respect of his government and board colleagues, is fortified by good health and an abundance of energy.

11

Cold-war defence cooperation: organizations and activities

At the June 1945 meeting of the Permanent Joint Board on Defence, devoted largely to a discussion of Canadian–American postwar defence cooperation, General G.V. Henry, senior United States Army member, suggested: (1) that Canada become a member of the 'military family of American nations' envisaged in the Act of Chapultepec; (2) that the board examine the continuing value to North American defence of the facilities developed during the war in Northwest Canada; and (3) that serious thoughts be given to the standardization of Canadian and American equipment and forces.[1] The reply of the Canadian Section, given by General A.G.L. McNaughton at the September 1945 meeting of the board, was: (1) that participation in the inter-American military system was a political question; (2) that the value of the facilities in the Canadian Northwest might very well be included in a general military estimate of the situation in northern North America; and (3) that a real case for standardization of material and organization between Canada and the United States could be made only if it were part of a larger program of standardization and coordination of military supply operations between the United States and the British Commonwealth as a whole.[2]

Both sections of the board agreed, however, that it would be helpful if both a new appreciation of North American defence requirements and a revised Canadian–American defence plan – to replace the wartime plan, ABC-22 – were prepared. The chiefs of staff of both countries agreed. Accordingly, on the concurrence of the board and the approval of the two governments, in February 1946 the Military Cooperation Committee (briefly discussed earlier) was established and by late spring of that year had completed its twofold task.

The committee's appreciation began by referring to North America's deteriorating defensive position. Before the war the broad oceans and the wide expanses of the Arctic had guaranteed immunity from direct attack. Now that immunity was being 'whittled away' by technological advances in weapon construction and delivery. By 1950 the enemy (unnamed but unmistakably the Soviet Union) would be able to launch all-out attacks on the populated centres of Canada and the United States, using not only long-range bombers armed with atomic weapons but also rockets and guided missiles launched both from submarines and from Arctic bases seized for that purpose. As a deterrent and a defence against such contingencies, the joint estimate recommended

that Canada and the United States cooperate in the construction of an effective air defense system including early warning, meteorological, and communications apparatus, a network of air bases deployed as far forward as possible from probable targets, sufficient numbers of fighter interceptor aircraft to inflict unacceptable damage upon the attacker, and adequate anti-aircraft defenses suitably deployed. In addition to the air defense system, the requirements for North American defense were said to include: (1) a program of air mapping and photography; (2) air and surface surveillance to give warning of infiltration or attack; (3) anti-submarine patrol and naval patrol of the sea approaches; (4) garrison and mobile forces to defend against lodgments; and (5) a command structure suitable to the needs of joint Canadian–American defense of the continent. All these, the planners considered essential, but the most urgent measure was the air defense system.[3]

The committee's Basic Security Plan, dated 5 June 1946, outlined the joint tasks which would need to be undertaken by the armed forces of the two countries, together with the division of responsibility for those tasks, and contained brief sections on implementation, preparatory measures, coordination, cooperation, and revision. Significantly, the PJBD was assigned the task of carrying out a periodic review of all revisions.

The appreciation and the plan were approved by the Canadian chiefs of staff and by the appropriate authorities in Washington. The Canadian cabinet, however, was not inclined to accept such an integrative program. As King and his advisers pointed out, implementation of the committee's proposals would cost a great deal of money, money that Canada could ill afford to devote to defence. Nor were they greatly enthusiastic over an American suggestion that the United States might be prepared 'to assume an equitable proportion of the cost' of the facilities located on Canadian soil.[4] Under the constraints of war, the prime minister had permitted the Americans greater control over facilities in the northern and northwestern parts of Canada than either he or his close advisers had thought desirable.[5] The wartime cooperation had left a legacy of 'Canadian aversion to the presence of American forces in Canada and extreme sensitivity to the potential derogation of Canadian sovereignty.'[6] The American proposals, it was feared, would make deep inroads upon Canadian territory and possibly Canadian resources. Both the appreciation and the security plan had been based primarily on American intelligence. With neither the appreciation nor the American proposals for air defence were the Canadian General Staffs in complete agreement.[7] There was also the objection, King averred, that the security plan was too bilateral. It was most important that there be 'the fullest exchange of views with the British on the whole question of defence.' It was equally important that nothing be done that might properly be viewed by the Soviet Union as provocative.[8]

The Canadian authorities did, however, agree that the continent was in truth, as Pentagon spokesmen insisted, 'wide open at the top'; that Soviet bombers and submarines did present a potential threat to North America; that Canada, acting alone, could not do what was necessary to protect itself; that Canada could derive definite benefits from cooperating in matters of defence with its powerful neighbour to the south; and that, in any event, since the Americans insisted that Canadian cooperation was essential to their own security, it would be inadvisable for the Canadian government to return a totally negative reply.[9] Accordingly, the prime minister did what he frequently did when confronted with a difficult decision: he simply procrastinated. At a cabinet meeting, held 9 May 1946, he asserted that he would not let the Canadian council accept the committee's proposals or a related PJBD recommendation (examined below) until after he had 'had a chance to discuss aspects of them with the British.'[10] The following month, after having talked with Attlee, Lord Addison, and Ismay in London, he advised his colleagues that the British had 'admitted that they could not hope to hold their own against Russia without the aid of the U.S.' He then added that it would be necessary 'to re-orient all our ideas about protection.' Nevertheless, he still thought that the 'whole matter needed the fullest possible discussion' and that the cabinet should not 'be rushed in settlement on what was to be done.'[11]

By late summer it was obvious to concerned persons on both sides of the boundary that if the continental defence issue was to be satisfactorily resolved it would have to be dealt with 'at the very highest level.'[12] In October King travelled to Washington for conversations with President Harry S. Truman. He assured the president that his government would be willing to cooperate with the United States on common defence problems, but 'had to watch particularly the question of our sovereignty.' He suggested that the whole question of publicizing cooperative moves should be carefully considered, care being taken 'not to give the Russians a chance to say we were trying to fight them.' The outcome of the conference was an understanding that further steps to work out defence plans would be 'taken up through Ministers and on a diplomatic level rather than by the services.'[13]

The suggested further steps were taken in December when nine high-ranking officials from the u.s. Departments of State and Defense travelled to Ottawa for lengthy discussions with eight top-level Canadian civil servants on various aspects of the continental defence issue. The Americans, while admitting that the Russians probably were not planning a direct attack on North America, emphasized the great danger of a 'misunderstanding or miscalculation' and urged the importance of advance planning and preparations. At the same time, they indicated a good understanding of the political problems that defence cooperation raised for Canada and suggested that early cooperative moves emphasize mapping and meteorology. The Canadians, for their part, impressed with the moderation of the American position and genuinely eager to be helpful, agreed that cooperation could and should proceed along the lines indicated by the American spokesmen.[14]

While the extended debate over the Military Cooperation Committee's Security Plan was in progress American spokesmen, mainly in the PJBD, were pressing Canada for other important, politically difficult concessions. These included: the maintenance by the United States of substantial permanent air forces, including heavy bomber groups, at the base at Goose Bay, Labrador (rented from Newfoundland by Canada); the opening of new weather stations in the Arctic islands; the continued operation by the United States of existing weather stations in Northeastern Canada; the operation of the Northwest Staging Route; the maintenance in a serviceable condition of far northern air fields; and the provision of facilities for various exercises and training programs in Canadian territory. The Canadian authorities agreed to permit their defence-obsessed neighbours to continue to operate (and in some cases to reopen) weather stations and some airfields established during the war, but deferred decisions with respect to Goose Bay, some airfields, and the establishment of new far northern weather stations.[15]

Especially disturbing to the authorities in Ottawa was Washington's vigorous pressure for Canadian acceptance of a list of general principles of continental defence cooperation recommended by the PJBD in November

1945, which some of King's advisers thought highly unsatisfactory. For example, Heeney suggested that the proposals went 'far beyond a working paper for the instruction of joint planners' and contained 'a number of fundamental military obligations.'[16] Later the board toned down the document, which eventually emerged as its 35th Recommendation. It called for 'close cooperation' between the armed forces of the two countries with respect to the interchange of military personnel, standardization of equipment and methods of training, joint manoeuvres and tests, reciprocal use of military facilities, national mapping and surveying, and free and comprehensive exchange of military information.

The amended draft was acceptable to the Canadian Chiefs of Staff Committee, as well as to the authorities in Washington, but met with vigorous opposition from the Canadian cabinet. Warned by Hume Wrong that approval of the recommendation might be interpreted both at home and abroad as equivalent to a Canadian–American alliance directed at the Soviet Union and as an obstacle to cooperation with Commonwealth countries, the ever-wary prime minister concluded that he would delay action on the recommendations until after he had had a chance to discuss defence questions with the British.[17]

As noted above, King had his talk with the British authorities, but he still withheld his approval of the 35th Recommendation. In the end it was a compromise proposed by the American members of the PJBD that opened the way to affirmative Canadian action. This was additions to the recommendation that defence projects were to be under the supervision of the country in whose territory they were carried out and were to confer no permanent rights or status to the other country. On 14 November the prime minister obtained the cabinet's approval of the revised recommendation and the following day secured 'renewed approval' of the document.[18]

The key question then became whether the newly approved principles of cooperation should or should not be publicized. Wrong, concerned over likely unfriendly Soviet reaction, recommended against publicity. Official Washington was also opposed to any public references to the recommendation. King and his cabinet colleagues, however, believed that the recommendation should be publicized.[19] With them a major consideration appears to have been a desire to correct the distortions that had appeared in the newspapers both in the Soviet Union and in North America regarding the defence talks and agreements. On the one hand, it had been reported that large-scale defence projects were being constructed in the Canadian North, and, on the other hand, that the American government had demanded military bases in the North and had been turned down by Ottawa.[20]

Parliament was soon to reconvene and Opposition members were certain to insist on a government statement on defence. To clear the atmosphere, publication of the recommendation seemed imperative. Reluctantly the American officials agreed; accordingly, on 12 February 1947 the gist of the new accord was outlined in a joint statement released simultaneously in Ottawa and Washington.[21]

The statement explained that 'in the interests of efficiency and economy' the two countries had decided to continue the wartime collaboration of their national defence establishments in the postwar period 'for peacetime joint security purposes.' The collaboration, which would 'necessarily be limited,' would be based on the following principles: (1) exchange of officers and men so as to familiarize each country with the military establishment of the other; (2) cooperation and exchange of observers in connection with the development and tests of material of common interest; (3) encouragement of common designs and standards in arms, equipment, organization, and methods of training; (4) mutual and reciprocal availability of military, naval, and air facilities in each country; (5) each country to continue to provide for the transit through its territory and territorial waters of military aircraft and public vessels of the other country; and (6) as an underlying principle, all cooperative arrangements to be carried on without impairment of the control of either country over all activities within its own territory. Each country would determine the extent of its collaboration and either might at any time discontinue collaboration on any or all of the six principles.

Implementation of the joint statement may be said to have got under way the following month with the announcement by C.D. Howe that during the next three years Canada would build nine new weather stations[22] above the Arctic Circle. The stations would be under Canadian control, but the United States would contribute to their cost and maintenance and would supply some trained personnel. A few weeks later the Canadian public was informed that the government had accepted a recommendation of the PJBD for the establishment of two 'lighthouses' in the Far North equipped with LORAN (long-range aids to navigation). In July 1947 extensive conversations were conducted among American, Canadian, and British personnel looking towards the standardization of arms and equipment. Early autumn found numerous Canadian, as well as British, officers and men attending American Army, Navy, and Air Force schools and colleges, while a limited number of Americans were in attendance at similar institutions in Canada and Britain. By early 1948 the interchanging of military observers and technical information had become a regular practice. Later that year units of the Canadian and the American navies engaged in joint exercises in the vicinity of Pearl Harbor. In February 1949 the press reported that arrangements were being worked out for the construction of a vast radar and aircraft interceptor network across North America.[23] In short, the two North American neighbours, with their British ally, seemed to be 'going all out' in their efforts to strengthen their own defences and, indirectly, those of the Free World in general.

Appearances, however, were deceptive. Even as early as 1949 certain deficiencies in the joint effort were glaringly apparent. Other deficiencies would eventually make their appearance. Of the deficiencies of 1949 one of the most striking was the absence of adquate machinery for coordinating the defence efforts of the various countries of the North Atlantic area. Confronted by Soviet expansionism, each country had made a modest attempt to build up its own defence forces, but nothing had been done to coordinate the individual efforts. In an attempt to remedy this situation, Britain, Canada, and the United States sponsored the creation of the North Atlantic Treaty Organization (based on a treaty signed 4 April 1949), committed to 'collective defense ... for the preservation of peace and security.'[24]

As integral parts of the new organization's elaborate intergovernmental machinery, five regional planning groups were set up to formulate military plans for the defence of the various regions. One of these was the Canada–United States Regional Planning Group, charged by the NATO Council 'with the responsibility for planning the defence of North America, and for providing strategic support and reserves for the NATO forces in Europe.'[25]

Significantly, at a meeting called in January 1950 to consider the steps necessary to establish the Canada–United States Group, the Canadian and the American chiefs of staff discussed the wisdom and feasibility of transferring all of the Permanent Joint Board on Defence's planning functions to NATO. The American spokesmen expressed strong opposition to such a move. The Joint Board, they pointed out, was set up to perform permanent defence planning functions, whereas NATO was based on a twenty-year treaty. The jurisdiction of the board extended to the Pacific Ocean, as well as to the Atlantic, whereas the Pacific was excluded from NATO's defence area. There were also grounds for doubting whether the European allies should be allowed access to American intelligence, research, and development information. There was the further danger, the American authorities contended, that if the air defence of North America 'became a NATO matter, and the extent of the facilities allotted to continental defence was revealed to the European partners, pressure could develop to strengthen the European defences at the expense of North American defence.' Most important of all, the air-defence forces were so closely linked to the protection of the American Strategic Air Force that any multilateral control of the protection of that force might lead to attempts to control it. Although the Canadian chiefs of staff were under political pressure to bring North American defence measures directly under NATO control, they accepted the logic of these arguments and went along with the American view. The final result was that continental defence planning continued to be the responsibility of the PJBD and the Military Cooperation Committee.[26]

This, however, was not the end of proposals to link up NATO more closely with North American defence. The matter was raised again in 1952, when the NATO Council decided that all of the European regional planning groups should be converted into military commands, each headed by its own commander. When Canadian spokesmen suggested that perhaps the Canada–United States Regional Planning Group should also be converted into a NATO command, American representatives demurred.[27] Significantly, the European members of NATO showed no inclination to support the Canadian proposal, all of them seeming quite content to leave to Canada and the United States the defence of North America.[28] More interesting still, when the Canadian authorities came to realize that the introduction of the European pattern of command to North America would probably entail the appointment of an over-all American commander for all defence planning for both Canada and the United States, their enthusiasm for the proposal quickly subsided.[29] Thereafter little was heard of such talk until the creation of NORAD in 1957.[30]

Except that it has a separate chairman, the Canada–United States Regional Planning Group has the same membership as the Canada–United States Military Cooperation Committee.[31] To 1951 the Chiefs of Staff Committee of the group, composed of the Canadian Chiefs of Staff Committee and the United States Joint Chiefs of Staff, took an active part in the work of the organization. But in that year it delegated most of its duties to the Regional Planning Committee, a working group drawn from the office force of the chiefs of staff.

Through the years the Regional Planning Group and the Regional Planning Committee has each held an average of three meetings per year, sometimes in Europe in conjunction with the NATO Council meetings, sometimes in Ottawa, and sometimes in Washington. The group reports to NATO's Military Committee, which, in turn, reports to NATO's Defense

Committee and to its Standing Group. It is expected to keep NATO members fully informed regarding 'air and missile defense arrangements made by the United States and Canada, and more specifically by the military Cooperation Committee.'[32]

The chief usefulness of the Regional Planning Group, it is generally conceded, has been as a coordinating agency – to coordinate the regional interests of both countries in NATO and to keep Canadian–American plans for the defence of the North American continent, particularly against air attack, continuously under review.[33] For example, following the outbreak of the Korean War, the group held a five-day meeting at the Pentagon for the purpose of proposing changes in the master plan for North American defence. Although no details of the plan were divulged, a joint announcement stated that the Canadian–American blueprint was 'being coordinated, as appropriate, with other regional planning groups of the North Atlantic Treaty.'[34] The group, frequently through combined meetings with the Military Cooperation Committee, also played a part in planning the construction of the radar screens, built in 1953–7. Since that time it has continued to give continuous study to the defence plans of the North American region.

Despite its activities, most observers are of the opinion that the group has never been of any great significance.[35] This is due in part to the fact that its functions are quite limited; that it has no assigned forces or command functions and thus has very little to do. More importantly, the authorities in Washington have always made it emphatically clear that they do not wish to see the group's functions increased since they prefer to have most matters relating to North American defence handled by NORAD and other bilateral Canadian–American defence arrangements.

The period of the Cold War was to spawn other agencies to deal with Canadian–American defence problems: the Joint United States–Canada Industrial Mobilization Committee, created in 1949; the Joint United States–Canadian Civil Defence Committee, established in 1951; NORAD (the North American Air Defence Command), set up in 1957; the Canada–United States Ministerial Committee on Joint Defence, created in 1958; and the Senior Committee on Defence Production–Development Sharing, established in 1960. Each of these will be discussed in the following chapters. Here a few additional comments, in the nature of a summary evaluation, may be hazarded relative to the roles played respectively by the Military Cooperation Committee and the Permanent Joint Board on Defence in dealing with the matters discussed in the preceding pages.

On the credit side, it cannot be denied that the MCC carried out in a most expeditious manner the drafting of its military appreciation and its Basic Security Plan. Nor can it be denied that the members demonstrated a good understanding of the new technology of war that had made obsolete the concept of self-sufficiency for either North American country. However, because of their military training and their focusing too narrowly on strictly military questions, they gave inadequate attention to the hard facts of Canadian nationalism, Canadian politics, and the very real concern of King and his advisers over safeguarding Canadian sovereignty.[36] Because of these deficiencies, it is not surprising that it was the diplomats and top civil servants (more flexible in their approach and more aware of Canadian fears and misgivings than the military officers) rather than the MCC who were able to alleviate the Canadian concerns and open the way to Canada's acceptance of the appreciation and the security plan.[37]

The PJBD members (some of whom, it will be recalled, also serve on the MCC) likewise demonstrated a good knowledge of the new technology of war and the problems of North American defence. The board served as a very effective forum for discussing both the question of revising the Basic Security Plan and the matter of drafting guidelines to govern the peacetime defence cooperation of the two countries. But its original draft of what later became Recommendation 35 was not particularly to its credit. True, it quickly rectified that mistake and prepared a draft more in keeping with Canadian views and concerns. And, of course, it was the compromise brought forward by the American Section of the PJBD (designed to safeguard Canadian jurisdiction over its own territory) that produced a draft that Mackenzie King was later to label 'an important document,' and a far-reaching sequel to the meetings with Roosevelt, at Ivy Lea and later at Ogdensburg.[38] Thus, on balance, the board's record carried more credit than debit items.

12

NORAD: origin and agreement arrangements

Over the years champions of NORAD (the North American Air Defence Command) have insisted that the formal establishment of that integrated Canadian–American air defence headquarters was in no sense a radical innovation but merely 'the last step' in the coordination of the air defence of the continent that had been in progress since 1946.[1] Although there is, as will be indicated shortly, considerable validity to that argument, it should be noted that no cooperative Canadian–American moves have aroused greater Canadian concern and controversy than the establishment and continued maintenance of the joint air command. Some of the reasons will be considered later; here a few comments may be in order regarding the pre-NORAD coordinated efforts.

As we have already observed, several of the American proposals of the immediate postwar period for air defence cooperation were, when first presented, rejected by the Mackenzie King cabinet.[2] The prime minister did not like the bilateral nature of the proposals and their potential threat to Canadian sovereignty, and he and his advisers questioned the need for extensive air defence arrangements. Soviet bombers, they contended, were too limited in range and carrying capacity to pose any serious threats to North America. Furthermore, only the United States possessed atomic weapons. Thus for a time the prime minister agreed to only a modest cooperative effort. But the champions of a comprehensive Canadian–American air defence were both determined and persistent, and the course of events added weight to their arguments. In September 1949 came the explosion of an atomic device in the Soviet Union, followed shortly afterwards by the unveiling of Soviet long-range bombers. August 1953 brought the detonation of the first Soviet hydrogen bomb. Not only the populations and industries of North American but also SAC (the American Strategic Air Command), upon which the Western Powers principally rely for deterrence, now were vulnerable.

The emergence of this threat provoked a vigorous debate on air defence between the champions of offensive action and the proponents of defence. The first school of thought insisted that it was foolish to spend money on an air defence system since if even a few planes armed with atom bombs got through they would be capable of inflicting enormous devastation on North America. It would be much more sensible, they contended, to apply the money to strengthening and enlarging SAC, since 'SAC's ability to retaliate instantly and decisively against the U.S.S.R. remained the surest, perhaps the sole, guarantee against a central atomic attack by Moscow.'[3] The second school of thought, while agreeing that it was important to maintain an effective strategic deterrent force, insisted that it was also essential to protect SAC bases; otherwise, the Soviet Union might be tempted to launch a pre-emptive attack against both SAC and the population centres of North America.

Not surprisingly, for a time the United States Air Force spokesman accepted the doctrines of the offensive action school of thought and, accordingly, minimized the importance of such projects as civil defence and air surveillance and warning. Eventually, however, most of them concluded that, along with an increase in the offensive air power of the United States and Canada, it would also be helpful if the two countries mounted a major air defence program, involving the detection, tracking, and interception of enemy aircraft. Reluctantly and with deep misgivings, Prime Minister King and his cabinet colleagues eventually came to the same conclusion. Accordingly, between 1951 and 1957 the North American neighbours pooled their scientific and financial resources to build three electronic warning networks: (1) the Pinetree radar line, along the border, (2) the Mid-Canada electronic screen, along the 55th parallel, and (3) the Distant Early Warning radar line, extending from Alaska through Baffin Island along the 70th parallel. Later the three networks and other surveillance systems were linked up with semi-automatic ground environment control installations (SAGE) equipped with computers to give instant warning to the American and the Canadian air defence commands and to direct any battles that might need to be fought against manned bombers.[4] Agreements were also reached for coordinating the national air defence efforts with respect to such matters as consultations between the two national air force commanders, the adoption in many areas of similarity in control techniques and equipment, the entrance of American fighter squadrons into Canada for peacetime training, joint air exercises, and the exchange of information.

Airmen of both countries, however, insisted that much more was needed. In particular, they emphasized the need for an integrated command for the air defence of the continent. Their general line of argument was that the geographical area to be defended was so vast, the equipment and techniques to be employed so complicated, and the need for rapid decisions likely to be so urgent, that it simply did not make sense for Canada and the United States each to continue to maintain its own separate air command. They stressed that the existing arrangements were being rapidly outmoded by the increase in the speed of bombers, by the conversion of defence elements from manual to automatic control, and, in particular, by the newly constructed electronic networks. Only a single authoritative command, they insisted, would be able to take full advantage of these technological advances and, at the same time, engage in the joint planning that was so essential to an effective air defence.[5]

In 1953, immediately before retiring as chairman of the Joint Chiefs of Staff, General Omar Bradley recommended that a joint air command with Canada be set up. A year later Congressman Sterling Cole, chairman of the House Armed Services Committee, urged the establishment of Canadian–American defence arrangements comparable to those created by the NATO accord of 1949.[6] Although he received little support from the Eisenhower administration, the congressman did not abandon his campaign. Encouraged, no doubt, by the creation a few months earlier of the Continental Air Defense Command (giving the United States a unified North American air command), in January 1955 Cole repeated his recommendation to Secretary of Defense Wilson and Admiral Radford, chairman of the Joint Chiefs of Staff, upon their appearance before his committee. Both, however, thought it politically inexpedient to raise with the Canadians such a question at that time.[7]

Wilson and Radford had, of course, pinpointed a basic problem. For Canada, the proposal to establish a unified air defence command raised questions of major national and political significance. Since the United States, given its superior manpower, financial, and technological resources, could be expected to dominate such an organization, would its creation have an adverse effect upon Canadian sovereignty and independence? Would the Canadian people be willing to see their armed forces operating under American operational control? Did the government dare to take the inherent political risks?

In both countries the air defence commanders 'made vigorous represen-tations to their respective chiefs of staff regarding the inadequacy of the separated command structure.'[8] And in June 1955 Air Marshall C.R. Sle-mon, the Canadian Air Force commander, either deliberately, or unthink-ingly, helped to pressure the Canadian cabinet into making a decision when he publicly affirmed that a unified North American air command was 'inevitable.' The minister of national defence hastened to assure members of Parliament that Slemon was not speaking for the government but was simply stating a trend in military thought. The American neighbours were not pressing Canada to agree to the establishment of a supreme command. The two countries 'were working closely and harmoniously together and there was no need for any change.'[9] Despite these assurances, in May 1956 a Canada–u.s. Military Study Group – consisting of senior officials of the three services and scientific agencies of both countries – was set up to explore the operational and technical problems which might be expected to result from the establishment of a joint command. Not surprisingly, the study group recommended 'the establishment of a joint headquarters to provide for the operational control of the air defence of Canada and the United States.'[10] After minor modifications, the recommendations were approved early in 1957 by the chiefs of staff of both countries and by Secretary Wilson. Seemingly all that remained to be done was to obtain official Canadian approval and to put the integrated command into opera-tion, which the American Joint Chiefs of Staff hoped could be effected by mid-year, when the last of the electronic networks would be operational.

The Americans, however, had not taken into account the political situa-tion in Canada. A national election was in the offing; the Liberals were expected to be returned to power, but Prime Minister St Laurent and his advisers chose to take no unnecessary chances. Although the matter of approving the agreement had originally been placed on the agenda for the 15 March meeting of the Cabinet Defence Committee, it later was removed and was not discussed by the comittee or by the cabinet as a whole. The American authorities, however, were informed that this failure to consider the accord had not been due to any objections to it but rather to the preference of the ministers to postpone the cabinet discussions until after the election.[11]

The Liberals, of course, did not win the election; instead, it was the Conservative government of John Diefenbaker that had to decide whether or not to approve the integrated command arrangement. The new govern-ment, a critic has charged, 'handled the important agreement with slap-dash informality.'[12] And, in truth, the agreement appears to have been approved without much study or discussion on the part of the Conservative ministers. The course of events, apparently, was as follows. Immediately after the election, General Charles Foulkes, chairman of the Chiefs of Staff Committee, approached George Pearkes, the new minister of defence, with arguments for the early establishment of the integrated command. Pearkes, a military man, required no great amount of convincing. Like many of his fellow Canadians of that era, he was firmly convinced that the air defence of North American had become a single, indivisible problem and that Canada would be unable to remain neutral in an American–Russian war; accordingly, he readily endorsed the integrated command proposal and urged Diefenbaker to give it his prompt approval. The prime minister, after, at most, only informal consultation with other ministers, and without submitting the matter to the Cabinet Defence Committee or to the entire cabinet, agreed to convey the government's affirmative decision to Secretary of State Dulles upon his arrival in Ottawa on 27 July. On 1 August the two governments announced that they were that day establishing the North American Air Defence Command (NORAD) as an aid to the strengthening of the defensive forces of the continent.[13]

The prime minister's hasty action appears to have been due in part to his acceptance of advice that what was involved was 'a relatively unimportant agreement' – nothing more, in fact, than 'the latest in a series of improvements in the implementation of a policy which had long been agreed upon.'[14] A second factor seems to have been his belief that what he was doing was little more than implementing a decision of his predecessors.[15] Most important of all, undoubtedly, was the pressure exerted upon Pearkes and the prime minister by the top Canadian military leaders.

The Canadian military officials themselves, well informed observers are convinced, were under pressure from their American counterparts.[16] But it is doubtful that much pressure was needed. As G.F.G. Stanley and other writers have noted, from the close of the Second World War onward, the Royal Canadian Air Force had maintained very close relations with the United States Air Force and had adopted American strategic thinking as well as American managerial and control techniques.[17] The RCAF representatives were eager to get the integrated arrangement in operation as soon as possible. They believed in the joint concept; they wanted to obtain for Canada a voice in the formulation of air defence policy; they had participated actively in the agreement's negotiation and were very much concerned to avoid the embarrassment that would have resulted if the news leaked out that the United States had approved the agreement and Canada had not. Accordingly, they urged the government to act without delay. As

General Foulkes later frankly admitted: 'Unfortunately I am afraid we stampeded the incoming government with the NORAD agreement.'[18]

In the United States the announcement that an integrated air command was to be established, although evoking only mild public interest, was greeted by observers as a sensible and timely move. Nor is that surprising. Most of them, no doubt, assumed that, 'with the setting up of NORAD, control of the continental air defense system had to all intents and purposes passed to the United States as the major partner in the combined command.'[19] Because the announced arrangements did not take the form of a treaty, or even an exchange of notes, it was not submitted to the American Senate for its advice and consent and was, in fact, largely ignored by both houses of Congress.

In Canada, however, it was an entirely different story. Although the general public showed no great concern,[20] Liberal and Cooperative Commonwealth Federation members of Parliament demanded full and exact information regarding the nature and scope of the new understanding. When informed that what had been agreed to was merely an interim arrangement, designed to serve until a more permanent one could be drafted, they wanted to know whether the formal agreement would be submitted to Parliament for its consideration.[21] The ministers replied that since NORAD was, in fact, only an 'amplification of and extension' of NATO, the government saw no reason for bringing the proposed exchange of notes before Parliament – particularly so since other important understandings, such as the Ogdensburg and the Hyde Park agreements, had been consummated without Parliament's participation. This conclusion, however, was unacceptable to Opposition spokesmen. As a consequence, the prime minister, most reluctantly, agreed that the integrated command arrangement should be discussed in detail and 'given full publicity in the house.'[22]

The notes, exchanged 12 May 1958,[23] outlined in some detail the principles that were to govern the future organization and operations of NORAD, stated that the question of the financing of expenditures connected with the operation of the integrated headquarters would be settled 'by mutual agreement between appropriate agencies of the two Governments,'[24] and then asserted: 'The North American Air Defense Command shall be maintained in operation for a period of ten years or such shorter period as shall be agreed by both countries in the light of their mutual defense interests, and their objectives under the terms of the North Atlantic Treaty.'

In the parliamentary debates that followed the exchange of notes, Opposition members not only criticized the government for the procedure that it had followed in the drafting and the adoption of the NORAD accord but also raised numerous questions about the organization itself. One of these was why it had not been placed directly under NATO control. Not caring to admit that a major reason had been the refusal of the United States to accept such an arrangement, Conservative spokesmen simply stressed the close NORAD–NATO relationship. Thus they cited the assertion of the NORAD agreement that 'the Canada–United States Region is an integral part of the NATO area' and its affirmation that CINCNORAD, the NORAD commander-in-chief, was to bear in mind Canadian–American 'objectives in the defense of the Canada–United States Region of the NATO area,' and went on to argue that the NORAD Region was 'a command in relation to the Canada–United States regional planning group.'[25] In reply, Opposition spokesmen acknowledged that CINCNORAD reported to the chiefs of staff of the two countries, who, through the Canada–United States Regional Planning Group, reported to the Military Committee of NATO. But they emphatically denied that NORAD was an integral part of the NATO military structure. NORAD did not derive its authority in any way, shape, or form from NATO; nor was it in any way subject to NATO control.[26] This, however, might yet be remedied if the government would direct its efforts towards bringing the joint air command within the NATO framework. When the prime minister indicated no inclination to do so, CCF members of Parliament introduced a motion that the government 'give consideration to the taking of such steps as are necessary to integrate these agreements [sic] within the structure of NATO.'[27] The motion, however, was ruled irrelevant by the Speaker and NORAD's relationship to NATO continued as a limited, indirect one.

Commentators have expressed doubts both as to whether the European members of NATO would have either the time or the inclination to take an active part in the Canadian–American defence region, and as to whether it would, in fact, be in Canada's interest for them to do so.[28] Nevertheless, it is perhaps unfortunate that the Canadian negotiators did not make a greater effort to bring NORAD within the NATO structure. Canadians concerned for the preservation of their country's sovereignty have always indicated a decided preference for multilateral over bilateral alliances and arrangements, feeling that there is 'security in numbers.'[29]

A second criticism of the NORAD arrangement voiced by numerous members of Parliament was that it made Canadian defence policy subservient to SAC. Although recognizing that SAC has an offensive, rather than a defensive, role and is maintained and controlled by the United States, the critical members argued that if it were ever called upon to attack enemy forces, it would undoubtedly be acting on information obtained through NORAD's communications system. Thus NORAD and SAC were, in truth, integral parts of a larger military organization which includes both offensive and defensive arrangements. Moreover, NORAD's only important function appeared to be to protect SAC's bombers and missile-launching sites.[30] Government spokesmen readily agreed that NORAD and SAC were parts of a single defensive system. They also admitted that the plans and activities of the two organizations would have to be coordinated. But they insisted that it was grossly misleading to assume that, by joining NORAD, Canada was taking unto itself a measure of responsibility for SAC.[31]

Possibly the most emphasized argument of Opposition members was that the government had, in effect, abdicated its authority to declare war and had placed Canadian air security in the hands of an American Air Force officer. As proof, they cited a press conference statement by General Earl E. Partridge, the CINCNORAD, that he had the approval of the president of the United States 'to use, without reference to anybody, any weapon at our disposal if there is a hostile aircraft in the system.'[32] Defence Minister Pearkes heatedly denied that the Canadian government had surrendered its right to declare war and challengingly questioned 'whether that is the arrangement existing between General Partridge and the President of the United States.' In the event of an immediate attack across the DEW line, there would be consultation with the government of Canada 'by telephone or other means' prior to the sending of Canadian interceptors into the air. A few days later the minister suggested that perhaps there was confusion in the use of the word 'consultation.' There would always be consultation in the planning stage but it might be better to use the word 'clearance' with respect to 'the operational stage.' Early in January 1958 he admitted that the Canadian air defence commander at St Hubert, Quebec, through whom, at that stage, the CINCNORAD was to control Canadian forces, could, without consultation with the Canadian government, order such forces into action in accordance with the 'rules of engagement' which had been in force since 1951.[33] (Later, with the introduction of SAGE, the chain of command ceased to be national and came to be directed from CINCNORAD to subordinate binational headquarters.[34])

These successive admissions by the defence minister seemed to imply that, if a surprise attack occurs over American or Canadian territory, one man, the CINCNORAD or his deputy, will have the responsibility of issuing the order to meet force with force. And that, of course, is what common sense dictates. Any enemy attack is likely to come so suddenly that there is not likely to be time for extensive consultations, even by telephone. The commander must be able to throw instantly his defensive forces against the attackers. These will include such tactical defence weapons as guided missiles and fighter interceptor planes, but not nuclear bombs or missiles, which may be loosed only upon the authorization of the president and (over Canada) of the prime minister.

As the critics contended, this is a formidable, potentially dangerous, power placed in the hands of NORAD. But the power must be exercised under a number of important limitations. In the first place, the 'plans and procedures' followed by NORAD in wartime, the notes of 12 May 1958 affirm, 'shall be formulated and approved in peacetime by appropriate national authorities and shall be capable of rapid implementation in an emergency.' In the second place, 'any plans and procedures recommended by NORAD which bear on the responsibilities of civilian departments or agencies of the two Governments' must be referred to those agencies and departments and may be the subject of intergovernmental coordination. In the third place, the NORAD commander and his deputy must abide by detailed, secret 'terms of reference,' which may be modified only with the approval of the high political authorities of the two governments. In the fourth place, no change can be made in the status of either country's forces until the required level of alert has been declared. In the fifth place, CINCNORAD is responsible to the Canadian Chief of the Defence Staff and the Joint Chiefs of Staff of the United States, who, in turn, are responsible to their respective governments. Finally, the agreement also includes the following significant provision (incorporated into the exchange of notes at Canadian insistence): 'The two Governments consider that the establishment of integrated air defense arrangements of the nature described increases the importance of the fullest possible consultation between the two Governments on all matters affecting the joint defense of North America, and that defense cooperation between them can be worked out on a mutually satisfactory basis only if such consultation is regularly and consistently undertaken.'

The consultation was expected to take place at three different levels: heads of government, chiefs of staff, and diplomatic. It would, the prime minister affirmed, be conducted 'throughout the days of peace' and would be 'intensified in times of emergency.' Since the time available for consultation during an emergency might be short, it was of the highest importance to the Canadian government that it be consulted as early as possible concerning any circumstances which could conceivably commit Canada to war or impede the maintenance of the joint cooperative effort.[35]

Opposition spokesmen also approved of the inclusion of the consultation clause in the agreement. Consultation, they asserted, which is highly essential between countries of unequal power and influence, had always been important in dealing with Canadian–American problems. Now, in view of the integration of the two air defence commands, it was more important than ever. Without consultation Canada might very well find itself blindly following American-formulated policies or even, willy-nilly, becoming involved in American wars. But, they cautioned, before the ministers congratulated themselves too profusely on getting the consultation provision written into the agreement, it would be well to wait and see whether it was actually implemented.[36] As the Cuban missile crisis (discussed in the following chapter) was to demonstrate, these admonitory words proved to be both astute and highly relevant.

Despite the critical questions raised, the outcome of the parliamentary debate was a foregone conclusion. Notwithstanding their dislike for various aspects of the arrangements, most members agreed that the integrated command was desirable. Accordingly, after more than a month of intermittent debates, the Commons approved the accord by a vote of 200 to 8.[37] The government spokesmen, however, had done such an ineffective job of explaining the new arrangements, and the debate had been so acrimonious and inconclusive, that the Canadian public was left confused and disturbed, which, in turn, contributed to the growth in the late 1960s of considerable dissatisfaction with NORAD and to demands for Canada's withdrawal.[38]

13

NORAD: functions, organization, and early difficulties

At the outset the primary responsibility of the North American Air Defence Command was to protect SAC (the American-maintained Strategic Air Command) from enemy bombers and to minimize damages to population centres in the Continental United States, Alaska, and Canada. This continues to be its most basic function and includes surveillance and detection of all unknown aircraft in the NORAD area and the interception and, if necessary, the destruction of any enemy bombers seeking to penetrate North American air space. Since 1958, however, the joint air command has acquired additional responsibilities. One of these is to maintain surveillance over and detect any hostile intercontinental ballistic missiles that may be launched against North America across the northern reaches of the continent. This it is expected to do through its BMEWS (Ballistic Missile Early Warning System) installations, located at Clear, Alaska; Thule, Greenland; and Flyingsdales Moor, England. At present neither NORAD nor the United States, acting independently, has any real defence against the ICBMS. The joint air command has, of course, no control over SAC; nor does it have any responsibility for the defence of the waters surrounding the continent, although its coastal radars do provide a detection and warning capability against submarine-launched ballistic missile attacks. Since late in 1960 NORAD has also had operational control over the space surveillance network for detecting and tracking satellites (SPASUR) developed by the United States Navy and for SPACETRACK, an American Air Force system incorporating the National Space Surveillance Control Center, which receives, analyses, and catalogues orbital data received from numerous world-wide sensors.[1]

CINCNORAD (the commander-in-chief) is in charge of the integrated headquarters. The second in command is the deputy commander. The appointment of both officers must be approved by the Canadian and the American governments. In theory, CINCNORAD could be from either country, for the notes of 12 May 1958 merely provide that the commander and his deputy 'will not be from the same country.' Thus far all of the NORAD commanders have been citizens of the United States, and it is reasonable to assume that as long as that country provides the bulk of the personnel and financing it will also supply the commander. The NORAD staff must be 'an integrated joint staff composed of officers from both countries.' During the absence of CINCNORAD, command passes to the deputy commander.

Narrowly viewed, NORAD is merely a headquarters structure, consisting of the central headquarters at Colorado Springs and the various regional headquarters scattered throughout the United States and Canada. It has no assigned combat units, no weapons, and, except for a modest budget, no funds of its own. These are all derived from the component services placed under its operational control, which at the peak in 1961 consisted of 248,000 service personnel but in 1978 had dropped to approximately 53,000 (exclusive of the United States unified Alaskan Command), made up of 10,500 from the Canadian Armed Forces Air Defence Command and the bulk of the remainder from the United States Air Force Aerospace Defense Command and the United States Army Air Defense Command, but with small contingents from the United States Navy and the Marine Corps. Also provided was a modest arsenal of defensive weapons consisting of air-to-air guided missiles, nuclear air-to-air ballistic rockets, and interceptor aircraft. Canada contributed three fighter interceptor squadrons and the United States twenty-one – down from an early high of nine Canadian and thirty-nine American squadrons.

Despite its limited jurisdiction, NORAD does have far-reaching responsibilities. These include not only the formulation of operational concepts and plans for the employment of air defence resources, but the exercise of 'operational control' over the units and individuals under its jurisdiction – defined by the exchange of notes as 'the power to direct, coordinate, and control the operational activities of forces assigned, attached or otherwise made available.'

Significantly, although CINCNORAD has the authority to move temporary reinforcements from one area to another – even across the international boundary – he can make no permanent changes of station 'without approval of the higher national authority concerned.' His responsibilities are also limited in that administration, discipline, internal organization, and unit training are prerogatives of the component commanders.

To facilitate NORAD's operations, the continent is divided into regions.

At the outset there were eleven regions; later the number was reduced to eight. Five of the eight include both American and Canadian territory and are serviced by American and Canadian personnel. As is indicated below, the regions are soon to be realigned. Along with that may go changes in the distribution of functions. At present each regional commander is responsible to CINCNORAD for the air defence of his geographical region. He also 'monitors and coordinates the air action, plans the use of assigned forces, and supervises the methods and procedures by which an air battle would be fought in his area.'[2]

Since April 1966 NORAD's command and control facilities have been located in a hardened facility in Cheyenne Mountain, near Colorado Springs, built and financed entirely by the United States at a cost of $142,400,000. It is to the combat operations centre of this complex that the computers of the regions transmit information of various sorts, where the data are analysed and correlated and presented in the form of constantly updated displays. It is from the Control Center that the first warning of an impending attack would go out to the two governments, to SAC, to civil defence workers, and to the North American people in general. It is likewise from there that control of the air battle would be directed.

On the military level NORAD, it is generally agreed, has been an unqualified success. The NORAD commander and his deputy have always gotten along well together, and relations between the rank-and-file of the Americans and of the Canadians at headquarters have consistently been excellent.[3] The government in Washington has never attempted to dictate to the deputy on the occasions when he has been in charge of the NORAD headquarters; nor on such occasions has his authority ever been questioned by American officers or men.[4]

At the political level the record has been a mixed one. During the Mideast crisis of July 1958 – when American military forces were sent into Lebanon to avert a feared takeover of the country by pro-Nasser groups – the previously agreed upon NORAD procedures were implemented to the letter. During the week preceding the dispatch of the armed forces, there was, according to John Diefenbaker, 'the closest consultation on the highest governmental level as well as between the Chiefs of Staff of the two countries.' After consulting with his staff, the NORAD commander recommended to the chiefs of staff that the defence forces under his operational control be placed on 'a state of readiness'; the chiefs, in turn, approved and transmitted the recommendation to the top government authorities. They gave their approval and the NORAD forces were brought into position to be able to act on a moment's notice.[5]

Quite different was the course of events during the Cuban missile crisis of October 1962. Because of his desire to retain the element of surprise in his dealings with the Russian leaders, President Kennedy, before deciding on his course of action, held nothing that could properly be called 'consultations' with the Canadian authorities or any of the other NATO leaders. Instead, on Monday, the 22nd, he sent special emissaries to four NATO countries – Britain, France, West Germany, and Canada – to inform the leaders of those countries that he proposed to impose a naval and air quarantine on the shipment of offensive weapons to Cuba and to force the Soviet Union to remove the ballistic missiles.[6] The emissary to Canada was Livingston Merchant, former United States ambassador to that country, who in a meeting with Diefenbaker and two of his cabinet colleagues, Howard Green and Douglas Harkness, read aloud to them the text of the speech that the president was scheduled to give on television one and a half hours later that evening, showed them blow-ups of the photographs taken of the missile bases, and answered their questions. The president did not request any specific actions or assistance from the Canadian authorities; but it is reasonable to assume that he hoped for, and expected to receive, the same type of cooperation that the Diefenbaker cabinet had accorded the Eisenhower administration during the Lebanese crisis.

Shortly after the delivery of the president's speech a message from NORAD headquarters was received by the Canadian chiefs of staff saying that all of the American forces assigned to NORAD had been placed on an alert technically described as 'Defcon 3' and recommending that the RCAF components also be alerted.[7] Both the Canadian military leaders and Defence Minister Harkness agreed that this should be done, but Prime Minister Diefenbaker chose to delay some forty-two hours before giving his approval.

The delay, which disturbed many thoughtful Canadians – including the Opposition leader, L.B. Pearson[8] – and incensed many officials south of the border, probably had no perceptible negative effect on the American government's military posture. The Canadian interceptors then assigned to NORAD were not armed with nuclear weapons and were therefore of limited use. More important still, Harkness, acting on his own authority, put all of the Canadian forces 'on what amounted to a full alert (except for announcing they were on alert) before the Cabinet authorized such a measure.'[9] No less importantly, immediately after the commencement of the crisis, the Canadian government took a number of actions designed to support the American position, the most important being the withdrawing of permission for Russian planes en route to Cuba to fly over Canadian territory or to land at Canadian airfields and the searching of all aircraft from other Communist countries on their way to Cuba to make sure that they were not carrying war-like materials.

However, there were several actions which had they been taken promptly would have appreciably strengthened the military stance of the Kennedy administration. Among these would have been the equipping of American interceptors at Canadian bases with nuclear warheads, the dispersal of American interceptor squadrons to Canadian airfields, and the free movement of SAC bombers armed with nuclear weapons over Canadian territory and their use of Canadian airfields. Whether the United States actually asked permission to take these measures is a moot question. Some competent writers have asserted that the United States made requests that were rejected by Canada;[10] other writers, equally competent, have expressed doubts that such requests were actually made.[11] What can be affirmed with certainty is that the prime minister's cooperation was less complete, and more grudgingly given, than many citizens of the United States or of Canada would have desired or expected.

The reasons for Diefenbaker's negative attitude probably were many and varied. Pierre Sévigny says the prime minister misjudged 'the seriousness of the situation ... and the absolute determination of his followers to stand side by side with their American neighbours.'[12] That, undoubtedly, was true. Other contributing factors appear to have been the prime minister's desire to avoid any action that might tend to aggravate an already volatile situation; his notorious reluctance to make decisions; his distrust of the military; his fear that to permit American planes armed with nuclear weapons to deploy to Canadian airports would intensify the debate already building up over the question of Canada's nuclear policy; his fear that Canadian opinion would not approve a policy of Canadian support for American action; his strained personal relationships with President Kennedy; his belief, emphatically supported by Green, that Canada should not meekly follow a policy 'made in Washington' but should adhere to a distinctively Canadian policy;[13] and, perhaps most important of all, his resentment at the president's failure, as he viewed it, to implement the consultations called for by the NORAD agreement.

Was the president, in truth, censurable for his failure to carry out bona fide consultations? Various commentators have affirmed that he was.[14] It can, of course, be argued that the risks of a leak would have been too great to make feasible consultations with all members of NATO and OAS. But did not Canada – which had integrated its economy and its air defence so completely with that of the United States – merit special consideration?

What of the much-touted 'special' Canadian–American relationship? More important still, what about the NORAD provision calling for regular and consistent consultations? Undoubtedly effective action during the Cuban confrontation called for speed and secrecy,[15] but could there not have been detailed discussions between representatives of the two countries during the weeks and days leading up to the crisis climax? Had Diefenbaker been fully informed regarding all aspects of American policy toward Cuba and afforded an opportunity to make the president aware of his own views regarding that policy, his response in October 1962 might have been more positive. However, one of the facts of life is that during national emergencies Great Powers are not disposed to consult with smaller partners. Does that mean that the NORAD consultation provision is impossible of implementation? Not necessarily. Perhaps all that is required is full and detailed consultations during the development of an emergency, with the number and degree of consultations at the climax left to be determined by the circumstances.

One of the significant consequences of the crisis was to call pointed attention to the urgent importance of a Canadian decision with respect to nuclear weapons. At issue were two interrelated questions: (1) whether Canada should acquire nuclear warheads for its six squadrons of CF-104s assigned to the 'strike' role in NATO and for the Honest John weapons system that had been purchased for its NATO brigade group; and (2) whether it should acquire nuclear warheads for its Voodoo interceptors for use under NORAD and for the missiles of the two Bomarc B anti-aircraft missile bases that had been built at North Bay, Ontario, and at La Macaza, Quebec. Although the Diefenbaker government had never given written approval to the acquisition of nuclear warheads, it had signed an agreement on 22 May 1959 calling for 'an exchange of nuclear information for mutual defense' and covering the training of Canadian troops in the use of some nuclear weapons.[16] It had also agreed in 1959 that the role of Canada's overseas air division in NATO should be changed from high level interception to one of strike reconnaissance, which implied the acceptance of nuclear warheads for the Canadian planes.[17] Moreover, it was generally recognized that the Bomarc B missiles in Canada would be virtually useless without nuclear warheads. More important still, during the negotiations for the Bomarcs the Canadian ministers had assured the American spokesmen that once the missiles were operational they would be armed with nuclear warheads. But for various reasons – including growth of much Canadian antipathy towards nuclear weapons, strong opposition of External Affairs Minister Green, and the reluctance of cabinet members to permit the entry of American troops into Canada to guard any atomic warheads that might be stored there – the government had not made a decision at the time of the eruption of the Cuban crisis.[18]

Early in 1963 the *Washington Daily News* alleged that Air Marshal Slemon, the NORAD deputy commander, was 'conducting an active campaign against the nuclear policy of the Diefenbaker government.'[19] The air marshal denied the charge, but there can be no doubt that both at that time and on earlier occasions he did attempt, at least indirectly, to influence the government to accept nuclear weapons.[20] Nor was General Lawrence Kuter, NORAD commander-in-chief, averse to exerting pressure when and where he could.[21] Such conduct on the part of the NORAD leaders was, of course, hardly in keeping with their assumed neutral position, but it is understandable. For months they had waited for the government to act, while morale at NORAD headquarters had noticeably declined.[22] When no decision was forthcoming, they spoke out publicly and sent off urgent notes to the service chiefs in Ottawa, who, in turn, put pressure on the ministers. The ministers, however, were unable to act 'without instructions from the top.'[23] It was a statement by General Lauris Norstad, recently retired commander of NATO (to the effect that if Canada did not accept nuclear weapons it would not be fulfilling its NATO commitments), followed by a press release of the Department of State, challenging the accuracy of certain of the prime minister's statements relative to defence cooperation, that finally, early in 1963, brought the nuclear issue to a head. Following the resignation of three of his ministers, Diefenbaker was defeated on a confidence vote in the House of Commons and then suffered defeat in the ensuing election. The new government, headed by Lester B. Pearson, promptly arranged for the entry into Canada of nuclear warheads.

Both the Cuban missile crisis and the nuclear arms issue made a profound impact on NORAD and on Canadian–American relations in general. Although pleased to discover that the authority of CINCNORAD was considerably less than they had assumed, many Canadians were disturbed at learning how inextricably NORAD had linked up their own air defence with that of their powerful southern neighbour, and increasing numbers of them joined CCF members and other early critics in demanding a termination of the agreement. The missile crisis, like the cancellation of the Arrow interceptor (discussed in a later chapter),[24] also vividly highlighted a basic problem of Canada's defence policy: 'the political frustration of having to accept and help to execute decisions taken in Washington which it is hardly able to influence, but which vitally affect its security.'[25]

For defence-minded Americans, both the Cuban and the nuclear arms issues raised the basic question of the reliability of Canada as a defence partner and caused Pentagon spokesmen to begin suggesting that it might be advisable for the United States not only to terminate the Defence Production Sharing Program but also to formulate an air defence policy not dependent on Canadian cooperation.[26] More serious still, following the two conflicts, the American military planners were increasingly inclined 'to take the security of North America more into their own hands.'[27]

14

NORAD: problems of obsolescence
and attempted solutions

Since the early 1960s NORAD's history has been largely 'one of perpetual
battle against shifting threat perceptions and technological obsolescence.'[1]
The basic problem has been, and continues to be, that NORAD and its
supporting communications system were designed to deal with nuclear-
armed Soviet bombers, whereas since the launching of Sputnik I, in October 1957, the most serious threat to North America has been posed by
ballistic missiles. Over the years each of the governments has had the
thankless task of deciding whether the threat from bombers was sufficiently
great to justify the retention of the NORAD system and, if so, what modifications were required to update it. The continual raising of these questions
has, in turn, afforded critics of NORAD with almost unlimited opportunities
to air their objections to the joint defence system. Although the criticisms
have come from both sides of the boundary, the most severe indictments of
NORAD have come, as will be noted later, from Canadians, many of whom
have found, and continue to find, much about the joint air command that is
objectionable.

In 1958 the Soviet Union had a thousand bombers, many of them capable
of penetrating to the heart of North America. With the development and
improvement of its ballistic missiles, the number of long-range intercontinental bombers in its arsenal gradually declined to a mere 140 in 1976.
Despite this decline, over the years USAF spokesmen, staunchly supported
by their Canadian counterparts, have consistently maintained that the
NORAD system was still needed to aid in protecting SAC and, thereby, in
assuring the United States of second-strike capability. If the anti-bomber
defences were dismantled, the Russian bombers would be afforded a 'free
ride' into their target areas. To critic retorts that it would be foolish for the
Soviet military leaders to use bombers since they have an almost unlimited

number of missiles, NORAD champions have usually replied that bombers are cheaper and more accurate, can carry a higher payload, and are more flexible than missiles. At the same time, beginning about 1963, American and Canadian spokesmen admitted that because of the decreased threat from bombers and the lessening of East–West tensions, it would soon be feasible to reduce somewhat the men, planes, and equipment assigned to NORAD. And in truth the cutbacks, which had started as early as 1960, were soon moving at an accelerated pace. During 1964–5 the two governments disbanded the Mid-Canada early warning network, reduced the number of interceptors assigned to NORAD, and consolidated those remaining into fewer squadrons. At the same time, they increased the potential efficiency of the NORAD forces during an emergency by introducing a back-up inter- ceptor control (known as BUIC).[2] Subsequently a number of Pinetree Line and DEW Line stations were phased out. By April 1972 the last of the Bomarc bases on Canadian soil had been closed.

While the bomber defences were being gradually reduced, American scientists and defence planners were energetically at work trying to perfect anti-ballistic missiles to deal with Soviet intercontinental ballistic missiles. In September 1967 the American secretary of defence announced that ABMs would be deployed at or near fifteen American localities. The pro- gram, however, aroused so much opposition that in February 1969 Presi- dent Nixon suspended it pending a review. The following month the presi- dent announced that for the time being he had decided to reduce the Johnson program to one installation in North Dakota and one in Montana and to set up machinery for halting all deployment if arms-control talks with the Soviet Union should make that desirable. By a very narrow majority, the Senate supported his request for a monetary appropriation and the revised program was set in motion.

Understandably, this American decision raised fundamental questions for Canada. Would not the deployment of ABMs upset the delicate balance of terror between the United States and the Soviet Union? Would the use of such a system increase the risk of Canada's becoming devastated either by Russian missiles or as a result of the effective operation of the American system? If there were good grounds for believing that such a system would promote North American security, should Canada cooperate in its de- ployment? If so, should some of the sites be located on Canadian soil? And should control be vested in NORAD? If Canada did not participate with the United States, should it develop a system of its own? In March 1969, on the eve of his departure for a visit with President Nixon in Washington, Prime Minister Trudeau advised members of Parliament that, although Canada had been 'notified' of President Nixon's decision, there had been 'no consultation in the sense that we might have been in a position to change the decision.' He thought Canada might have to participate in the American system if it wanted to influence Washington's stance. Later, after opposition spokesmen had urged him to assert Canada's right to be consulted with respect to American deployment of ABM s, the prime minister expressed the view that, since the American plans did not visualize placing the missiles under NORAD, the Canadian people could not properly complain if they were not consulted.[3]

At the conclusion of Trudeau's Washington visit a joint Canadian–American statement affirmed: 'Over the years the United States has regularly informed Canada of plans and developments in the ABM field; it has been agreed that this practice will be continued.'[4] This affirmation, plus the prime minister's assertion upon his return to Ottawa that his government's decision relative to the ABM system would be based upon its assessment as to whether such a system would more likely promote peace or war, may have offered some reassurance to concerned Canadians. But they could not have failed to note that, on the very eve of the prime minister's arrival in Washington, Defense Secretary Melvin Laird admitted to a Senate subcommittee that he could not say whether the Nixon administration would drop its plans to locate ABM sites at Grand Forks, North Dakota, and Great Falls, Montana, if Canada objected. His reply was interpreted by Senator Fulbright as meaning: 'You wouldn't give them a veto power. In other words, if they don't like it, they can lump it.' The secretary explained that, although the United States had always had 'a working agreement' with Canada covering deployment of the ABM system, there had never been 'an understanding under which Canada could veto the sites' of such missiles.[5]

The Nixon administration, of course, went ahead with its plans to build the two authorized ABM installations. Early in 1970 it requested funds not only to add missiles at the bases already approved but to start preliminary work on five more sites and to build defences around Washington, DC. Congress appropriated money for the sites under construction, but cut the preliminary work to two sites and vetoed defences for Washington. Thereafter the issue began to fade – particularly after the United States and the Soviet Union in 1972 agreed, in the accord on strategic arms limitation, to limit themselves to just two ABM installations apiece. In 1974 Nixon and Brezhnev reduced the limit to one site each. The following year, after American scientists had concluded that the American Safeguard system was not capable of stopping the new Soviet SS-19 missile, Congress voted to close down the entire facility except for its radar system (capable, it is stated, of detecting aircraft in the deep Arctic), which is to be permitted to remain in operation. The controversial ABM issue, had, however, left its unhappy imprint on Canadian–American relations. Once again, bitter Canadians noted, the Americans had moved blithely ahead with their own defence plans regardless of the serious consequences that implementation of those plans might have for Canada.

A second American project that has caused some uncertainty and controversy in Canada has been one to replace the existing air defence system with another, the Airborne Warning and Control System (AWACS). The present system, it is generally agreed, is deficient in three major respects. First, it is highly vulnerable to enemy-launched intercontinental ballistic missiles. Second, it has limited ability to track low-flying aircraft 'because the line-of-sight from radar to target is cut off at the horizon.' Third, the fixed radars of the existing system limit seriously the defence belt within which interceptors and missiles can be controlled. These weaknesses, it is contended, could be overcome by an AWACS system, which would extend the defence system 'outwards and downwards ... making its components less vulnerable.'6

The new system would require not only large and expensive aircraft, with large crews, but also sophisticated equipment for communication, computing, data storage and display. It would likewise require the installation of Over-the Horizon-Backscatter (OTH-B) radar and improved interceptor aircraft. However, it would permit a reduction in the SAGE system, in the ground-based radars, and in the interceptor bombers assigned to NORAD.7

Although Canada appears to have been 'in on the discussions' of the AWACS-OTH-B programs from 'the beginning,'8 the authorities in Ottawa have been unusually close-lipped as to exactly what Canada's role will be in the deployment and operation of the new programs. The general Canadian approach was well summed up by the Canadian minister of national defence early in 1975 when he stated that he was recommending to the cabinet that 'we continue to work with the United States in the development of the new system and that we learn of their thinking, we find out the cost, we find out where Canada can appropriately fit into the new systems.'9 Perhaps both concern over the cost – originally set at $12,300,000,000 for the entire system but now, no doubt, much higher – and a desire not to arouse further the ire of opposed individual Canadians and groups have caused the Ottawa authorities to discourage public discussion of the matter.

Regardless of any Canadian decisions, the United States is moving ahead with the production of AWACS aircraft and the construction of OTH-B sites.[10] It is, however, generally agreed that the system would work much more efficiently if AWACS aircraft and interceptors were permitted to use airfields in Canada; if serviceable portions of the existing electronic system were utilized; and if the entire system were placed under NORAD. Moreover, it would be less expensive for Canada to pay a reasonable share of the cost of the American-built system than to develop and maintain one of its own. Even if the bomber threat completely disappears, the AWACS-OTH-B system, the experts assert, would be quite useful for the surveillance of Canadian territory and coastal waters.[11] But to Canadians critical of NORAD and other integrated Canadian–American defence arrangements, any Canadian participation in the new warning system would be most objectionable.

Both the United States and Canada, most commentators agree, have benefited from their association in NORAD. The former was afforded access to Canadian territory during a period of time when such access was desperately needed. It has also benefited from the airspace, land, planes, manpower, and technical knowledge that Canada has brought to the partnership arrangement. Canada, for its part, through very modest financial outlays, has contributed to the strengthening of the American deterrent and thereby its own security. At the same time, by providing men, planes, and materials for the defence of North America, it has forestalled any possible need or excuse for American intervention in Canadian affairs for the purpose of preventing Canadian military weaknesses from becoming a threat to the security of the United States itself. It has, likewise, provided still another channel for making Canadian views on air defence known to American Air Force spokesmen and, in the opinion of some Canadians, for influencing the formulation of American defence policies.[12] And, of course, if NORAD and its associated communications facilities have helped to avert nuclear war – which would be difficult to prove or disprove – both Canada and the United States, as well as people everywhere, have greatly benefited.

Despite the benefits, since NORAD's very inception numerous Canadians have been critical of it and have seized every opportunity to urge that their country withdraw from it. They have been particularly vocal on the occasions when the NORAD agreement has been up for renewal, in 1968, 1973, and 1975, but have agitated constantly for the termination of Canada's involvement.

Some of the objections have been largely reiterations of those raised by Opposition members of Parliament in 1958: Canadian defence policy has been made subservient to SAC, Canada has become a military satellite of its powerful neighbour, and so on.[13] But other arguments have also been advanced: integrated defence has contributed to a strengthening of American control over Canadian industry;[14] NORAD is likely to draw Canada, willy-nilly, into American wars; the advent of intercontinental and submarine-based ballistic missiles has made the NORAD system obsolete; since the Americans, in their own interest, must protect Canada, why not leave the defence of the continent to the United States?[15] More significantly, some critics have also challenged the common assumption of the 1950s that Canadian interests and American interests are identical. They have pointed out that Americans and Canadians have had widely divergent views with respect to Communist Cuba, Nationalist China, and Vietnam, and that this difference of views in turn has led to different assessments regarding threats to North America and world peace.[16] The consultation clause of NORAD, they add, offers no assurance that distinctive Canadian aims and views will receive an adequate hearing. Consultations all too frequently turn into briefing sessions, with the Americans doing all of the briefing. In any event, the United States, a great imperialist power, has no intention of allowing its defence and foreign policies to be determined in concert. All that is expected of Canada is acquiescence in, and support for, American policies and actions.[17]

The first renewal of the NORAD agreement – effected by an exchange of notes 30 March 1968, carried out quietly, almost furtively, after discussions of the matter by the PJBD and by a joint negotiating team[18] – made three important changes: (1) it was to run not for ten but for only five years; (2) whereas the notes of 1958 called for a review of the terms of the agreement upon the 'request of either country at any time,' the notes of 1968 provided not merely for a review but for a termination of the agreement upon the request of either government 'following a period of notice of one year'; (3) while the earlier notes were silent on the subject of defence against missiles, the later ones specifically affirmed that the agreement did not involve 'in any way a Canadian commitment to participate in an active ballistic missile defense.'

Approximately a year after the first renewal, Prime Minister Trudeau issued a statement to the press setting forth in broad outline 'A Defence Policy for Canada' that specifically rejected 'any suggestion that Canada assume a non-aligned or neutral role in world affairs.'[19] Canada would 'continue to co-operate effectively with the United States in the defence of North America.' To that end, the cabinet would 'seek early occasions for detailed discussions with the United States Government of the whole range of problems involved in our mutual co-operation in defence matters on this continent.' To the extent that it was feasible, the government would attempt 'to have those activities within Canada which are essential to North American defence performed by Canadian forces.' The 'order of priority' for Canadian armed forces would be: (a) 'the surveillance of our own territory and coast-lines, i.e., the protection of our sovereignty'; (b) the defence of North America in cooperation with the United States; (c) 'the fulfillment of such NATO commitments as may be agreed upon'; (d) the performance of such international peace-keeping roles as Canada may assume.

The joint discussions were duly held, one immediate result being an agreement for Canada to take over from American forces the control centre at Melville, near Goose Bay, Labrador, thereby giving the RCAF the responsibility for the surveillance of the air space of Canada's Atlantic approaches. Along with that move, Canada's CF-101 interceptors assumed a greater role in carrying out interceptions and identification missions over Eastern Canada.[20] In 1972 the minister of national defence indicated that the Canadian government was preparing to use its CF-104 aircraft, based at Cold Lake, Alberta, to do surveillance in the Prairie area. It was also 'taking a careful look at what, if anything, could be done against the submarine-launched ballistic missile.'[21]

By an exchange of notes, dated 10 May 1973, the two governments agreed that the NORAD accord should be extended without alteration for a period of two years. The indicated reason for the short-term extension period was to allow 'additional time ... to examine the component elements of the concept for a modernized air defence system now under development.'[22]

In January 1975 James A. Richardson, national defence minister, advised the House of Commons Standing Committee on External Affairs and National Defence that most of the uncertainties of 1974 had been largely resolved. Because the agreement in principle reached between the United States and the Soviet Union in 1974 envisaged the inclusion of long-range bombers within the common ceiling of 2400 intercontinental delivery systems, it seemed unlikely that any major increase would occur 'in the Soviet bomber threat to North America in the next decade.' As a consequence, the United States had decided 'to proceed with modernization of its air defence forces on a much more modest scale than was earlier considered.' Canada, in turn, had decided 'to proceed during the next few years with a joint civil-military system of airspace surveillance and control.' Thus the air defence of both countries had matured to the point where consideration should be given to renewing the NORAD agreement 'for a longer period in order to provide a stable basis for carrying present plans into effect.' The minister then summarized five reasons why he believed Canada should renew the agreement: (1) the continuation of a bomber threat, although now only 'minimal'; (2) the need for peacetime surveillance and control of Canadian airspace; (3) the enhancement of Canada's sovereignty by partnership with the United States in NORAD; (4) the conviction of the government that if Canada were not in the joint air command it would still need similar forces and capabilities, and the expense of providing them would be greater than its present contribution to NORAD; and (5) the equally strong conviction that Canada's cooperation with the United States in North American defence was 'a major positive element in the over-all relations which exist between the two countries.'[23]

The Commons Committee also concluded that, 'on the basis of broad security, political and economic considerations,' it was in Canada's 'present interest' to remain in the joint air command.[24] Since the American authorities strongly favoured NORAD's continuation, an understanding was soon reached that the agreement should be renewed for five years but with a realignment of the command's regional boundaries.[25] Although the realignment has not yet been effected, the plan contemplated is that, instead of having, as at present, five of the eight regions astride the boundary, Continental United States will be divided into four regions and the whole of Canada into two. This, it is held, will facilitate joint military and civilian aircraft control for both countries.[26] It will also, of course, help to achieve an objective much favoured by Canadian political leaders of having operations in Canadian airspace controlled from centres in Canada and carried out by Canadians.

Fortunately, NORAD's effectiveness under conditions of nuclear attack has not yet been tested. However – except for Canadian procrastinations at the time of the Cuban crisis – alerts have been carried out speedily and efficiently. No less importantly, tens of thousands of aircraft flying over North America are identified each day by NORAD's radar screens and interceptors, while a daily average of more than 12,000 observations on approximately 1600 objects have been recorded by the sensor network of the Space Detection and Tracking System. The joint air command provides both countries with valuable information regarding radioactive fallout, and it cooperates closely with air-sea rescue agencies. Furthermore, its annual operating cost has been quite modest, amounting in recent years to about $150,000,000 annually for Canada and $1,120,000,000 for the United States.[27]

Despite these and other benefits that the two countries have derived from NORAD, the organization's future is most uncertain. For one thing, if the bomber threat continues to diminish, as seems likely, Canadian airspace will become much less important to the defence of the United States and its retaliatory force. Once that threat completely disappears, most of NORAD's remaining functions could be adequately discharged by the United States alone.[28] Each country could handle its own air and water surveillance responsibilities, with only close coordination of the two national efforts. The proposed new alignment of air defence regions and the recent Canadian moves to establish its own joint civil-military system of airspace surveillance and control may very well be important first steps in the direction of substituting a coordinated type of control for the NORAD system of integration.

Numerous Canadians have long objected to the integrative features of NORAD.[29] If it should be determined that the dissolution of the joint command would not weaken North American security, increasing numbers of Canadians are likely to support such a move. Although they would be reluctant to see hundreds of millions of dollars spent on the development of a sophisticated all-Canadian AWACS-OTH-B system, they might conclude that the greater freedom of action that a national system would make possible would be worth the monetary cost.

Certainly NORAD no longer commands the measure of support accorded it in 1961 and 1964, when roughly two-thirds of all Canadians polled approved of 'Canada's defence becoming merged more and more with the U.S.'[30] American involvement in Vietnam, the growth of Canadian nationalism, and doubts regarding the organization's military value are some of the factors that have combined to erode the earlier substantial support accorded the joint air command system.[31] And even the Canadian government authorities who have favoured continued Canadian membership in NORAD appear to have been motivated less by military than by political and economic considerations. For example, in his appearance before the Commons Committee, Richardson stressed the point that, since 'our American friends' attached 'considerable importance' to the NORAD agreement, Canadian willingness to renew it would have 'a positive impact on Canadian-U.S. relations at a time when a number of difficult issues have to be settled between our two countries.'[32] The secretary of state for external affairs, Allan J. MacEachen, in his comments to the committee, suggested that the Americans 'would view very seriously the termination of arrangements which in their view add to the effectiveness of that defence.'[33] And the committee itself admitted that, in reaching its affirmative conclusion, it 'was impressed by the argument that a Canadian decision to withdraw from NORAD at this time would be interpreted at home and abroad, not as an isolated development, but as evidence of a possibly major change in the orientation of Canadian foreign policy.'[34] Two years previously the question of the likely impact upon the Defence Production–Development Sharing Program of a Canadian withdrawal from NORAD had been brought up at the committee hearings. Richardson's reply had been that, although no direct questions had been raised along those lines, if Canada withdrew 'it would be unlikely that ... a defence-sharing agreement would continue in its same form.'[35] In one of its reports the committee had commented on the same question but had concluded that it was conceivable that the production program 'would be maintained even if Canada decided to withdraw from NORAD.'[36]

Would Canadian withdrawal from NORAD result in American retaliation against Canada? Since the integrated air command is no longer viewed by Washington officialdom as vital to the defence of the United States, the correct answer, one suspects, is 'probably not.' But, as the Commons Committee pointed out in 1973, American reaction would largely depend on how and why the withdrawal was made: 'While a decision to terminate Canadian participation in NORAD would not necessarily damage Canadian–American relations if made on rational grounds, bilateral relations would be likely to suffer if the debate were conducted in a vituperative manner which called into question the fundamental principle that relations between the two countries must remain close and harmonious.'[37]

15

Defence-production sharing

Although defence-production sharing between Canada and the United States is commonly thought of as having started in 1959, following the Diefenbaker government's cancellation of the Arrow project,[1] in reality that program, like cooperation in military defence, dates from the Second World War. It traces its antecedents to the Roosevelt–King informal Hyde Park Agreement of 20 April 1941. To help alleviate a critical Canadian balance of payments problem and, at the same time, to speed up the production of urgently needed military supplies and equipment, the two political leaders accepted and publicly affirmed 'the then revolutionary ... principle'[2] that 'in mobilizing the resources of this continent each country should provide the other with the defense articles which it is best able to produce, and, above all, produce quickly, and that production programs should be coordinated to this end.'[3]

The accord, implemented by five separate Canadian–American joint economic agencies established between 14 May 1941 and 22 August 1943, contributed so significantly to the mobilizing of North American resources and the winning of the war[4] that it is not surprising that the two governments agreed in May 1945 to continue the general principles of the Hyde Park Declaration 'into the post-war transitional period.'[5] Unfortunately, in the frenzied rush of both countries to demobilize following the termination of the war, this agreement was overlooked and the joint agencies that might have been utilized were dismantled and only the Permanent Joint Board on Defence was left to promote cooperation in defence production and standardization of arms and equipment. But, largely no doubt because of the pressures of the Cold War and the urgent pleas of Canadian spokesmen for a revival of the Hyde Park-type of cooperation, on 12 April 1949, through an exchange of notes, the Joint United States–Canada Industrial Mobilization Committee was created, consisting of two members from each country, to promote the exchange of information and the coordination of the views of the two governments in connection with planning for industrial mobilization.[6] For more than a year the committee accomplished very little. This was partly due to certain restrictive American laws, including one that debarred the sale of American weapons, munitions, and materials to foreign buyers unless the articles in question had been declared surplus to the needs of the American Armed Forces[7] and another, a 'Buy American' Act, specifying that American military supplies were to be purchased only within the United States except when it was 'in the national interest' to buy them elsewhere because stocks were not domestically available, or costs were out of line with foreign prices, or an emergency existed.[8] A second obstacle to effective defence production cooperation was the pressures exerted upon Congress and the administration by powerful American mining and manufacturing interests, who insisted that American industry could produce all the defence items needed for the nation's rearmament program.[9]

With North Korea's invasion of South Korea on 25 June 1950, and the great increase in the Defense Department's demand for military supplies of all kinds, the complacent American attitude of 'business as usual' received a terrific jolt. Meeting in Ottawa some six weeks later, the Joint Industrial Mobilization Committee, in a statement reminiscent of the Hyde Park Agreement, asserted that Canada and the United States should 'co-operate in all respects practicable, and to the extent of their respective executive powers, to the end that the economic efforts of the two countries be coordinated for the common defense and that the production and resources of both countries be used for the best combined results.' To facilitate these objectives, it set forth a 'Statement of Principles for Economic Cooperation' calling for the development of a coordinated Canadian–American program of requirements, production, and procurement; coordinated controls over the distribution of scarce raw materials and supplies; consultation before imposing economic controls; free exchange, where feasible, of technical knowledge and productive skills; and the removal, as far as possible, of 'barriers which impede the flow between Canada and the United States of goods essential for the common effort.'

Some eleven weeks later the decisions of the committee were officially approved by the two governments in a signature-affixing ceremony held in Washington on 26 October 1950.[10] More important still, significant steps were taken to implement the new-style 'Hyde Park Agreement.' Thus, early in November the United States placed a $10,000,000 order for naval guns with Sorel Industries, at Sorel, Quebec, and both countries imposed strict controls over the use of steel and both agreed to restrict consumer credit. The following month the American authorities announced that the ceiling for United States purchases in Canada for the fiscal year 1951 was being raised from the pre-Korean War figure of $25,000,000 to a new maximum of $100,000,000. Certain supplies imported from Canada were granted exemption from the 'Buy American' Act and improved arrangements were worked out to grant Canadian firms access to classified information about American defence projects.[11] Most important of all, Canada began rapidly to standardize its arms and other equipment on the United States pattern, shipping much of its stock of British-type weapons to its European allies.

On through 1952 and into 1953 the coordinated defence production programs continued at a lively pace. Both military goods and scarce raw materials were produced in impressive quantities. Reciprocal procurement was boosted, and a large measure of cooperation was introduced into such fields as price stabilization, the determination of production priorities, and the control over the export of scarce commodities. And American purchases of arms and equipment in Canada came close to approximating Canadian purchases from the United States. With, however, the ending of the Korean hostilities in July 1953, vested American interests began demanding once more preferential treatment for domestic producers. The Eisenhower cabinet, composed largely of businessmen, although kindly disposed towards Canada, was not inclined to fight very hard for the 'Principles for Economic Cooperation,' especially since the Canadian government itself seemed to favour domestic industry in defence contracting.[12] The Industrial Mobilization Committee, which might have been expected to spearhead the fight for continued economic cooperation, quietly went into a sleep – from which it has not yet awakened[13] – and American arms purchases from Canada steadily declined. By 1954 the old pre-Korean War pattern had been restored, with Canada regularly spending more on purchases in the United States than that country was spending north of the border.

The decline in American purchases, however, was only relative. More important still, the Canadian defence industry quickly demonstrated that it was not only vigorous and enterprising, but was strong enough to compete with American industry in the manufacture of many defence items. Thus, by the mid-1950s it was

producing a wider range of more sophisticated military equipment than it ever had. Canada had produced no aircraft engines during World War II, but by 1957 it was producing the R-1340 and R-1820 piston and Nene, Orenda and Iroquois jet engines. It had developed an advanced electronics industry. It was selling to the U.S. at least six kinds of aircraft: the F-86 and CF-100 fighters, Harvard and T-34 trainers, and Beaver and other transport aircraft. In short, while it remained dependent upon the U.S. for many of its military needs, by the mid-1950's Canada was in a position not only to produce most of the military equipment needed for its own forces, but also to compete on a selective basis for U.S. orders.[14]

Ironically, this expertise of the Canadian defence industry eventually became a source of embarrassment to the Canadian government. This came about when the government authorities in 1953 – with totally inadequate consideration of all the cost and construction factors involved – contracted with A.V. Roe of Canada Ltd. to produce an all-weather jet interceptor aircraft for Canada's air defence. The original thought was that only the airframe would be developed in Canada; the engine, the fire control system, and the weapons would be obtained from the United States or from Britain and the United States. It was also hoped that the United States, and possibly other of Canada's NATO allies, would purchase a number of the new planes. In the end, due to circumstances too complicated to detail here, all of the component parts were produced in Canada, with, of course, an enormous increase in construction costs over the original estimates. The plane – labelled the CF-105, but popularly referred to as the Arrow – made its test flight 25 March 1958. Its performance was excellent, but by that date the dominant opinion in the United States, as well as in Canada, was that the greatest threat to North America was no longer manned bombers, which the Arrow had been designed to counter, but rather intercontinental missiles, against which the interceptor could offer no defence.[15]

In September 1958, in a statement to the press, Prime Minister Diefenbaker announced that, because of new developments in the missile field, the government had decided: (1) not to put the Arrow into production 'at this time' but to continue its development pending a new review of its future in six months; (2) to discontinue immediately production of the radar and rocket weapons systems designed for the Arrow; (3) to purchase from the United States for introduction into Canada the Semi-Automatic Ground Environment (SAGE) system and the Bomarc surface-to-air missiles that went with it; and (4) to open at once discussions with the American authorities looking towards the participation by Canadian industry in the development and production of equipment for North American defence.[16] Late in February 1959 – when it became painfully evident that there would be no foreign market for the Arrow; that production solely for Canada's limited needs would be prohibitively expensive; and that, in any event, the Arrow had been made largely obsolete by the rapid development of electronics and guided missiles – the prime minister advised the House of Commons that work on the interceptor would be terminated at once and that Canadian air defence would be based on equipment obtained from the United States.[17]

As numerous writers were quick to point out, this statement of policy carried immense implications for Canada.[18] The government, in effect, was admitting that Canada could not carry out the independent development of sophisticated weapons, and that any such weapons as it might thereafter wish to acquire would have to be obtained from the United States or some other outside source. This, in turn, raised various difficult questions. Would a Canadian defence industry be able to survive? Would closer economic integration with the United States result in a weakening of national control over the Canadian economy? And would Canada be able to maintain its political independence if the government relinquished control over vital defence decisions?

Understandably enough, Diefenbaker and his ministers were not able to provide reassuring answers to these and other troublesome questions. Perhaps none was possible. That there were disadvantages and risks involved in linking up the Canadian economy more closely with that of the United States was readily apparent. For one thing, economic dependence might, unavoidably, lead to a loss of Canadian freedom to determine its own foreign and defence policies. In contrast, if Canada wished to continue making a contribution to the defence of North America, integration in defence production seemed to be the only satisfactory option open to the Diefenbaker government. As has already been indicated, in August 1957 a joint command for North American air defence (NORAD) had been set up. That required each country to obtain some expensive, sophisticated military hardware. Since Canada was no longer able to develop major weapons systems for its own forces, the logical alternative was to obtain the needed systems from the United States. But that, in turn, as Canadian spokesmen repeatedly asserted, made it imperative that Canadian defence industry be accorded easy access to American markets. Although they had been less than enthusiastic over earlier Canadian proposals of defence production sharing, and were still under tremendous pressures from the Munitions Lobby in Washington to reserve the American market for American industrialists,[19] the president and his advisers now acknowledged both the logic and reasonableness of Canada's position. Nor is that surprising. Given their preoccupation with 'the Soviet military threat,' they logically concluded it was essential that Canada's very substantial defence production capability be fully utilized. Thus, even before the cancellation of the Arrow, Eisenhower assured the prime minister that the American government was prepared to work out production sharing arrangements with Canada.[20]

As it turned out, working out the provisions and procedures of the Defence Production Sharing Program proved to be a lengthy process, extending over a number of months, and the program itself eventually included a dozen or more directives, declarations, and agreements, 'all of which remain in force indefinitely subject to modification or termination at any time by mutual agreement or by written notice of the intention of one party to terminate them.'[21] But, like the Ogdensburg and Hyde Park agreements, the production program was launched in a most informal manner. On the occasion of Eisenhower's visit to Ottawa in July 1958 a general understanding was reached that such a program should be initiated. Detailed arrangements were then worked out by a bilateral committee at the level of deputy minister and assistant secretary. These were then approved by the Canadian minister of defence production, the American secretary of defence, and President Eisenhower. Then, without any treaty or exchange of notes, they were given practical effect in July 1960 when the American Department of Defense incorporated them into a revised directive entitled 'Defense Economic Cooperation with Canada.'[22]

The directive set forth as the major purpose of the program 'the policy of maximum production and development ... in support of closely integrated military planning between the United States and Canada.' This purpose was to be achieved through 'the best possible coordination of the materiel programs' of the two countries, including 'actual integration insofar as practicable' of their industrial mobilization efforts. As a corollary, the Department of Defense would attempt 'to assure Canada a fair opportunity to share in the production of military equipment and materiel involving programs of mutual interest' to the two countries 'and in the research and development connected therewith.'

Supplementing the directive was an informal accord by the terms of which the United States agreed to share the costs of the Bomarc guided missiles, the SAGE control and computing equipment, and the radar stations that were to be introduced into the Canadian defence system. In the construction of bases in Canada, work was to be carried out 'by Canadian construction companies employing Canadian labour and material.' When completed, the bases were to be manned by Canadian military personnel. Most important of all, a share of the work of producing the technical equipment financed by the United States was to be carried out by Canadian industry.

Responsibility for formulating and implementing the joint production program was assigned to the Senior Committee on Defence Production–Development Sharing, composed of members at the level of assistant secretary and deputy minister (along with supporting staff members) drawn from the American Department of Defense and the Canadian Departments of Defence Production, National Defence, External Affairs, and Finance. Although the committee has had no meetings since 1966, it had previously met twice a year, alternating between Ottawa and Washington, presided over by its two co-chairmen. It had no permanent secretariat but was assisted by a Joint Steering Group and various working groups. In addition to its general supervisory responsibility, the committee was expected to coordinate, as far as possible, the defence requirements, development, production, and procurement for the two countries, and, in particular, to see to it that applications of Canadian industrialists for defence contracts received prompt and proper attention. Following the discontinuance of the committee meetings, the coordinating and expediting responsibilities were handled first by person-to-person contacts of the civil servants and then, after 1972, by the Joint Steering Group, which meets annually.[23]

During the first half-dozen years of the program's operation it likewise commanded the attention of another joint agency: the Canada United States Ministerial Committee on Joint Defence created in September 1958. The origin, organization, and activities of that top-level organization will be discussed later.[24] Here, however, it should be noted that one of the functions it was expected to discharge was to help launch and then exercise general oversight over the Defence Production Sharing Program. And down to 1964, when it became inactive, it took this responsibility quite seriously. Thus at each of its four meetings (in 1958, 1959, 1960, and 1964) it gave extensive attention to the production program. At the fourth meeting it agreed to undertake a special study with respect to maintaining a rough balance between the two countries in the purchase of defence equipment in each other's country.[25] Following the abandonment of the committee meetings, the general supervisory function was discharged through informal procedures.

Understandably, administration of Defence Production Sharing has been both delicate and difficult. The industrialists of one country can hardly be expected to welcome the entry into the home market of competitors from another country. Legislators, sensitive to domestic interests and pressures, are likely to raise embarrassing questions as to why the manufacturers and workers of a foreign country should be accorded equality of treatment with those of the home country.[26] There is also a natural reluctance on the part of a great power to admit that items designed and manufactured in a small country can be comparable in quality to those produced at home. Adding to the difficulties at the outset were the restrictive American laws and regulations, such as the 'Buy American' Act, referred to above.

Despite the difficulties, through the combined and sustained efforts of the diplomats, the civil servants, and the defence contractors, Canadian contractors were soon granted a number of important concessions. The 'Buy American' Act was waived for all defence supplies made in Canada for American defence contracts. With a few exceptions, Canadian materials were exempted under the program from all American duties. Canadian manufacturers were granted access to classified information concerning weapons projects; and American military procurement procedures were modified to expedite Canadian bidding on American contracts.

A significant fact is that to 1966 the concessions all were one-sided. In that year the Canadian government lifted the tariff on all Canadian defence orders in the United States in excess of $250,000. Prior to that date Canada had yielded nothing in return for the significant concessions made by the United States – neither tariff reductions nor the acceptance of obligations to buy American military equipment. Nor is that surprising since the major objective of the program was to promote the development of a *Canadian* defence industry.

Despite the American concessions of 1959–62, many Canadians still were not satisfied. In order to compete effectively with American manufacturers, Canadian firms needed to be involved in the actual development of at least some of the defence articles. This need Canadian spokesmen, with the full support of the joint committees and working groups, convincingly argued in various meetings with representatives of the government in Washington. The eventual outcome was a formal agreement between the United States Department of Defense and the Canadian Department of Defence Production, signed in November 1963, setting up arrangements for participation by Canadian industry in American defence development projects on a cost sharing basis.[27] Private industry was authorized to undertake the development projects but the costs were to be shared by the American and the Canadian governments and interested Canadian firms.

The only reciprocal Canadian concession was a commitment, given by Minister of Defence Production Charles M. Drury to American Secretary of Defense Robert S. McNamara, that Canada would cooperate in keeping trade in defence items between the two countries in 'rough balance.'[28]

Canada, it is generally agreed, has derived numerous economic benefits from the operation of the program. For example, from 1959 through 1971 it sold defence supplies and equipment in the United States valued at $3,385,400,000, while the United States had sales in Canada totalling $3,024,200,000.[29] Although the balance in recent years has shifted in favour of the United States, Canada continues to sell vast quantities of defence items to its southern neighbour. No less importantly, by keeping a Canadian defence industry alive, the program has provided jobs to some 15,000 Canadian workers, as well as profits to more than 150 companies (even though many of them are American-owned). The program has enabled Canadian industry to keep abreast of advanced technology in such fields as electronics and aerospace and to undertake 'a variety of highly advanced, and sometimes very profitable, programs on behalf of the u.s. military,' such as the AN/GRC-103 radio relay system 'developed by Canadian Marconi Ltd. and sold in substantial quantities to the u.s.'[30]

From the military viewpoint, the Defence Production Sharing Program has, undoubtedly, served well American interests. It has made possible a greater dispersal of North American defence industries, which, even in this nuclear age, is still highly desirable.[31] It has promoted standardization of military equipment. And it has enabled the United States to obtain from Canada numerous items not readily procurable from American sources.

The program, however, has been severaly critized in both countries. For example, a few years ago concerned Americans regularly complained that defence production sharing was depriving thousands of American workers of jobs and, at the same time, was contributing to American balance-of-payments problems.[32] They also occasionally added the pointed reminder that Canada was not buying enough American equipment to maintain the 'rough balance' called for by the Drury–McNamara agreement of 1963. To help restore the trade balance, in 1971 Secretary of the Treasury John Connally urged Canada not only to eliminate its tariffs on American defence exports but to purchase the American-produced Lockheed Orion to replace its obsolete Argus patrol planes.[33] Connally's exit from government service and the improvement in the American balance-of-payments position (following the termination of hostilities in Vietnam) combined to moderate the pressure on Canada, but disgruntled American legislators and industrialists can still be found who would like to see the program either terminated or significantly modified.

Even more numerous and emphatic have been the Canadian objections. Thus it has been contended that the program has seriously restricted the Canadian government's freedom of action in the conduct of the nation's foreign policy;[34] that it presents an ever-present threat of Canada's being pulled into a war economy;[35] that it has promoted some segments of the economy at the expense of other segments;[36] that it has promoted the takeover by the United States of Canadian firms in the defence industry;[37] that it has served to protect inefficient Canadian industry;[38] that it has undermined Canada's role 'as an international arbitrator and negotiator';[39] and that, in any event, the program runs counter to Canada's traditional policy of avoiding economic integration with the United States.

Still another Canadian criticism of a few years ago was that changed conditions had made the program obsolete. In the forties and fifties, and even in the early sixties, all North Americans had assumed that the military equipment produced under the cooperative program would always be used against a common enemy. But during the years 1965–73 the United States waged war against North Vietnam, a country that Canada did not consider an enemy. Although the Canadian government consistently refused to permit military equipment to be shipped directly to Vietnam, many such items exported to the United States eventually found their way to southeastern Asia.[40] Since they viewed American military actions in Vietnam as both ill-advised and immoral, concerned Canadians demanded that their government terminate at once the cooperative program. To such demands the usual Canadian reply was that, since the bulk of Canadian sales to the United States was component parts, rather than finished products, it was impossible to know how much of it found its way to Vietnam; that by affording Canada an opportunity to obtain essential defence equipment at the lowest possible cost, the cooperative program served well Canada's own national interests; and that, in any event, stopping the sale of Canadian defence materials would have little impact on the American war effort but would, undoubtedly, have far-reaching adverse repercussions upon continental defence cooperation and upon Canadian–American relations in general.[41]

Not surprisingly, with the ending of direct American participation in the Vietnamese War, the most vociferous Canadian objections to the defence production sharing program ceased. But many Canadians are still critical, particularly those who take seriously Prime Minister Trudeau's argument that Canada should lessen its dependence on the United States by seeking additional contacts with other countries. If the United States again becomes involved in a war not supported by Canadian public opinion, the vehement Canadian objections of the Vietnamese War era are likely to be revived. However, if in the years ahead the United States avoids involvement in other Vietnamese-types of conflict and, at the same time, no longer feels any special need for Canadian defence items, the strongest objections to the continuation of the joint program may well come from south of the border.

In short, the future of the defence production–development sharing program is clouded in uncertainty. But one conclusion can be safely affirmed: the authorities of neither government are likely to move precipitately in terminating the joint arrangements. They will be restrained not only by their appreciation of the benefits that the arrangements have already brought to both countries, but also by the knowledge that their defence production economies are now so closely intertwined that serious political, as well as economic, repercussions would result from any sudden ending of the cooperative effort.

16

Civil defence and emergency preparedness

Although some Canadian–American cooperation in civil defence (that is, non-military defence) occurred during the Second World War,[1] it was the outbreak of hostilities in Korea, in June 1950, and the rapid worsening of Soviet–Western relations that provided the major impetus to the launching of a significant cooperative civil defence program. Canadians and Americans, it was widely assumed, were confronted with the very real possibility that, with little or no warning, Soviet bombers would launch an all-out thermonuclear attack against their continent. Although the primary targets would probably be American military installations and industries, bombs aimed at Detroit, Seattle, or Minneapolis might fall instead on adjoining densely populated areas in Canada; or the deadly fallout from bombs released over American territory or from those shot down in the Canadian North might extend downwind over Canada's towns and cities. And even if, by some miracle, the bombs and fallout missed Canada completely, if American cities were devastated the Canadian people would undoubtedly insist on going to the aid of their neighbours. Thus common sense dictated that, before the bombs started falling, the two countries arrive at an understanding with respect to the types of assistance that each would provide the other during an emergency and how their civil defence efforts might be most effectively coordinated.

The cooperative scheme first seriously considered was the integration of the civil defence plans of the Canadian provinces with those of the adjacent states through the device of regional compacts negotiated directly by the provinces and states. Thus an Ontario representative participated in talks looking towards the creation of a northeast civil defence arrangement, while representatives of Saskatchewan, Alberta, and British Columbia joined spokesmen of seven states in discussions relating to the establishment of a western mutual assistance program.[2] But the authorities in Ottawa took a dim view of these proposed arrangements. It was all right for the provinces to get together with the states for informal talks, a Canadian spokesman explained, 'but any formal pacts will be made through the u.s. State Department and the Canadian Government.'[3]

In conformity with these Canadian views, early in January 1951 Congress passed and the president signed a bill authorizing the Federal Civil Defense Administrator to 'give all practicable assistance to states in arranging, through the Department of State mutual civil aid between the states and neighboring countries,' and to coordinate the civil defence activities of the departments and agencies, not only with each other but 'with the activities of the states and neighboring countries.'[4] Less than three months later, on 27 March 1951, through an exchange of notes, the two national governments entered into a formal Joint Civil Defence Mutual Aid Agreement.[5]

'As far as possible,' the agreement affirmed, the civil defence activities of the neighbouring countries 'should be coordinated for the protection of persons and property from the result of enemy attack as if there were no border.' Except for 'matters of broad government policy,' for which the diplomatic channels would be appropriate, the normal channel of communication with regard to civil defence would be between the Co-ordinator of Civil Defence in Canada (or any successor authority) and the Administrator, Federal Civil Defense Administration, in the United States (or any successor authority). The federal civil defence authority of each country would keep the other informed about developments under consideration or actions taken with respect to such matters as organization, equipment, training, public information, and arrangements with state, provincial, and municipal authorities. It would also exchange personnel at the working level and offer training facilities to students designated by the other country. Appropriate legislation would be sought and instructions would be given 'in connection with customs, immigration, integration of services and facilities and other matters whether under federal, state, provincial or municipal jurisdiction.' The federal civil defence authorities would empower the state and provincial authorities to 'confer together' and to sanction cooperation between border municipalities. The cost of civil defence assistance provided by one country in connection with an attack upon the other country would be 'reimbursed by the country attacked.'

Significantly, to help implement this cooperative program, the agreement established a Joint United States–Canadian Civil Defence Committee to consist of 'the Federal Civil Defense authorities and such other members as may be designated by them.' The committee was empowered to establish such working groups and subcommittees as might be necessary and to recommend to the two governments such action as was 'considered desirable to insure the closest cooperation.'

The organizational meeting of the committee, attended by eight Canadian and six American representatives, was held in Washington on 28 April, 1951. The delegates, vowing their determination to work out arrangements for an easy exchange of people and equipment 'so there will be no obstacles in the way of mutual assistance,'[6] discussed such topics as medical care, special weapons defence and emergency welfare, the entry of the civil defence forces and materials of one country into the other, training, standardization, and interchange of equipment, communications and warning systems, and state-provincial mutual aid agreements.[7] They decided to set up task forces to study these topics and to meet again the following year to assess progress and to plan new courses of action.

In keeping with this understanding, the committee held annual meetings during the years 1952–8 and participated in the planning and discussions that led to such important joint enterprises as the construction of electronic screens across the central and northern parts of the continent;[8] the staging of joint air defence drills at various times and places along the border; and the drafting and putting into effect of a number of mutual aid agreements.[9] Nevertheless, for civil defence personnel on both sides of the border the seven-year period was one of disappointments and frustrations – disappointments at their failure to win general public support for their programs and objectives and frustrations at their inability to obtain the sustained backing of their respective governments.

Undoubtedly one reason for the lack of public support for civil defence was the frequent changes in the programs and procedures announced from time to time by the civil defence spokesmen. For example, in the early 1950s they stressed the importance of being prepared, in the event of a nuclear attack, for the wholesale evacuation of the urban populations. Later they came to place chief emphasis on guaranteeing to city residents the availability of blast shelters. Later still they concluded that only the people living near prime targets would need blast shelters; everyone else would require protection only from fallout radiation. Of course, these changes of emphasis were partly the result of changes in technology and military strategy, but, unfortunately, no one bothered to provide those concerned with adequate explanations.

A second, and even more compelling reason for the failure of many North Americans to support civil defence was their conviction that it was either completely useless or, worse still, potentially dangerous. Thus some of them were positive, as tens of thousands still are, that there can be no real defence against nuclear war, that, 'despite any conceivable civil defense program, this nation the United States, its population, its economic wealth, its social fabric – all that we speak of as our civilization – would be lost irretrievably after a nuclear war.'[10] Other concerned persons stressed the 'fantastic' cost of bomb shelters, the difficulties involved in staying in shelters for any length of time, and the impossible conditions certain to confront any survivors of a nuclear attack. Other critics feared that the expenditure of billions of dollars on bomb shelters would create among the people of the United States a 'Maginot Line mentality' – a belief that their country was so well prepared for nuclear war that it no longer needed to make large expenditures on military hardware. Still others feared that civil defence preparations would not only accelerate the arms race and encourage 'brinkmanship' diplomacy, but might, if carried too far, provoke the Soviet Union to launch a pre-emptive attack.[11]

These opposition arguments were, of course, emphatically rejected by the champions of civil defence. Thus they affirmed that shelters would not only provide substantial protection to lives and property but would greatly facilitate recuperation after a war ended. As for the cost, when the choice was between the loss of an additional fifty million people and the spending of thirty to fifty billion dollars, there could be no question that the North American people could finance the needed shelters. Since both the Soviet Union and Communist China already had ambitous shelter programs under way, they could hardly view North American shelters as 'provocative.' In fact, a Soviet pre-emptive attack was more likely to be precipitated by the lack, rather than the existence, of such shelters.

Unfortunately for its champions, civil defence was not uniformly supported by the officials in Washington. For example, during the early 1950s Pentagon spokesmen, in their eagerness to obtain as large appropriations as possible for 'active' defence, were opposed to the spending of more than a token amount of money on shelters and other forms of 'passive' defence. Although they eventually came to accept shelters as a useful supplement to the nuclear deterrent, there can be no doubt that their earlier negative position made more difficult the efforts of President Truman to win Congressional support for a sizeable shelter program.

President Eisenhower gave lip service to shelters, but, since he wanted to limit the powers of the federal government, wanted to balance the budget, and did not want to divert money from other types of defence or from foreign aid, he chose to place the responsibility for providing shelter protection largely on the states and individual house owners.[12] Nor was Congress at all helpful. From the fiscal year 1951 through the fiscal year 1957 the Federal Civil Defense Administration requested $1931 million and was given $398 million. By sharp contrast, during the same period the Department of Defense requested $300.3 billion and received $289.2 billion![13]

The Canadian story was not significantly different. Ignoring advice such as that tendered by James Eayrs that Canada set an example for the United States by launching a 'full-scale civil defence programme,'[14] successive Ottawa governments of the 1950s seemed content to leave the initiative to others. Thus they accepted American assessments of the effectiveness of new weapons and of the prospects of defence against them[15] and publicly affirmed that civil defence was largely the responsibility of the provinces and the municipalities.[16] Accordingly, their requests for civil defence appropriations invariably were extremely modest – never exceeding $4,500,000 annually for the period 1948–58.[17] This parsimonious policy, however, evoked hardly a ripple of protest from a largely apathetic public.[18]

The civil defence officials of the two countries, however, were anything but apathetic. Nor could they afford to be. In 1949 the Soviet Union had detonated its first atomic bomb; by 1953 it had developed not only a hydrogen bomb but also bombers capable of penetrating to the industrial heartland of North America. October 1957 brought the successful orbiting of Sputnik 1, ominously revealing the Soviet intercontinental ballistic missile potential and shaking the foundations of the earlier civil defence policy of evacuation. The previously assumed warning time of three hours was now reduced to a mere fifteen to twenty minutes. What evacuation could be carried out in that length of time? And why bother with either national or international civil defence exercises? Suspending without an official explanation the annual meetings of the Civil Defence Committee, the two governments turned to the consideration of new civil defence concepts and reorganizations.[19]

The first significant moves occurred in Canada, where to 1959 federal civil defence responsibilities had been divided among half a dozen or more departments. In that year a new agency, the Canada Emergency Measures Organization, was set up in the Privy Council Office and made responsible for coordinating all emergency planning not only with the agencies of the federal government but also for assisting and coordinating provincial activities. It likewise was authorized to develop programs directed towards the survival of Canada as a nation, while the Federal Civil Defence Division of the Department of Health and Welfare retained the responsibility for matters relating directly to the protection of the Canadian population against enemy actions. Two years later those particular duties were also taken over by the Emergency Measures Organization, while the Department of Health and Welfare, along with the Departments of National Defence and of Justice, was assigned some emergency measures responsibilities.[20]

Although President Eisenhower chose to emphasize 'massive retaliation' and to de-emphasize shelters, he gave civil defence a psychological boost in July 1958 when he issued an executive order merging the Federal Civil Defense Administration and the Office of Defense Mobilization to form the Office of Civil and Defense Mobilization, and giving the director of the new agency cabinet status and a seat in the National Security Council. Also that same year civil defence was made the joint responsibility of the federal, state, and local governments, whereas earlier the emphasis had been on the responsibilities of the state and local authorities. But this concentration of all civil defence functions in one agency did not work out very well. Because of meagre financial resources, OCDM concentrated 'on the more pressing operational aspects – the tangible hardware-type problems of civil defense – at the expense of more forward planning in mobilization and resources management for post-attack recovery.'[21] In an effort to remedy this situation and to secure Pentagon support and funds, on 20 July 1961 OCDM was split into the Office of Civil Defense (OCD) and the Office of Emergency Planning (OEP). OEP, located in the Executive Office of the President and represented on the National Security Council, in addition to 'advising the President upon the coordination of economic, industrial, and civilian mobilization in time of war,'[22] was expected to concern itself, free of all responsibility for operations, with the long-range policy and planning aspects of mobilizing the nation's resources for future national emergencies. At the same time, the prestige and the resources of the Department of Defense, in which the Office of Civil Defense was located, would be sufficient, it was hoped, to guarantee 'greater progress in the implementation of the civil defense program.'[23]

While these reorganizations were in progress, joint civil defence did little more than mark time. A Standing Planning Group, created in 1958, was able the following year to complete the draft of a province–state planning guide and to set up a pilot group to study civil defence problems in the Niagara Falls–Buffalo area, but little else of any significance was achieved during the years 1959–61.[24] In 1962, however, top civil defence spokesmen of the two countries held a couple of meetings for the purpose of reactivating cross-border consultation, fostering the exchange of information, and revising the agreement of 1951. Out of these meetings came three regional conferences in the spring of 1963 – attended by state, provincial, and local, as well as federal, spokesmen – convened to consider civil defence problems along the entire border. Questions raised at the conferences were discussed later that year in Toronto at a meeting of officials of the Canadian Emergency Measures Organization and the American Offices of Civil Defense and of Emergency Planning, after which assignments were made to agencies, working groups, and departments to investigate and report on problems in such fields as transportation, communications, radiological defence, and intergovernmental agreements. In due course studies were completed in these and other areas. Equally significantly, on 15 November 1963, a new agreement to replace that of 1951 was effected by an exchange of notes.[25]

As its title, 'Defense: Civil Emergency Planning,' indicates,[26] the new accord was much broader in scope than that of 1951, which had dealt only with civil defence viewed in the narrow concept of population survival. By 1963 that concept was viewed as outmoded. Now, everyone agreed, it was essential not only to ensure the immediate survival of the population but to guarantee, if possible, the survival of the organized governments, food supplies, natural resources, and industries upon which the welfare and existence of the people and national recovery from nuclear attack would ultimately depend. Moreover, the agreement of 1951 had made the top civil defence coordinator of each country the chief point of contact with respect to mutual civil defence matters. Now there were two top officials in the United States with significant responsibilities with respect to civil defence and related matters. No less important, there were scores of agencies – national, provincial, state, and municipal – actively interested in civil emergency planning. In short, as the new agreement noted, planning had 'reached a stage at which it would be mutually advantageous to revise the liaison arrangements between the two countries and to establish direct channels for detailed and technical consultation on civil defense, the use of resources in emergencies, and other aspects of civil emergency planning.' Accordingly, the two governments agreed to create a Joint United States–Canada Civil Emergency Planning Committee (to replace the earlier Joint Civil Defence Committee) to meet at least once a year and to consist of Canada's secretary to the cabinet and the director of the Canada Emergency Measures Organization, the American director of the Office of Emergency Planning, the assistant secretary of defence for civil defence and other representatives as might be designated. Joint secretaries were to be provided by the Departments of State and of External Affairs.

In addition to performing the two important functions assigned the earlier committee of establishing working groups and subcommittees and of making recommendations, the new committee – usually referred to as the Senior Committee – was empowered to arrange for direct communications between the civil emergency planning authorities of the two countries; to facilitate the exchange of information; and to make arrangements to facilitate civil emergency planning among public authorities in states, provinces, and municipalities adjacent to one another along the border.

Under the guidance of the Senior Committee, the two countries took a number of significant cooperative actions during the years 1963–6. These included conducting joint studies of the effects of nuclear attacks on the North American economy; establishing landline teletype communications between four headquarters regions in Canada and four corresponding regions south of the boundary; holding joint discussions with respect to supplies, welfare, health, manpower, and transportation; preparing lists of counterpart officers at the federal and regional levels; perfecting and coordinating operational systems for forecasting, monitoring, reporting, and evaluating post-attack radiation hazards; sharing information regarding warning systems; and exchanging views regarding the broadcasting of instructions to the public.[27]

During the same period the civil emergency organization of each country was able to chalk up some progress in dealing with distinctively national problems, thereby indirectly strengthening the joint effort. For example, in the United States the Office of Civil Defense, operating on a very modest budget, identified potential fallout areas in existing buildings with a capacity to shield 140,000,000 persons and succeeded in establishing and stockpiling in those buildings sufficient shelters to accommodate 70,000,000 persons.[28] In Canada the civil emergency officials developed a more professional attitude in their day-to-day work and learned better how to coordinate their own efforts with those of other government agencies. More significantly still, in both countries the staffs concerned with emergency measures began taking an active part in dealing with peacetime disasters. Thus American officials rendered highly useful services during the Alaskan Earthquake of 1964 and the hurricane emergencies of 1964;[29] and Canada's Emergency Measures Organization provided exceptional leadership in the spring of 1966 when thousands of military personnel, civil servants, and volunteers laboured successfully to prevent the Red River from flooding large areas of Manitoba, prompting an Ontario paper to remark that the test should have proved to a sceptical public that EMO was 'not just an agency organized to serve in the event of nuclear war' but could also lend aid during any disaster.[30]

The civil emergency agencies, however, were still confronted with formidable problems. Not the least of these was the continued apathy of the North American people with respect to civil defence programs in general and fallout shelters in particular, and the continued reluctance of their legislatures to appropriate sufficient funds for civil defence purposes. For example, because many members believed that the broad question of anti-missile defence should first be resolved before large additional expenditures were made on civil defence, the United States Senate refused both in 1963 and 1964 to appropriate funds to finance a 'pilot' program designed to provide shelters for ten million people.[31] In both countries the need to obtain the concurrence of the state, provincial, and municipal authorities for all important programs and actions frequently proved frustratingly difficult and time-consuming.

Even the agreement of 1963, which for a time had provided a satisfactory framework for civil emergency cooperation, became less satisfactory as joint planning was expanded to include many additional areas of government. Joint consultations in the resources field, which should have been continuous and comprehensive, tended to be sporadic, uncoordinated, and limited mainly to 'an examination of mutual support needs during the immediate post-attack period.'[32] Increasingly, representatives of the two central governments came to feel that more detailed guidance was needed; while American spokesmen pointed out that the existing agreement did not contain sufficient legal authority to allow their individual departments to proceed with the type of cooperative planning originally visualized.[33] These deficiencies were discussed by the Senior Committee at its annual meeting, on 21 April 1965, and an understanding was reached that a broader agreement should be negotiated. Officials in the Office of Emergency Planning prepared a first draft, which, when approved by the Department of State and other interested American departments, was transmitted to Ottawa, where it was reviewed not only by the Emergency Measures Organization but also by fifteen other agencies.[34] The eventual outcome was an agreement, put into effect 8 August 1967, replacing that of 1963.[35]

The new accord, it should be emphasized, enunciated no new statements of policy and made only minor modifications in the cooperative machinery. What it did do was to set forth in a lengthy annex principles and planning goals to provide 'more detailed guidance for ... the two governments in the development of compatible plans for mutual support in the event of armed attack on [the North American territory of] either country.' The list includes such principles as the following: if the normal application of law in either country causes delays or hardships, 'appropriate alleviation' may be requested of the other country; in areas of common concern, attempts will be made to ensure that 'the plans of the two governments for the emergency use of manpower, material resources, supplies, systems and services shall, where feasible and practicable, be compatible'; each government 'will use its best efforts to facilitate the movement of evacuees, refugees, civil emergency personnel, equipment or other resources into ... or across its territory'; each government will avoid, as far as possible, a 'levy of any national tax on the services, equipment and supplies of the other country when the latter are engaged in civil emergency activities on the territory of the other, and will use their best efforts to encourage state, provincial and local authorities to do likewise'; each government will provide 'adequate security and care for the personnel, equipment and resources of the other country entering its territory by mutual agreement in pursuance of authorized civil emergency activities'; each government will encourage and facilitate 'cooperative emergency arrangements between adjacent jurisdictions on matters falling within the competence of such jurisdictions.'

The Senior Committee was to continue but with a changed membership. Representatives of the Departments of State and of External Affairs were made full-fledged members instead of joint secretaries and the secretary to the cabinet was dropped as a member. The other members were to be, for Canada, the director general of the Canada Emergency Measures Organization and, for the United States, the director of the Office of Emergency Planning (later renamed the Office of Emergency Preparedness) and the director of civil defence. The Committee Secretariat was to be provided by the Canada Emergency Measures Organization, the Office of Emergency Planning, and the Office of Civil Defense. The committee was to meet at least once a year and, in addition to the functions specified in the agreement of 1963, was to be responsible for *supervising*[36] United States–Canada cooperative civil emergency planning and arrangements generally, including making recommendations as required to the two governments and providing guidance as required to their departments and agencies, concerning civil emergency plans, cooperation, and mutual assistance.

The signing of the new agreement gave a temporary boost to transboundary cooperative moves. Thus, under the guidance of the Senior Committee, British Columbia and Washington state signed a 'Letter of Understanding' setting forth principles and procedures for provincial–state cooperation both in formulating plans for dealing with civil emergencies and in rendering 'all possible help to the other' during times of actual emergency. An identical 'Letter of Understanding' later was signed with Montana by both British Columbia and Alberta; while New Brunswick and Quebec each, in turn, entered into informal arrangements with Maine covering civil defence training and equipment transportation.[37] More significantly still, the Canadian minister of national health and welfare and the American secretary of health, education and welfare signed an 'Understanding' designed to facilitate the effective employment of all available health personnel of both countries during an emergency.[38]

The accelerated pace, however, was not to continue. In the early 1970s 'reorganization fever' once again struck south of the border. In 1972 the Office of Civil Defense was abolished and its functions transferred to a new organization, the Defense Civil Preparedness Agency, directly responsible to the secretary of defence. The following year the Office of Emergency Preparedness was abolished and some of its functions were turned over to the newly created Federal Disaster Assistance Administration, set up in the Department of Housing and Urban Development, and some to a new organization, the Office of Preparedness (later renamed Federal Preparedness Agency), established in the General Services Administration. Largely, no doubt, because of these reorganizations, combined with increasing American preoccupation with Vietnam, in 1972 both the Senior Committee and its elaborate hierarchy of supporting committees discontinued their meetings. Civil defence personnel in the two countries did, however, keep in touch; and all indications now point towards a renewal of the meetings in the immediate future.[39]

Just how useful the cooperative arrangements would be in dealing with a nuclear holocaust it would be difficult to say. Fortunately thus far they have not been subjected to an actual test. It must be said, however, that the Cuban missile crisis of 1962 appears to have caught the Canadian government authorities considerably 'off-guard.' Reford quotes a minister as having said: 'I went home on Tuesday night, after we had been discussing the crisis in Cabinet all day, and I realized I had no idea what I should do if the missiles were actually fired. I felt like a fool. But I did not know where I should go, or what my responsibilities would be. Nor did I know what would happen to my Department – where my Deputy Minister would be and so on. We were all in the same boat, and after the dust had settled, we raised Cain about it.'[40]

Another nuclear confrontation would, no doubt, find the governments and peoples of both countries better prepared than they were in 1962; but one can not be dead certain on that point. Certainly no North American can derive any reassurances from two incidents of recent years. One of these was a false warning of an imminent attack, inadvertently released from the emergency warning centre at NORAD headquarters in 1971; the second was a false alarm caused by a siren malfunction of the Ontario emergency measures system in 1974. On each occasion the overwhelming majority of the people who heard the warnings demonstrated no understanding what-soever of what was expected of them.[41] The national civil emergency planning officials, unquestionably, understand how in the event of a nu-clear attack the cooperative effort is supposed to be initiated and carried forward. The general pattern has been spelled out in dozens of agreements. One wonders, however, whether either the people or their local govern-ment authorities actually know what they are supposed to do or what assistance they are expected to give, or receive from, the neighbouring country.

What of the future? One thing that seems reasonably certain is that in the years ahead the civil defence officials are likely to devote increasing atten-tion to peacetime emergencies. This is partly because both Canadians and Americans have clearly indicated that they appreciate the assistance that the civil emergency agencies have provided during natural disasters in recent years, and partly because the civil defence officials (who in the past have always had difficulty convincing the taxpayers that the civil defence organizations were actually worth what they cost) are likely to emphasize the non-nuclear disaster functions as one way of improving their public images and of obtaining larger appropriations.[42]

The future of the nuclear disaster preparedness activities is more difficult to forecast. Most political leaders in both countries, along with the majority of North Americans, still seem largely unconcerned over the lack of any worthwhile civil defence preparations for dealing with nuclear warfare. The dominant viewpoint seems to be that of the Canadian minister of national defence, Barnett Danson, who in 1977 unabashedly stated: 'On civil defence, our policy is one of deterrence. We do not see that civil defence contributes to deterrence.'[43] Not surprisingly, the Canadian Emergency Measures Organization (now called Emergency Planning Canada) has seen its annual appropriations reduced from $11,900,000 in 1967–8 to $3,700,000 in 1977–8![44] Similarly, civil defence appropriations in the United States dropped from a peak of $207,000,000 in 1962 to a new low of $71,000,000 in 1977.[45]

There are, however, indications of increasing American concern over recent developments in the Soviet Union: its accelerated missile construction program; its increased attention to the dispersal of industry; and its huge expenditures on shelters and civil defence in general, said to approximate $2 billion annually.[46] No less significantly, in November 1978 the United States Civil Defense Director announced that President Carter had approved the launching of a crisis location program which, as its main component, involves preparations for mass evacuations from the cities.[47] Recently, however, little has been heard about the new program. The 1979 civil defence budget is a mere $98 million, less than the estimated cost of one BI bomber,[48] and the American public is still largely apathetic. If the new SALT agreement is not ratified, an active interest in preparedness may develop both in the United States and in Canada – especially since most military experts hold that fallout shelters both supplement and support active defence systems. If the agreement is ratified, the North American governments are likely to continue largely ignoring preparedness for wartime emergencies.

For both countries one obvious need is the launching of a broader and more intensive information program on all aspects of civil emergency planning. The people need to be fully informed both about why such planning is needed and about what is expected of them during times of emergency. A second need would seem to be wider federal support. The recruiting and equipping of military personnel are not left to the states or provinces. If, as both the civil and the military authorities insist, civil defence is an integral part of the defence effort of each country, it would seem logical for the two national governments to take over as many of the civil defence responsibilities as is compatible with their respective federal systems of government.[49]

A suggestion advanced by a European civil emergency planning expert is that 'at least the planning of a uniform and common non-military defence of the North American continent ... be transferred to NORAD ... (whose air and sea-forces and anti-aircraft artillery are already integrated).'[50] From the standpoint of efficiency, the proposal has much to commend it. But, from a practical standpoint, it probably is unrealistic. For one thing, Canadian nationalism is much too strong to allow NORAD any significant role in Canadian civil emergency planning. Already there is concern in some Canadian quarters that, in the name of civil emergency cooperation, Canadian resources may be pre-empted by the United States.[51] At the same time, it is hard to quarrel with the expert's conclusion that civil defence will never constitute any real deterrent to an attack on North America until non-military defence preparations reach a 'high standard' in both countries.[52]

If the Canadian and the American peoples should conclude – as they may very well – that civil defence is making no significant contribution to deterrence, they may insist that the civil defence personnel abandon their efforts directed towards preparing for nuclear war emergencies and direct all of their time and resources towards dealing with non-nuclear disasters. Should that happen, there would, of course, still be need for Canadian–American cooperation in civil emergency planning and operations.

17

The Canada–United States Ministerial Committee on Joint Defence

An interesting innovation of the 1950s was the creation of two joint cabinet committees: the Ministerial Committee on Trade and Economic Affairs, established in 1953, and the Ministerial Committee on Joint Defence, set up in 1958. Of course, joint committees were used during the Second World War, but they were composed not of cabinet members but of top civil servants. Furthermore, they were actively engaged in operations, whereas the committees of recent years have been concerned with the exchange of information, the solution of problems, and the coordination of sometimes divergent national policies.[1]

The creation of the Canada–United States Ministerial Committee on Joint Defence was agreed to during President Eisenhower's visit to Ottawa in July 1958 and the institutional arrangement was formally established by an exchange of notes on 29 August and 2 September of that year. Unfortunately, neither the joint statement, dated 10 July 1958, announcing that the committee was to be set up[2] nor the later exchange of notes[3] gives a very clear indication as to exactly what functions it was expected to discharge. The statement merely affirmed that the committee would 'consult on matters bearing upon the common defense of the North American Continent, which lies within the North Atlantic Treaty area' and would, 'in a supervisory capacity, supplement but not supplant existing joint boards and committees'; and the Canadian note of 29 August (officially proposing the committee's establishment) simply specified three broad general functions:

1. To consult periodically on any matters affecting the joint defense of Canada and the United States.
2. In particular, to exchange information and views at the Ministerial level on

problems that may arise, with a view to strengthening further the close and intimate cooperation between the two Governments on joint defense matters.

3. To report to the respective Governments on such discussions in order that consideration may be given to measures deemed appropriate and necessary to improve defense cooperation.

The reasons for the committee's establishment are also not altogether clear, but a major one appears to have been the determination of the two leaders, particularly of Prime Minister Diefenbaker, to maintain at all times civilian control over all activities and decisions pertaining to North American defence. This was made quite explicit in the assertion of the joint statement of 10 July that it was important that matters of defence 'be subject to civilian decision and guidance,' and it was implied in the comment of the Canadian note of 29 August that 'it was recognized that the agreement of the two governments to integrate air defense arrangements increased the importance of regular consultation between them on all matters affecting the joint defense of Canada and the United States.'

Pressure by the military authorities had, of course, been one reason for Diefenbaker's hasty approval of the NORAD agreement in 1957 – an action that had gotten him into serious political difficulties.[4] He, it may be assumed, was determined to avoid similar difficulties in the future. Moreover, by the summer of 1958 many Canadians were beginning to fear that the chiefs of the services in both Canada and the United States were becoming too influential.[5] They learned from press reports that discussions relating to significant questions of defence were sometimes initiated by the service chiefs and carried far towards completion before either the Permanent Joint Board on Defence or cabinet members were brought into the negotiations, and that on a few occasions Canada's military leaders had made 'far-reaching private agreements with the Pentagon.'[6] Astute politician that he was, the prime minister undoubtedly recognized that the Canadian public believed that the time had come to subject the service chiefs to proper ministerial control.[7]

A second reason for the committee's creation appears to have been the belief of Canadian cabinet members that the country's defence relations were becoming so complex that the Permanent Joint Board on Defence could no longer adequately deal with them – particularly with the political and economic aspects. A top-level committee, it was believed, not only would be able to exert a restraining influence upon the service chiefs but would also keep a watchful eye on all aspects of defence cooperation.

A third reason for the prime minister's initiative seems to have been his desire to facilitate cabinet-level discussions regarding the integration of defence production. As has already been indicated, in the years prior to the committee's creation, the Canadian authorities had waged a not too successful campaign to obtain for their industrialists a larger share of American defence orders.[8] The PJBD had supported the Canadian efforts, but its members were not drawn from the top levels of government. The Joint Industrial Mobilization Committee, set up in 1949 and reactivated in 1951, although never formally abolished, had long ceased to operate. A new committee at the ministerial level, the prime minister no doubt concluded, might succeed where the other joint agencies had failed.

A fourth reason for the committee's establishment appears to have been the existence of the Ministerial Committee on Trade and Economic Affairs. It is true that that organization had not yet been strikingly successful as a consultative agency, but the prime minister appeared to believe that many Canadian–American ailments could be alleviated by more frequent consultations and more joint agencies,[9] and President Eisenhower seemed 'willing to apply the particular brand of ointment recommended by Diefenbaker.'[10] After all, a cabinet committee to deal with economic problems had been set up during the president's last visit to Canada. Why not climax this particular visit by agreeing to establish a complementary cabinet committee to deal with defence questions?[11]

The agreement of 29 August–3 September provided that the committee would consist, from Canada, of the secretary of state for external affairs, the minister of national defence, and the minister of finance; from the United States, the secretary of state, the secretary of defence, and the secretary of the treasury. As the need arose, either government might also from time to time designate 'other appropriate cabinet members.' The organization would meet 'once a year or more often' as might be 'considered appropriate and necessary,' alternating between Washington and Ottawa, with a Canadian member presiding in Ottawa and an American member in Washington.

Except for rotating the chairmanship between the American secretary of state and the Canadian secretary of state for external affairs, none of these stipulations has been strictly adhered to. The most serious deviation has been the infrequency of the meetings. Instead of meeting 'once a year or more often,' the organization has had a total of only four meetings: in 1958, 1959, 1960, and 1964. The reasons for, and significance of, this deviation we shall come back to later, but the point should be emphasized that the committee has had only one meeting since 1960. A second, much less significant, deviation has been the locale of the meetings. Of the four, the first was in Paris, during the regular annual meeting of the NATO Council; the second was at Camp David, the presidential retreat in the Catoctin Mountains in Maryland; the third was at Montebello, Quebec; and the fourth was in Washington. As for participants, for Canada in 1958 they were the secretary of state for external affairs, the minister of national defence, and the minister of finance; in 1959 a fourth member, the minister of defence production was added; in 1964 the delegation was still further enlarged by the inclusion of the associate minister of national defence. By contrast, the United States has had only three representatives on each occasion. In 1958 and in 1964 they were the secretaries of state, of defence, and of the treasury; in 1959 the under secretary of the treasury substituted for his chief; and in 1960 the under secretary of state 'filled in' for Secretary Herter.

At each meeting senior military and civil officials – including the Canadian Chiefs of Staff Committee, the chairman of the United States Joint Chiefs of Staff, and the chairmen of the Permanent Joint Board on Defence – have served as advisers to the cabinet members. The Canadian ambassador to the United States and the American ambassador to Canada have also regularly attended. On each occasion an agenda has been prepared in advance and a record has been kept of the proceedings.

The discussions in the Committee on Defence, we are assured, have been frank and lively but totally lacking in acrimony. They have also been conducted, as the Canadian secretary of state for external affairs has testified, in a most informal manner: 'There is no big table with one group lined up on one side of the table and the other group opposite them, with briefs and so on.'[12] 'We were able to sit around in the lounge of the main building and discuss views frankly on a man to man basis, with both sides feeling free to make any complaints or any suggestions.'[13]

As for the topics considered, here we have only general and, it is reasonable to assume, incomplete information. True it is that with the exception of the first, each conference has issued a communiqué at the close of the discussions. But, as Judy LaMarsh has observed with respect to the communiqués issued at the end of dominion-provincial conferences,[14] these have been bland, innocuous statements, obscuring any lack of agreement, and omitting all references to contentious matters. Nevertheless, the communiqués when supplemented by information pried out of individual ministers before and after the meetings by resourceful news reporters, do provide at least some inkling of the topics that have occupied most of the time of the participants. Not surprisingly, they remained pretty much the same from meeting to meeting, namely: (1) the nature of the threat to North America, (2) the progress of cooperative measures designed to improve the defences of the continent, (3) ways of making NATO more effective, (4) arms control and disarmament proposals, (5) defence-production sharing between the two countries, and (6) a review of the machinery for consultation on defence matters.[15] At the fourth meeting Canada's peace-keeping activities and 'the situation in southeast Asia' also came in for special attention.[16]

How useful have these discussions been? Have they really served any worthwhile purpose? Different observers have had different views on these questions. The participants – especially the Canadian ministers – have been loud in their praise of the meetings. For example, Canada's secretary of state for external affairs, Howard C. Green, referred to the second meeting as 'very beneficial' and the third as 'particularly helpful.' It would not 'be possible,' he affirmed, 'to bring about such frank exchanges of views in any other way.'[17] In a similar vein, his colleague, George P. Pearkes, minister of national defence, concluded an enthusiastic report on the second meeting, with its high-level participants and its 'most intimate discussions on all defense matters,' with the assertion: 'I suggest that is top level consultation.'[18]

In support of the enthusiastic position of the participants, it must be said that the meetings have provided the two countries with a most useful high-level forum for exchanging information and for airing their grievances, generally with a considerable amount of publicity. The committee's role in promoting defence-production sharing and development has already been summarized.[19] Of equal note was its efforts in behalf of fuller consultations in NATO, a concern which began in 1959, when Howard Green, in a press conference in Washington the day before the opening of the second session of the committee, stated that there was an urgent need for a thorough discussion within the NATO Council of such important matters as negotiating with the Soviet Union and went on to recommend that the Council, scheduled to meet 15 to 17 December, be reconvened after the gathering of the American, British, French, and West German political leaders on 19 December.[20] At the conclusion of the discussions Secretary of State Herter informed the press that a meeting of the full NATO Council would be held following the conference among the heads of governments of the four big NATO members, and the committee communiqué asserted: '... the ministers reaffirmed their common desire and intention further to strengthen consultation in the North Atlantic Council generally and in particular with respect to preparations for forthcoming negotiations with the Soviet Union.'[21] The second NATO Council meeting was convened and the members unanimously supported the position adopted a few days earlier by the four Allied leaders with respect to Berlin and negotiations with the Soviet government.[22]

Because it opened up to Canadian ministers an additional channel of communication with the knowledgeable and influential American cabinet members, the committee has no doubt been more useful to Canada than to the United States. But it is reasonable to assume that both countries have benefited from the verbal exchanges.

There is, however, a negative side to the ledger. For example, Arnold Heeney has suggested that the raising by an American spokesman at the 1960 committee meeting of the issue of a proposed American embargo of Castro's Cuba had unfortunate consequences. Because there had been 'no diplomatic preparations whatever' for the discussion of this particular question, 'the Canadian ministers reacted coldly.'[23] At the same meeting the crude intervention of one of the United States military advisers in presenting an appreciation of Soviet intentions and of the capabilities of the American deterrent shocked Green and confirmed 'his worst suspicions of the malign influence of the Pentagon.'[24] From that particular meeting onward, according to Heeney, relations between Ottawa and Washington gradually deteriorated.[25]

Nor should the fact be overlooked that the committee was not even convened during the Cuban missile crisis and therefore rendered no consultative function at that time; and that the committee was not able to resolve an issue of special concern to the United States, viz., whether Canada would or would not accept nuclear weapons. The basic facts of the nuclear arms controversy have already been summarized.[26] Here attention is focused on the rather modest role played by the Committee on Defence.

At the committee's first meeting the Canadian delegation, according to General Foulkes, one of the participants, 'put forward a proposal in which the United States would supply nuclear weapons for Canada.' This proposal, the general notes, 'was approved in principle, and both sides agreed to have it put in writing later. Nothing was signed, but a draft agreement was made up at the time.'[27] Disagreement within the Canadian cabinet, however, developed and the matter was again included on the committee's agenda, at the Camp David meeting in 1959. There 'the logjam was temporarily broken' when the participants agreed that the Canadian forces should be provided with nuclear weapons.[28] But the agreement did not hold. Diefenbaker was not ready to take a definite stand on what had now become a very controversial issue. Agreement was almost reached when Secretary Gates held private talks in Ottawa in connection with the third meeting of the committee. But the prime minister still was not convinced of the need for positive action. Thereafter matters gradually moved from bad to worse. Bitterness engendered over the arms issue, Canada's procrastination during the Cuban missile crisis, and the growth of personal antagonisms between President Kennedy and the prime minister brought Canadian–American relations to the lowest point in years. This, in turn, had a highly adverse impact on the joint machinery of cooperation. Thus the Committee on Defence was not convened at all during the most difficult period of the controversy, that is, from the summer of 1960 through 1963. And it was, of course, only the change of party control in Ottawa in 1963 that finally ended the impasse and opened the way for Canadian acceptance of nuclear arms.

Thus the critics may properly ask whether anything can be said in defence of an organization that fails to resolve the really difficult issues and does not even meet when defence relations are most in need of attention. The answer, it seems, is that three things can and should be said: (1) it was not the committee, but rather the Canadian government, that had difficulty arriving at a decision; (2) the committee, as noted above, did help to find answers to other important questions; and (3) it was primarily antipathies between the chief executives of the two governments, rather than any inherent deficiences of, or disillusionments with, the committee, that kept the joint agency from meeting during the last thirty-one months of the Diefenbaker era. Significantly, following both the Kennedy–Pearson meeting of 10–11 May 1963 and the Johnson–Pearson talks of 21–2 January 1964, public announcements were made that a meeting of the committee would soon be convened,[29] and, of course, a meeting was held in July 1964.

With respect to the meeting of 1964, little has been said or written and most of that has been highly critical. Thus Bruce Phillips of the Washington bureau of the Hamilton *Spectator* wrote:

The first meeting in four years of the Canada–u.s. cabinet committee on defence ... created the impression that once every four years is far too frequent.

The meeting apparently was a gross waste of everybody's time.

By all accounts it consisted mostly of exceedingly general discussions which pointed nowhere in particular.

But the question arises whether such meetings have any value if people leave with the feeling that they have wasted their time.[30]

Peyton Lyon noted that the meeting 'confirmed that there were no disputes beclouding continental defence – a pleasant change.' He thought, however, that 'a day-long meeting with men as pressed as Secretaries Rusk and McNamara may not have been necessary to confirm the obvious.'[31]

Although these evaluations are perhaps a bit harsh, the fact seems to be that the participants in the committee's fourth meeting were not presented with any challenging problems. The nuclear arms issue had been resolved, at least temporarily; trade between the two countries in defence production items had achieved a 'rough balance' – all that Canada could reasonably ask; both governments were in favour of an effective arms control and disarmament program; NATO's affairs seemed in reasonably good order; the Americans were deeply appreciative of Canada's peace-keeping activities; and the Canadian delegates accepted, with sympathy and without challenge, the explanation of American objectives in Southeast Asia.[32] Not surprisingly, the communiqué issued at the close of the meeting – unlike the previous committee communiqués – made no reference to the convening of a future meeting. The unstated, though implied, assumption seemed to be that the next meeting would be convened when needed.

Whether another meeting will ever be held is entirely unpredictable. At the moment the probability seems quite remote. For one thing, continental defence is a less active issue today than it was at the time of the establishment of the committee, and the general consensus seems to be that 'there has to be something very important to decide before you have a ministerial meeting.'[33] No less importantly, the failure of the two governments to convene the committee during the critical period of the nuclear arms controversy encouraged the expanded use of other channels for consultation: the service staffs, the PJBD, the diplomatic services, the ministerial meetings of NATO, contacts between the responsible ministers themselves, and, during 1964–8, numerous heads-of-governments meetings. These other channels, in the opinion of influential persons both in Washington and in Ottawa, may just as well continue to perform the needed consultation function.[34] In the third place, it is at least arguable that the basic premise upon which the committee was created (that ministers would be able to participate regularly and effectively in joint meetings) was of questionable validity. It is, in truth, extremely difficult for busy cabinet members to find the time 'to look into the detailed technical problems of defence.' If they cannot find the time, then there can be no really worthwhile negotiations or even exchange of views. This elementary fact, unfortunately, was lost sight of during the nuclear arms controversy – the outcome being the fiasco of the early 1960s.[35]

The Canada–United States Ministerial Committee on Trade and Economic Affairs

Canada, it is generally agreed, took the initiative that led to the establishment of the Ministerial Committee on Trade and Economic Affairs.[1] The proposal for such a committee was first revealed publicly by Prime Minister St Laurent when he visited President Eisenhower in May 1953, and the committee's composition and terms of reference were formulated by a working group in Ottawa composed of representatives of interested departments of the Canadian government and of the American embassy.[2]

That the Canadian authorities should have been interested in such an organization is not surprising. As has already been indicated, the Canadian economy has long been heavily dependent upon trade with, and capital from, the United States; thus any significant decisions or actions on the part of that country may have a tremendous impact on its less populous neighbour. Unfortunately for Canada, during the second year of Eisenhower's first term of office, under pressure from regional interests, members of Congress began agitating for additional import restrictions on such Canadian products as frozen fish fillets, oats, and dairy products. They likewise began demanding a doubling of the American tariff on lead and zinc, the production of which had been expanded in Canada at the special urging of the American government.[3] No less disturbing, the president's chief cabinet officers seemed to have no conception of what American tariff policy meant to Canada or just how important Canadian markets and raw materials were to the American economy.[4] For years Canadian imports from the United States had regularly exceeded exports to that country in a ratio of roughly four to three – generally amounting in monetary terms to about one billion dollars annually. Now there was a very serious danger that American tariff changes would be granted or quotas would be imposed that would still further tilt the trade balance in favour of the United States. New machinery and procedures for exchanging information between the two governments and, if possible, for assuring a Canadian voice in American decision-making, seemed obvious needs. For thirteen years the Permanent Joint Board on Defence had rendered a useful service in dealing with mutual defence problems. Why not, Canadian spokesmen asked, try the expedient of a joint agency for economic problems? President Eisenhower, eager to demonstrate that he was genuinely interested in Canada's economic life, readily accepted the Canadian proposal.

The committee, an exchange of notes of 12 November 1953 explained, was 'to consider matters affecting the harmonious economic relations between the two countries' and, in particular, 'exchange information and views on matters which might adversely affect the high level of mutually profitable trade which has been built up.' It was 'to report to the respective Governments on such discussions in order that consideration may be given to measures deemed appropriate and necessary to improve economic relations and to encourage the flow of trade.'[5]

The notes stipulated that the committee should consist, for Canada, of the secretary of state for external affairs and the ministers of finance, trade and commerce, and either the minister of agriculture or the minister of fisheries; and for the United States, of the secretaries of state, treasury, agriculture, and commerce. In 1961, however, the American government proposed, and the Canadian government concurred, that, in view of the 'great and growing interest in matters concerned with the development and exchange of energy resources,' the secretary of the interior should be added to the United States membership. Similarly, in 1963 the Canadian government proposed, and the American government concurred, that the Canadian membership be expanded to include the head of the newly created Canadian Department of Industry,[6] now merged with the Department of Trade and Commerce. Thus, although the committee theoretically consists of nine members, in practice its membership has varied from meeting to meeting. For example, occasionally each country has had only three or four cabinet members in attendance, while on other occasions the total number of participants has exceeded ten because of the inclusion in the American delegation of the under secretary of state, the president's special trade representative, and the chairman of the President's Council of Economic Advisers and the inclusion in the Canadian delegation of the governor of the Bank of Canada, the minister of justice, the minister of national revenue, the minister of energy, mines and resources, and the minister of the environment.

The committee, it should be noted, has no permanent secretariat and has never made any attempt to carry on its work in a collective capacity on a year-round basis. This, of course, means that its meetings are of fundamental importance. In recognition of this fact, the authorizing agreement stipulated that meetings were to be held 'once a year or more often, as may be considered necessary by the two Governments.' But, like the similar provision in the exchange of notes establishing the Ministerial Committee on Joint Defence, this particular provision has been flagrantly ignored. To November 1970 the meetings were held on an average of once every fifteen months. Since then none has been held. The committee, however, has not been abolished. Furthermore, its record of achievements is quite creditable. In fact, as recently as 1969 a high external affairs official characterized it as 'probably the most important of all the joint Canada–U.S.A. organizations.'[7] Thus it merits more than cursory attention.

Although at the outset formal agendas were not used,[8] during the sixties agendas were regularly drafted and usually were fairly closely adhered to.[9] Preparation of the agenda was primarily the responsibility of the Department of External Affairs and the Department of State, with some assistance from the two embassies. The civil servants also had the responsibility of drafting position papers for their respective delegations and for briefing the individual cabinet members.

The topics dealt with have normally fallen into two broad categories: (1) those of concern to other countries as well as to Canada and the United States, such as the expansion of trade on a multilateral basis, the reform of the international monetary system, and the trade and development problems of the emerging nations; and (2) those of interest primarily to the two North American countries. The second category has included a great number and variety of topics, of which the following may be viewed as typical: the agricultural surplus disposal policies and activities of the two countries; American restrictions on the importation of oil, lead, zinc, cheddar cheese, flaxseed, and linseed; Canadian restrictions on the importation of turkeys, peas and other agricultural products; Canadian attempts to encourage the exportation of automobiles and automotive parts; attempts of the United States to discourage American capital outflows; the development of a continental energy policy; the control of water pollution in the Great Lakes; the improvement of the Alaska Highway system; and an American request 'that Canada accord official recognition to Bourbon whiskey as a distinctive product of the United States.'[10]

Each delegation has generally been accompanied by fifteen to twenty-five civil servants, most of them recruited from the departments represented at the meetings but some drawn from other agencies. For example, in 1966, when the committee was considering a Securities and Exchange Commission proposal to extend its regulations to certain Canadian companies whose shares were traded over the counter in the United States, a member of the SEC was present; similarly, in 1968, when balance-of-payments problems were being discussed, Louis Rasminsky, governor of the Bank of Canada, was one of the Canadian advisers. The Canadian ambassador to the United States and the American ambassador to Canada were regularly in attendance. Although an adviser has occasionally been asked to review developments in a given field, the experts, as a rule, have not participated in the formal discussions. Their usual role has simply been that of supplying their respective delegations with information.

Each meeting has usually been opened by wide-ranging reviews by the American secretary of state and the Canadian secretary of state for external affairs of recent developments in international relations. These, in turn, have sometimes been followed by reviews of economic developments in the United States, given by the secretary of the treasury or the chairman of the President's Council of Economic Advisers, and, in Canada, by the minister of finance or by someone else concerned with financial matters. Afterwards have come comments on the speeches and questions, followed by discussion of agenda items and other related matters.

Although, as indicated below, meetings later came to be rather formal and structured, in the beginning the discussions were very free and wide-ranging. A member could bring up any question of immediate interest or importance and obtain for it a general airing. Officials of External Affairs have sometimes thought that the Canadian delegates were 'too polite and deferential' to the Americans and 'too silent and reserved' on issues of special concern to Canada;[11] but other observers assure us that participants on both sides have generally set forth their views frankly, bluntly, and forcibly, and, not infrequently have engaged in 'very tough, hard bargaining.'[12]

Significantly, the committee has never used formal voting. Its procedure has been to arrive at agreements through a free and frank discussion of each issue. Occasionally the solution of a problem has been found during the informal exchanges that follow the formal meetings. More often, the committee has referred the unsolved problems for further study by United States and Canadian officials or to a joint working group, thereby adding an impetus which might not otherwise have existed.

Immediately preceding the committee's second meeting, the Ottawa correspondent for *The Economist* expressed doubts as to whether it would be able to achieve any worthwhile results. His reasons were: (1) the lower status and responsibility of an American cabinet member compared with that of a Canadian member, and (2) the negative position that Congress and American interest groups were likely to take of any attempts to change American economic policies.[13] As it turned out, these predictions did not materialize. The American cabinet members did sometimes find it convenient to assert that the 'facts of life,' i.e. American political realities, would not permit them to make the trade or other concessions desired by Canada.[14] But, when they were really interested in seeing changes made, they usually did not let fear of adverse congressional or public opinion deter them from giving their approval. The result was a multiplicity of decisions on a great variety of matters. In fact, the joint communiqués issued at the close of the meetings are replete with affirmations: 'The Committee agreed,' 'it was agreed,' and so on.

Not surprisingly, during its period of activity the committee came in for not a little negative criticism. Thus American critics complained of the inability of the members to give adequate attention to Canadian–American issues, the frequent changes in the committee's composition, the inadequate briefing of the American delegates and their failure to present a coordinated American position, and the 'premature and intense preoccupation of all concerned' with the joint communiqué.[15] For their part, Canadian critics argued that all too frequently the American spokesmen viewed the committee as merely 'an instrument for enlisting Canadian support for American policies,'[16] that the meetings were used as platforms for the delivery of set speeches, and that the joint communiqués were so vague and general as to be virtually meaningless.[17]

There is much validity to the above criticisms, but there is also validity to the statements of many observers and former committee participants who insist that, for both countries, the positive features of the meetings outweighed the negative. One of the positive features was that difficult problems were anticipated and resolved before they reached crisis proportions;[18] a second was the opportunity afforded the participants to get acquainted, thereby facilitating later telephone calls and personal conferences; a third was the early access provided each country to the policy thinking of the other country; and a fourth was what Robert Schaetzel, former American ambassador, has called the 'cross fertilization' of ideas among the delegates. By listening to other views and being obliged to explain and defend their own positions, they were supplied antidotes to their own narrow specializations.[19] A fifth positive feature was that the face-to-face meetings 'inhibited the normal tendency of the politicians toward self-serving political hyperbole.'[20] A sixth was that preparations for the meetings and the meetings themselves forced the American authorities to do some serious thinking about Canada and Canadian–American economic relations. Finally, the meetings laid the groundwork for new programs, such as the Auto and Auto Parts Agreement, resolved a number of difficult issues, and took the initiative in the creation of several joint working groups.

An example of the committee's success in resolving a long-standing vexing problem was the concessions won by the Canadian ministers at successive committee meetings with respect to American practices in disposing of agricultural surpluses abroad. The first was an agreement in 1954 to consult 'and not interfere with normal commercial marketings';[21] the second was an American pledge, given in 1957, not to operate barter sales in such a way as to interfere with normal purchases of wheat by importing countries;[22] and the third was an understanding, arrived at in 1959, that a joint working group of wheat experts from the two North American countries should hold quarterly meetings 'in an attempt to solve periodically any problems involving wheat and flour.'[23] Largely because of the implementation of these agreements, by 1961 American policy in disposing of agricultural surpluses had ceased to be a major issue in Canadian–American relations.

The creation of the wheat and flour working group in 1959 was noted above. In 1963 the committee established 'a technical working group' to consider financial questions arising out of United States legislation designed to improve its balance of payments position.[24] The following year it created a group 'to prepare a programme of studies relating to trade in all kinds of energy' between the two countries.[25] In 1967 the committee set up the Technical Committee on Agricultural Marketing and Trade Problems to consider questions of trade in agricultural products between the two countries; and two years later it created a working group to deal with problems relating to the movement of Canadians into the United States. Then in 1971 – following the last meeting of the Ministerial Committee on Trade and Economic Affairs – the two governments established the United States–Canada Trade Statistics Committee to reconcile the gap between the statistics dealing with the flow of merchandise, trade, and services compiled by Canada and those compiled by the United States.

These working groups, staffed with experts drawn from interested departments of the two governments, have sometimes been able to suggest solutions to problems that have baffled both ministers and diplomats. Note, for example, the record of the Trade Statistics Committee. At the end of 1970 American statistics showed an American trade deficit with Canada of $2.1 million, while Canadian statistics placed the deficit at $1.04 billion.

With computers and open minds, the civil servants tackled the difficult problem. By January 1973 they had agreed on a figure for 1970; by November of the same year they had reconciled the figures for 1971. In the same manner they have continued to the present their helpful work of analysis and reconciliation.[26]

At other times the outcome has been less gratifying. Thus the Balance of Payments Group (or committee as it usually is called), struggled valiantly from 1963 through 1968 to find policies and procedures that would lighten the effect of the trade and financial policies of each country on the other, but to little avail. Two difficulties, it seems, were that the members 'were positioned too far below the top policymaking level to command serious attention on either side' and that the Canadian government shied away from joint decision-making, preferring to resolve issues as they arose through personal relationships.[27] Similarly, the Technical Committee on Agricultural Marketing and Trade Problems, after an undistinguished three years of operations, was replaced in 1970 with an 'agricultural trade consultation procedure.' But the two working groups did have the beneficial result of educating the American officials and cabinet members with respect to the close linkages between the American and the Canadian economies.[28]

If, as the author believes, the Ministerial Committee on Trade and Economic Affairs did, in fact, do an effective job, the question logically arises as to why no meetings have been held since November 1970. Knowledgeable observers have put forward a variety of reasons. They usually start with the 1970 meeting which, because of inadequate preparations on both sides and clashing personalities, was, according to one account, virtually a 'disaster.'[29] After that came elections or impending elections in both countries and the suddenly imposed Nixon restrictive policies of August 1971, which not only effectively demolished the long-existing special relationship between the two countries but ushered in months of tension and strained relations. As Arnold Heeney has observed, when relations are cool, cabinet committees seldom meet, even though one might assume that that is precisely when they should be meeting. But the fact of the matter is that such organizations can operate effectively only when there exists some common ground and an all-around desire to find solutions to difficult problems. Thus, it is quite probable that a major reason the two governments chose not to hold committee meetings during the tension-charged months following the launching of the Nixon New Economic Policy was because they feared that the difficult issues of the day, such as the auto agreement, defence-production sharing, and energy sales, would be exacerbated by the publicity regarding the meetings.

Another negative factor was that, by the late 1960s, bringing together eight or ten cabinet members for two to three days had become a major undertaking – particularly for the American members, preoccupied as they usually were with responsibilities in various parts of the world. Furthermore, considerable patience and tolerance are required of a cabinet member to sit around a conference table listening to speeches and comments on topics of little interest to himself personally. As Rufus Smith has put it: 'I could not see Henry Kissinger sitting down for three days to deal with a problem. He is not that kind, he does not sit still that long.'[30] On the other hand, Kissinger and other American cabinet members might be agreeable to holding relatively short conferences with their opposite members on matters of special interest to themselves. And that brings up another factor of some importance. During the early 1970s, when the committee was not meeting, other modes of communication were developed. For example, between November 1970 and the end of 1973 two 'summit' meetings were held between Prime Minister Trudeau and President Nixon and a number of one-to-one conferences were held between individual cabinet members. Following Ford's succession to the presidency, the pace of the meetings was quickened. Thus there not only were exchanges between Ford and Trudeau but one-to-one conferences numbered in the dozens between Canadian and American cabinet members. In addition, there have been several discussions participated in by three or four ministers and supporting officials from each country to deal with individual pressing issues such as energy sales.

What of the future? Will, and should, the committee be revived? Even though the political atmosphere is more favourable than it was in the early 1970s, the inclination to renew the meetings seems lacking. Thus in 1977 a spokesman of the Department of State said that he did not 'expect mechanism used in the past to be revived.' He thought Canadian and American officials might be discussing 'new methods of periodic consultation' that would make unnecessary formal meetings of ministerial committees.[31] Two years earlier the Canadian secretary of state for external affairs asserted that because of the number and variety of the one-to-one contacts, 'the joint ministerial committee meetings are less suited to today's demands of this relationship.' He then added: 'I feel it is questionable, given the present demands upon ministers, whether it is necessary, let alone possible, to hold joint ministerial committee meetings between Canada and the United States in the nineteen seventies.'[32]

Significantly, as part of a general assessment of the joint Canadian–American machinery, the Canadian Standing Senate Committee on Foreign Affairs concluded that, given 'the structural form it has recently taken,' the ministerial committee 'serves no constructive purpose and may even be counter-productive.'[33] The reasons for the senators' negative conclusion was that they believed the committee had lost many of the characteristics that at the outset had made it a valuable organization, i.e., its unstructured meetings, its informality and limited attention to publicity, and its success in dealing with issues before they required decisions. Over the years more and more time had been spent on the joint communiqués; set speeches, with an eye on the press, had come to be the rule; while excessive publicity had eventually nullified 'the original exploratory and consultative purpose of this channel.'[34] The senators did not recommend that the joint agency be abolished. On the contrary, they observed, seemingly with satisfaction, that it 'would be available if it were decided by both sides to revive it in its original form or to call it for any special purpose.'[35]

If the cabinet members could be convinced that they could find the time required for the meetings (and it is significant that each country has a joint economic committee with a number of other countries), it might be desirable to revive the committee. In addition to supplementing the diplomatic and other one-to-one contacts, it provides benefits not attainable by the other contacts. When and if the meetings are revived, there would be definite advantages in adopting a recommendation made by Robert Schaetzel, viz., that the committee have two items for each meeting, the first, a discussion of the state of the world, and the second, an item of major interest to the two countries. It might also be helpful to 'rule out any use of the committee as a town meeting at which specific grievances are aired and then, inevitably, rebutted.'[36]

Also helpful would be the creation of a subordinate committee at the deputy-assistant secretary level to meet fairly frequently and to supply information and assistance to the senior committee. But even if the Committee on Trade and Economic Affairs is not revived, it would still be advantageous to have a lower-level committee for fact-finding and issue-probing purposes. Members of such a committee would, no doubt, have less trouble than cabinet members in finding time for meetings and, even though they would be expected to steer clear of policy questions, they might very well be able to render significant assistance to the diplomats and civil servants in dealing with the flood of Canadian–American economic issues continually demanding the attention of all levels of government.

19

The Canada–United States Interparliamentary Group

The Canada–United States Interparliamentary Group, established in 1959, has been characterized as 'novel in the relationships between the two countries'[1] – and indeed it is. As we have observed, over the years Canada and the United States set up numerous joint boards, commissions, and committees to exchange information or to deal with problems on the administrative and cabinet levels. But to 1959 they had established no organization to provide liaison between the two national legislatures or to help in a general way in the promotion of mutual understanding; and that, in the opinion of many North Americans, especially Canadians, was a serious deficiency. Even though the primary responsibility in each country for the formulation and conduct of foreign policy rests with the executive authorities, the role of the national legislators, particularly members of Congress, has always been considerable. Also, of course, since about 1973 the influence of Congress has tremendously increased at the expense of the presidency.[2] Thus in many areas of vital concern to Canada, such as tariffs, quotas, transportation and the disposal of agricultural surpluses, the decisive influence rests not with the president but with Congress.

Compounding the problem for Canada in the pre-1959 years was the fact that members of Congress, although consistently well disposed, were often abysmally ignorant about their northern neighbours. Department of State officials could usually be depended upon to do what they could to enlighten the legislators, but under the American system of government, based on the principle of separation of powers, the ability of administration spokesmen 'to influence or coerce a Congress which has views differing from its own is markedly limited.'[3] The Canadian diplomats, who might have been expected to do some explaining on Canada's behalf, found their freedom of action so restricted by the niceties of diplomacy and the insistence of the

Department of State that business be conducted through proper channels that they usually refrained from making direct contacts with members of Congress.[4] Under the circumstances, it is not surprising that the legislators not infrequently overlooked Canadian interests and opinions and responded instead to the pressures and demands of interest groups and their own constituents.[5]

On one occasion Lester B. Pearson, then ambassador to the United States, half seriously suggested that Canada should have a diplomatic representative to Congress as well as one accredited to the president. The Department of State, it is reported, did not appreciate his too clever remark,[6] but he had made his point. With the establishment of the Interparliamentary Group, Canada obtained not the additional ambassador suggested by Pearson but an even two dozen of them!

The influences and events leading up to the creation of the joint organization extended over a period of years. The first significant moves were taken in 1943 when plans were formulated for occasional joint meetings between committees of the two national legislatures to discuss trade, postwar reconstruction, and other mutual problems.[7] The pressure of more urgent matters prevented the implementation of these plans during the war, but the basic idea in a modified form was revived in the immediate postwar period when Arthur Vandenberg of the American Senate and Norman Lambert of the Canadian Senate held two or three discussions on the establishment of a continuing Canadian–American parliamentary organization. In May 1952, on the invitation of an ad hoc committee of the Canadian Parliament, a small congressional delegation visited Ottawa for informal discussions with members of Parliament on matters of common Canadian–American interest. At the close of the conversations it was agreed that a delegation of Canadian legislators would be invited to visit Washington for the purpose of cooperating in the establishment of a permanent organization. But, because of the difficulty of finding a mutually convenient date and for other reasons, the expected invitation was never extended. The following year President Eisenhower promised W.M.L. Robertson, government leader in the Canadian Senate, that he would help to arrange an organizational meeting, but again no positive actions followed.[8]

An additional and powerful stimulus, it was obvious, would be required to get the project off the ground, and that eventually was provided by the shocking discovery by influential members of Congress that all was not well with Canadian–American relations, that, in truth, the 'fences' along the famous 'unguarded border' were urgently in need of some extra attention.

As preliminary moves, the House Committee on Foreign Affairs authorized Representatives Brooks Hays, of Arkansas, and Frank M. Coffin, of Maine, to undertake a special fact-finding mission to Canada, and the Senate Foreign Relations Committee scheduled a day of hearings on 'United States policies respecting Canada.'

The Hays-Coffin Report and the Senate hearings[9] made it unmistakably clear that an erosion of major proportions had occurred in the traditionally excellent relationships between the neighbouring countries. The stated causes were many and varied: American practices in disposing of surplus agricultural commodities; American tariff laws and administration; the magnitude of American direct equity investments in Canada; congressional 'witch-hunting' that besmirched Canadians; 'the fear of being swept along, in the stream of a foreign policy which the Nation cannot control, over the brink of nuclear war';[10] Canadian concern over possible loss of sovereignty under the existing bilateral defence arrangements; the natural concerns and fears of a small nation obliged to live beside a great world power; and, perhaps most important of all, a general American tendency 'to take Canada for granted' and a failure to understand or appreciate its 'proud heritage, its economic and political problems and its special relationship with the United Kingdom.'[11]

To help allay Canadian fears and concerns and to halt a further deterioration in relations, Hays and Coffin, among other things, called for a greatly increased 'Congressional awareness' of 'the vital role which Congress plays in determining United States–Canadian relationships.' As one way of achieving that objective, they urged the inauguration of periodic visits to each country by the parliamentarians of the other country.[12] The same general concept received enthusiastic approval both from individual senators and from witnesses appearing before the Foreign Relations Committee.[13] More significantly still, Prime Minister Diefenbaker gave the idea his prompt and whole-hearted approval.[14] The proposal was discussed by President Eisenhower and Prime Minister Diefenbaker on the occasion of the president's visit to Ottawa early in July 1958. Later that month Senator Aiken introduced (for himself and Senator Mansfield): (1) Senate Concurrent Resolution 108, calling for the establishment of subcommittees by the Senate and the House to study the desirability and feasibility of instituting periodic discussions between Canadian and American legislators, and (2) Senate Resolution 359, calling for the establishment of a subcommittee by the Senate Foreign Relations Committee (to accomplish in the Senate the same purpose in the event the House failed to act on Senate Concurrent Resolution 108).[15] On 8 August both resolutions were approved by the

Senate without a dissenting vote. Congress adjourned before the House of Representatives could act on the Senate resolution but the chairman of the House Committee on Foreign Affairs (now called the Committee on International Relations) assumed the initiative of appointing a committee of four to represent the lower chamber in any discussions that might be held with the Canadian parliamentarians.

Complementing the action of the American legislators, on 12 August Diefenbaker officially and formally proposed the formation of a group of Canadian members of Parliament to discuss with appropriate representatives of the executive and legislative branches of the American government the question of an interparliamentary organization. The proposal was heartily approved by all of the party leaders in the House of Commons, and a recommendation along the same lines received unanimous assent in the Canadian Senate.[16] Following further discussions among the legislators of the two countries, on 9 January 1959 nine Canadian legislators journeyed to Washington to meet eight of their American counterparts for the purpose of organizing the proposed joint agency. The outcome was a unanimous recommendation that there be 'a continuing relationship between the parliamentarians of the two countries'; that the organization be called the Canada–United States Interparliamentary Group; that the next meeting be held in Canada; and that a committee composed of four of the conferees (Senator George D. Aiken and Representative Edna F. Kelly of the United States, and Speakers Mark R. Drouin and Roland Mitchener of Canada) prepare an agenda for that meeting from a list of topics suggested by the delegates.[17]

On 18 February 1959, Mrs Kelly introduced House Joint Resolution 254, authorizing American participation in the new group, providing procedural guidelines, and authorizing the appropriation of funds for the expenses of the American delegations.[18] Significantly, the resolution evoked some highly critical comments from a few members of the House. Two or three raised the question of the monetary cost. Already the United States was a member of the NATO Parliamentarians' Conference and the Interparliamentary Union. Would not the creation of a Canada–United States interparliamentary committee be the opening wedge for the establishment of similar organizations between the United States and other of its NATO allies and then with most other countries of the world? Already thousands of dollars of the taxpayers' money were being spent by legislators travelling 'all over the world' to attend interparliamentary conferences, accompanied by their wives and sometimes by their children. Where would it all end? In any event, was not adequate consultation machinery already in existence? And would not other countries interpret the congressional action as giving Canada favoured-nation treatment?

Most members, however, supported the resolution, pointing out that the Canadian–American relationship was unique; that multiple-member organizations such as the NATO Parliamentarians' Conference did not afford the type of 'down-to-earth' informal discussions that a Canada–United States group would provide; and that other countries could not reasonably take offence if the United States felt unable to set up similar organizations with them.[19] The resolution passed the House on 15 April and the Senate, with amendments, on 1 June, and was approved by the president on 11 June 1959, becoming Public Law 86-42.

In the meantime, the recommendations of the organizational conference had been considered in the Canadian Parliament. There the comments had been almost wholly favourable. True it is that the leader of the Opposition, L.B. Pearson, had called attention to what he viewed as formidable obstacles to the effective operation of the new organization, particularly certain differences between the parliamentary and the congressional forms of government. For example, American legislative committees had an independent existence and can exert influence 'even in spite of the executive,' while the same cannot be said of Canadian committees. Another obstacle, he feared, was the failure of the organizers to provide for the day-to-day consideration of Canadian–American problems. The new organization might become important, or it might become 'almost all window dressing.'[20]

The group's initiators were fully aware that launching and successfully operating the new organization would not be easy. Officials in the Departments of State and External Affairs had made it abundantly clear that they did not view with enthusiasm the group's creation.[21] Business between governments, they pointed out, had to be conducted at diplomatic and executive levels. For Canadian politicians to talk to their American counterparts (or, conversely, for American politicians to talk to their Canadian counterparts) about subjects under diplomatic review might complicate rather than simplify negotiations. There was also the very real danger that party differences might be aired in the meetings, to the mutual embarrassment of governments and legislators. Still another danger, it was pointed out, was that a national delegation might presume to speak for its national legislature or the group as a whole presume to speak for the two governments, again with resulting embarrassments, as well as misunderstandings and complications.

Interestingly enough, the members of the organizing conference appear to have assumed that the joint agency would contribute directly to the formulation of policy in each country. Thus a summary of the proceedings prepared by American staff officials stated that the delegates had agreed that the '*conclusions and recommendations*' of the organization should be 'transmitted to the respective legislative bodies and the respective executive branches of government by each national group according to its own constitutional procedures.'[22] By the date of the group's second meeting (25–8 June 1959), however, the majority of the legislators had concluded that the organization should not make recommendations but should limit its objectives to the exchange of information, and to serving as a forum for the discussion of mutual problems and as a mechanism for promoting better understanding.[23] These became and continue to be the major goals.

Significantly, neither the organizational meeting of January 1959 nor that of June of that year attempted to lay down detailed guidelines regarding the organization of the group or its procedure. The American delegates were most eager that its creation should not set a precedent for the creation of similar groups with other countries. Accordingly, they recommended that the group be organized and operated with a maximum degree of informality. Although they realized that implementation of this proposal would necessarily limit any policy-making influence that the group might exert, the Canadian parliamentarians did not demur. Acutely aware, as they always must be, of the dominant role assigned the cabinet under their form of government, and the correspondingly insignificant role open to backbenchers, they probably welcomed the American proposal. In any event, the two delegations readily agreed that the organization be kept informal; that no constitution be adopted; that rules of procedure be kept to a minimum; and that no minutes of proceedings be prepared.[24]

The organizational conference suggested that for the second meeting 'twenty-four from each country would be an appropriate number.'[25] Later the American law of 11 June 1959 specified that 'Members of Congress not to exceed twenty-four' should constitute the American delegation. Thus, the membership of the group was fixed at and has continued at twenty-four, although on several occasions actual attendance has fallen well below that figure.[26] However, because leaders of Congress have for a number of years followed the practice of appointing alternates, occasionally the United States has had more than its normal quota of participants.[27]

The American delegation generally consists of twelve members from the Senate and twelve from the House of Representatives; for Canada the usual composition is six from the Senate and eighteen from the House of Commons. Officially, delegates from the American Senate are appointed by the president of the Senate and delegates from the House by the Speaker. In practice, the Senate delegates have generally been selected by the majority and minority party leaders, with major assistance from the chairman of the Senate delegation. Similarly, the majority leader, the minority leader, and the chairman of the House delegation each normally plays some part in the selection of House delegates, although the dominant role is usually that of the Speaker. Until 1974 the Canadian delegates were selected by the party leaders of the individual chambers. Since that date they have been chosen by the Elected Executive of a continuing association of members of Parliament interested in participating in group meetings.

Because members of the American Senate have many responsibilities and little free time and, in any event, usually have only a limited interest in Canadian–American affairs, there has never been any real competition among members of that chamber for places on the Senate slate of delegates to the group meetings. Quite the contrary, the problem often has been one of finding persons available for service. For similar reasons, the same has also been true, although to a lesser degree, of members of the House of Representatives. If desirous of attending a meeting, they too have generally been able to obtain appointments.

With Canadian members of Parliament the situation has usually been significantly different. For them participation in a meeting not only opens up new sources of information and valued contacts, but also brings prestige and favourable publicity. Moreover, they have fewer committee and other prestigious job activities than their American counterparts. Thus they have always coveted assignments as group delegates. But because of Canadian traditions of strict party control and the difficulty of establishing 'objective schemes of qualification according to merit, ability, and interest' prior to the introduction of the new selection procedures of 1974 assignments to the Canadian delegations often were made primarily on political grounds.[28] In the words of Judy LaMarsh, appointments were viewed as 'rewards for good behaviour' – as bribes to members 'to be good little boys.'[29] Now the political factors, although still present, are less important than the qualifications of members for dealing with agenda topics.

In both legislatures the selection process has always made provision for equitable party representation. Thus in the United States the party in control of a chamber normally has seven places on the national delegation, while the opposition has five; in Canada the party in control also usually has two representatives more than the other large party, but, as a rule, two places are reserved for the New Democratic party and one for the Social Credit party. But in each country considerations other than politics and party membership have also usually been given some consideration. These have included a member's desire to participate; a member's geographical proximity to the Canadian–American border; the importance of giving a large number of members an opportunity to serve on a delegation; and the need to preserve a measure of membership continuity. In addition, the governing American law requires that not less than four of the House delegation shall be from the Foreign Affairs (International Relations) Committee and not less than four of the Senate delegation from the Foreign Relations Committee.

The organizational conference decided that 'no less than two meetings shall be held each year, one in each country.' The American law specifies that the American members shall be 'appointed to meet jointly and at least annually and when Congress is not in session.'[30] In practice, neither the conference decision nor the American law has been adhered to. The meetings have rotated between the two countries, but only in 1959 and in 1961 have two meetings been held during a given year. No meetings were convened in 1963, 1971, or 1974. With these exceptions, the group has met annually, usually late in the spring. Most of the meetings since 1960 have been held while both Congress and Parliament have been in session.

That the group has not met more frequently, members of both legislatures agree, has been largely due to the difficulty involved in finding convenient dates for the meetings and adequate time for preparations and discussions. Aside from the Canadian Senate, members of both legislatures have been obliged to give high priority to party activities and elections. Also conscientious members do not like to absent themselves too frequently from their legislative chambers.[31] As for meeting when Congress and Parliament are not in session, that, the legislators insist, simply is not feasible.

Although neither side has ever had staff officials working full time on Canadian–American affairs, each has always had the services of a staff both in preparing for meetings and during the meetings themselves. In Canada six full-time officials of the Interparliamentary Relations Branch of the House of Commons devote all of their time to the seven parliamentary associations in which Canada participates. Since October 1968 a small, but expertly staffed, privately endowed organization, the Parliamentary Centre for Foreign Affairs and Foreign Trade, has also been available to advise members of Parliament relative to foreign affairs. In the United States it is to the staff of the House International Relations Committee and of the Senate Foreign Relations Committee that the legislators look for assistance in preparing for the meetings. On both sides these staff officials, along with the experts of the Parliamentary Centre, not only do research requested by members but obtain for them information and background papers from the executive departments of the government and arrange departmental briefings for them prior to the opening of a meeting.

Unfortunately, the staff services do not always guarantee well-prepared participants. For the legislators a major difficulty is that of finding time in which to make preparations. There are, of course, a thousand and one demands upon their time. Furthermore, occasionally a member is called upon at the last minute to substitute for another member who cannot conveniently participate. For the substitute member there, obviously, is little time for preparation. Also, aside from members drawn from the legislative committees and others with seniority privileges, notices of appointments to a group delegation have often been given only two or three weeks in advance of the convening of a meeting. More serious still, not infrequently the background papers have arrived only a day or two before the briefings, and the briefings have been few in number and limited in scope. For the legislators from the United States these deficiencies, though vexing, have never been serious. Through service on their legislative committees, access to excellent research facilities, and attendance at other interparliamentary meetings, they can generally be depended upon to have a reasonably good knowledge of at least some of the agenda topics. For the Canadian members, the situation has generally been quite different. Most of them will not have had extensive committee service, access to adequate research facilities, or previous experience at interparliamentary meetings. For them the background papers and briefings are of vital importance. Fortunately for them, since 1969 appointments to the group delegations have been made earlier and the briefings have been much more extensive than previously. For example, briefing sessions in preparation for the thirteenth group meeting (March 1970) were organized over a five-week period preceding the meeting and included discussions with senior officials from nine different government agencies. More importantly still, as one of a number of proposals approved in 1974 by an all-party conference of interested members of Parliament for improving the effectiveness of the annual meetings, the responsibility for leading the Canadian delegation and for guiding its activities between meetings was assigned to co-chairmen elected by the continuing association of parliamentarians referred to above rather than, as in previous years, leaving that task to the overworked speakers of the Senate and the House of Commons. This change, combined with the earlier appointment of delegates and fuller briefings than in previous years, has undoubtedly been an important reason why the Canadian delegations since 1974 have been unusually well prepared.[32]

The conference of 1959 recommended that the group meetings 'not always be held in Washington and Ottawa' and that the organization occasionally divide into smaller parties and 'visit areas of special interest.' During the first sixteen years of the group's existence the first of these recommendations was largely ignored. Aside from a meeting in Montreal in 1959, before 1975 all of the formal sessions were held either in Ottawa or in Washington. But at a meeting in Quebec in that year the delegates agreed that, as a general practice, 'meetings should be held outside of the capitals to ensure better attendance.'[33] In keeping with this resolution, the group met at Key Biscayne, Florida, in 1976; in Victoria in 1977; and in New Orleans in 1978.

Before 1975 most of the formal sessions were followed, and perhaps climaxed, by tours – participated in by most of the visiting parliamentarians and a few of the host members – to such places as Quebec City, Edmonton, Cape Kennedy, New York City, and Houston. Beginning with the meeting of 1975, the prevailing practice has come to be three days taken up largely with discussions followed by one day given over to organized tours of the host city.

So far as the conduct of the meetings is concerned, the usual practice is to have two plenary sessions, one at the beginning and one at the end, and three meetings of each of the two committees (three since 1975) into which the group has divided itself. The press is barred from all sessions, and ambassadors and cabinet ministers are admitted only to the opening session. In fact, the only persons normally present at the committee sessions other than the legislators are the staff officials employed by the legislatures, who take notes and prepare summaries of the discussions. The meeting in March 1970, however, marked an innovation when an assistant secretary of state, Philip Trezise, was invited to appear before the group to brief the delegates on significant developments in an important matter – establishing a precedent followed at several subsequent meetings.

The first plenary session is usually given over largely to the welcoming speeches and to a general discussion of Canadian–American relations. Then the committees organize and conduct their discussions, after which reports are prepared summarizing the proceedings and conclusions. Prior to 1975 these were worked out jointly and issued as press releases. Because they were jointly prepared, they 'tended to be cautiously worded and not informative'[34] and occasionally affirmed a greater measure of unanimity among the delegates than actually existed, as, for example, in 1970 when the communiqué asserted that there had been 'general agreement that a continental approach to all aspects of energy requirements, including water to be used in the generation of electric power, would be the most effective way to deal with the energy problems facing Canada and the United States.'[35] Since 1975 each side has prepared its own reports, one result being longer and more revealing documents.

Exactly how many topics have been discussed, and how much time has been devoted to each of those discussed, it is difficult to say. The reports and communiqués, however, indicate that literally dozens of topics have received some attention and that some of them have appeared repeatedly on the group's agenda. Some of the topics have related to global issues, such as aid to underdeveloped countries, NATO, and international disarmament. Others have been strictly bilateral in nature, among these being such sensitive issues as American investments in Canada, the pollution of boundary waters, labour strife on the Great Lakes, Canada's foreign ownership legislation, and American proposals for transporting Alaskan oil by tankers through Juan de Fuca Strait.

The group reports have regularly used highly laudatory words to describe the tone and atmosphere of the discussions: 'We discussed the issues in a relaxed and informal atmosphere of give-and-take natural for a meeting between friends'; 'the discussion was frank and animated, but was always carried on with a complete good humour and respect for divergent views'; 'discussions were conducted in a frank and informal manner and without regard to political affiliation.' And observers agree that, although the exchanges frequently are frank and sharp, they are never bitter or acrimonious and that members generally refrain from playing politics or from making chauvinistic appeals.[36]

Interestingly enough, disagreements arise within national delegations as well as between delegations. Thus Grattan O'Leary, veteran of eight group conferences, frankly admitted: 'I myself, when speaking on a particular subject, have often disagreed with my colleagues. This is true also of delegates from the United States.'[37]

Significantly, differences have arisen less frequently, or at least have been less frequently made public, within Canadian than within American delegations. The Canadian parliamentarians, viewing the meetings as opportune occasions for explaining and publicizing Canada's numerous grievances, have tended to coalesce 'to present a united front to the American delegates,' particularly with respect to bilateral problems. That this front has not been more consistently maintained has been largely due to the New Democratic delegates, who have occasionally felt constrained to express their disagreements with the views of some of their colleagues.[38] Because Canadian–American issues attract much less attention in the United States than north of the border and because Americans, in any event, usually have fewer grievances than their Canadian neighbours, American delegates have usually felt less need to present a common front and, as a consequence, have frequently expressed a broad range of views.

As for national differences, prior to 1973 Canadian participants frequently criticized American policy in Vietnam, while in 1970 American delegates were outspokenly critical of Canada's announced intention to act unilaterally in extending its territorial jurisdiction to 12 miles and in establishing pollution control zones in the Arctic more than 100 miles in width. In addition, there have been sharp exchanges over such issues as the admission of Red China into the UN and American proposals that Canadian waters be diverted southward.[39] Furthermore, some of the verbal exchanges of the most recent meetings appear to have been sharper and blunter than those of earlier years. Thus the press reported that at the fifteenth (1973) meeting the Canadian delegation, 'in tough, no-nonsense terms ... told ... shocked U.S. congressmen that Canada will give up nothing to help the U.S. out of its serious balance-of-payments mess.'[40]

What has the group accomplished? In considering this question, it is important to bear in mind the limitations under which the organization has always operated. Of first importance is that, under both the Canadian and the American governmental systems, the conduct of foreign affairs is primarily an executive responsibility. Being fully aware of this fact, the legislators – as the diplomats freely admit – have scrupulously refrained from conducting negotiations or from attempting to work out binding agreements.[41] More than that, since the group's second meeting the delegates have consistently abstained from making recommendations or even from passing resolutions or issuing policy statements. Furthermore, having no full-time staff, being composed for the most part of members without special interest or expertise in the field of Canadian–American relations, and meeting on an average of only once a year, the group is not well qualified to deal with urgent issues. In fact, during the many months of the nuclear arms crisis of the early 1960s it did not even meet, and most other really difficult issues (including the purchase of the Mercantile Bank by Citibank of New York, the cancellation of tax exemptions on advertising placed in Canadian editions of two American magazines, and the American equalization tax) have been resolved through the efforts of the diplomats or of the administrators. The reports of the conferences, although read by lower-ranking civil servants, seldom reach the top-echelon officials and ministers. In any event, over the years they have not been viewed as having much value because they have not disclosed 'the key communications between delegates – the informal ones' and their bland and general format has not shed much light 'even on the discussions in the working committees.'[42] Whether the new plan for summarizing the proceedings will provide appreciably more useful reports remains to be seen.

Nor have the group discussions had much of a direct effect on the national legislatures.[43] This probably has been partly due to the failure of either legislature to establish formal methods of evaluating the reports and the personal impressions of the participants. But it is also significant that except in the Canadian Senate – and there only in recent years – the reports have not been discussed in the legislatures and individual legislators have rarely mentioned the group to buttress their arguments.

It would, however, be erroneous to conclude that the group has been totally lacking in influence. Quite the contrary, it has had a significant impact both on the views and behaviour of individual legislators and on various aspects of Canadian–American relations. Thus the meetings have supplied Canadian parliamentarians with much-needed information on American policies and opinions and many other matters. At the same time, they have provided members of Congress with valuable political information regarding Canadian interests and grievances – information that enables them to evaluate more intelligently the vast quantities of information always at their disposal. They have given the legislators of both countries new insights into common problems, have helped to dispel misconceptions and unjustified fears, and have opened up 'contacts which have modified extreme reactions and prevented prejudicial legislation from being passed.'[44] They have likewise, on the testimony of A.E. Ritchie, former under-secretary of state for external affairs, been 'of the greatest value' to the Canadian embassy in Washington, by helping it to establish contacts with the American legislators which, in turn, have facilitated the settlement of 'many major questions.'[45]

As for the group's effect on specific aspects of Canadian–American relations, these, on the attestation of observers, have included the following: congressional rejection in 1959 of anti-Seaway and Chicago water diversion bills;[46] the procuring for Canadian industry of a progressively larger share of American defence contracts; the obtaining of an agreement to delay proposed American action to cut from $500 to $100 the United States tourist duty-free allowances;[47] the approval by Congress of an amendment to the United States Immigration and Nationality Act of 1965 to alleviate some of the problems caused employees of Canadian companies by the quotas of that Act; the clearing away of obstacles to the ratification of the Columbia River Treaty;[48] the working out of arrangements to allow Canadian pulp cutters to cross the boundary to work in Maine paper-mills; the arriving at an agreement on parallel legislation governing pilotage regulations on the St Lawrence Seaway; and the influencing of the two governments to refer to the ijc the question of the economic feasibility of the further development of the Richelieu–Champlain waterway.[49] The discussions have also been of great value, group champions assert, in helping Canadian parliamentarians to understand American policy with respect to such matters as the admission of Red China into the UN, the war in Vietnam, and the disposal of agricultural surpluses, and in helping American legislators to understand Canadian views with respect to such questions as the recognition of Red China, American investments in Canada, and trade with Cuba. With understanding, of course, generally goes greater toleration and often the dissipation of differences before they become deeply entrenched.

What of the future? Since the need for a forum for the discussion of mutual problems and the promotion of understanding is likely to increase as relations between the two countries become more complicated and problems more numerous, one cannot foresee a day when the group will not be needed. But, of course, it cannot simply rest on its laurels. In that connection, it is significant that, in its report of 1972 on *Canada–United States Relations*, the Canadian Senate Standing Committee on Foreign Affairs, after taking note of the important procedural modifications introduced a few months earlier, went on to urge 'that this effort to improve the functioning of ... the legislative link ... be further developed.'[50] That, most certainly, was sensible advice and, even though American legislators can be expected to oppose changes, as they did in both 1970 and 1973,[51] various aspects of the group's procedures most certainly merit careful reexamination. One is the selection of delegates. For example, it would be highly advisable for both countries to appoint more members with a special interest in, and knowledge of, the topics to be discussed. Thus a greater number of delegates might be recruited from the standing committees dealing with finance, trade, and energy matters. Both countries might also give more thought to obtaining greater continuity in their delegations. For Canada this would seem to be a matter of top priority. Thus for the five meetings held in 1964–8, only eight Canadian legislators attended more than three sessions, and seventy-three of them attended only one or two. By contrast, seventeen of the American delegates attended more than three sessions.[52] It is, of course, desirable that many members have the educational experience of participating in one of the group conferences, but it is perhaps even more desirable that each delegation include a sizeable number of members who have participated in several conferences. 'As a rule a member's effective contributions are made on the basis of the self-confidence and familiarity that come from attendance at more than one of these sessions.'[53]

It would likewise be helpful if all members could be advised of their appointments and be given detailed information regarding the agenda at least two or three months in advance of the convening of a conference. This should result in fuller and less hurried briefings and more adequate preparations. For both countries additional and more informative briefings would also be helpful. The same would be true of a joint subcommittee of the two legislatures or, if that were not feasible, a subcommittee in each of the legislative chambers, which could keep Canadian–American relations under regular and systematic study and serve as the nucleus of that chamber's annual interparliamentary delegation.[54]

The group would be well advised to continue the practice started in 1970 of emphasizing North American bilateral problems. It may also wish to drop the practice of including some of the same topics year after year on the agenda. For example, are such topics as Canadian trade with Cuba and China and the proposed development of a deep Richelieu–Champlain Waterway important enough to be given a place on the agenda four or five years in a row – especially when the time allocated for the formal discussions is extremely limited and many new topics calling for attention are continually arising?

It might likewise be desirable to reduce the number of items included on each conference agenda. This could make for a deeper probing of issues and a general raising of the quality of the discussions. The same would probably be true of the reduction by one-third or one-half in the size of the delegations. Alternatively, in the intervals between the regular group conferences, one or more one-to-two-day special meetings of smaller numbers of delegates might be convened, each focusing on a single topic. Significantly, a special one-day meeting convened in 1971 to discuss the Nixon administration's new economic measures met with such general approbation among the legislators that the delegates to the fourteenth annual meeting, 1972, 'agreed that if at any time one side wishes urgently to discuss any problem of mutual importance, it should approach the other side regarding the possibility of holding a special meeting.'[55] In keeping with that recommendation, a second special meeting was held in July 1973, following congressional approval of the Alaska pipeline. This plan of special meetings, convened on short notice to deal with crisis issues, most certainly does constitute 'a valuable additional mechanism for bilateral dialogues,' but there is still a need for regular special meetings.

A basic problem, most members as well as interested observers agree, is the matter of finding more time for formal committee discussions. Although most of the meetings have lasted for four days, to 1975 only six to eight hours usually were devoted to the committee discussions. Since that date the time given to such discussions 'has approximately doubled.'[56] But, with the meetings being held so infrequently, even this doubling of the discussion period still does not provide sufficient time to cover at all adequately a large number of topics. Holding two regular meetings a year is undoubtedly out of the question. The same probably is true of adding a day to each of the meetings. One possible solution would be to reduce the amount of time regularly devoted to social and sightseeing activities. These, at least in the past, have been quite extensive, involving receptions, dinners, luncheons, and tours.[57] Another possible approach is to follow a procedure, used both in 1976 and in 1977, of organizing breakfast discussions on topics not dealt with in the committee sessions.

Interestingly enough, some participants emphatically deny that the sightseeing trips may properly be regarded as 'junkets.' It is 'the informal contacts and discussions ... between individual delegates or groups of delegates,' Senator Macnaughton contends, 'that are the most directly useful aspect of these meetings.' If it is well arranged, the social program, he insists, 'provides ample opportunity for informal discussions among delegates – for those important occasions when delegates can explore attitudes underlying the official positions taken by one or other of our two countries.'[58] Perhaps so, but one wonders whether a bit of additional time could not be sliced off the social and travel programs for additional committee discussions.

It would also be helpful if all participants – particularly the American legislators – gave the discussions their undivided attention. Thus, following the twelfth meeting, one Canadian participant remarked: 'I had the feeling of great preoccupation on the part of the Americans with things other than the immediate cause of our being together,'[59] while on an earlier occasion another Canadian participant admitted that he not only was 'overwhelmed' by the social activities but also found it 'disconcerting' that various American participants kept going to and from their offices and leaving the meetings to make the quorum calls of their respective chambers.[60] It was largely to ameliorate this problem that Canadian parliamentarians for several years regularly recommended that the conferences be held outside the national capitals. As noted above, their recommendation finally won American approval; and we are assured that since 1974 attendance at all sessions of the meetings has greatly improved.[61]

In the opinion of the author, another matter of major importance is the establishment of more effective procedures for getting the reports into the hands not only of all of the legislators but also of the top executive authorities of the two countries. It would likewise be desirable to give the general public more information regarding the discussions. To achieve that objective, the participants might wish to consider permitting press coverage of some of the committee discussions.

A final suggestion is that in the title of the organization 'group' be changed to 'committee,' 'organization,' or 'conference.' As Senator Grosart has observed, there was adequate 'reason for the generic name in the early stages ... to stress the fact that it was an unofficial group,' but now that the organization has become well established and has acquired prestige and influence, there is 'merit in ... giving it a higher status than that of merely a group.'[62]

20

Conclusion

What has been the role of the intergovernmental machinery? The question, unfortunately, is one that cannot be answered with any degree of precision. Sometimes a joint institution has played only a supporting role, as when the Civil Defence Committee participated with the scientists and the military officials in the formulation of plans for the electronic detection screens. On other occasions, as when the International Joint Commission and its boards participated in the research that led to the signing of the Great Lakes Water Quality Agreement, the agency's role has been the dominant one. About all that can be said with assurance is that the role of each institution has varied with the times, the circumstances, the enterprise and vigour of its members, and the degree of confidence and support accorded it by the two governments. For example, because of the high esteem in which General McNaughton was held by both Canadian and American government authorities, the prestige and influence of the Permanent Joint Board on Defence probably was higher during the years of his chairmanship of the Canadian Section of the board, 1945 to 1959, than at any other time before or since. In contrast, the prestige and usefulness of the IJC sank to an all-time low during the 1920s because of the repeated appointment by the United States of elderly, poorly qualified politicians as commissioners.[1]

The history of some of the joint organizations has been one of great activity for a time, followed in some instances by a gradual decline and in other instances by a complete cessation of all activities. For example, the period of greatest activity of the International Boundary Commission was during the two decades following its creation in 1908, when much of the boundary was being surveyed, demarcated, and mapped. By the late twenties most of the difficult surveying, clearing, and mapping had been completed and the commission was able to discharge its remaining duties with a smaller staff.[2] Similarly, the PJBD was extremely active during the entire period of the Second World War but has had fewer important responsibilities since the termination of hostilities. The Joint Industrial Mobilization Committee, organized in 1949, has had no meetings since 1953; the Senior Committee on Defence production–Development Sharing kept quite busy for a time following its establishment in 1959 but has not met since 1965; the Civil Emergency Planning Committee, after obtaining new powers and a revised membership, terminated its meetings in 1972; the Ministerial Committee on Joint Defence, established with high hopes in 1958, held the last of its four meetings in 1964; and the Ministerial Committee on Trade and Economic Affairs, created in 1953, did an excellent job for ten to twelve years of exchanging information and tackling refractory problems but ceased its meetings in 1970.

In sharp contrast, during the past quarter of a century the activities of the IJC have greatly expanded. This has come about largely as a result of the increasingly large number of investigations it has been asked to make and the great amount of surveillance and monitoring it supervises. Particularly time-consuming have been its various activities relating to water and air pollution control and the maintenance of stable water levels.

The activities of the three bilateral fishery commissions have also shown a significant increase in recent years. For the Great Lakes Fishery Commission this has been principally because of an extension of its lamprey control program to increasing numbers of the Great Lakes tributaries; for the other two agencies, additional duties, along with expanded budgets and staffs, have resulted from accelerated research activities and the emergence of increasingly difficult conservation and regulation problems.

The continued growth of the defence production–development sharing program has, understandably, meant increased activity for the joint steering group that coordinates and expedites that program. At the same time, problems arising from a general expansion in the volume of Canadian–American trade and investments have resulted during the past fifteen years in the creation of various committees and working groups. Some of these have been quite active, and, as already noted, the Trade Statistics Committee has been highly effective.

The Interparliamentary Group seems to have found new vigour and usefulness after several years of indecisive drifting. From the outset the group served the helpful function of enabling the legislators of each country to learn more about the problems, interests, and aspirations of the other country, but it seemed always in danger of turning into a social, junketing club. Fortunately, at the insistence of Canadian parliamentarians, since 1974 the social and junketing activities have been subordinated to the serious business of analysing current issues. It now is serving a definite need and seems in no immediate danger of becoming obsolete.

The most successful of the joint institutions have been the commissions, i.e., the low-level agencies dealing with such matters as fisheries, parks, boundaries, and boundary waters. They are staffed by experts who are better qualified than most diplomats to deal with such technical problems as the establishment of the optimum water level for a boundary lake or the fixing of the size and character of a fishing appliance. They enjoy the additional advantages of operating under precise codes of law and principles set forth in formal treaties and/or written rules of procedure and of being free of rigid instructions and government interference. They are particularly useful for the collection and exchange of factual information and for reviewing and defining points of view. They, likewise, help to anticipate problems and to prevent issues from escalating into crises. By keeping issues on the lower levels, they are kept out of the news media and are resolved on the basis of the factual information available to the experts. From the technical viewpoint, NORAD, the Permanent Joint Board on Defence, and some of the other defence agencies have also been quite successful in the discharge of the functions for which they were created. They, however, have not won as widespread acceptance in Canada as have the more technically oriented agencies.

In view of the disparities between the two countries, questions logically arise as to just how beneficial the joint instruments have been from the Canadian viewpoint. For example, have Canadian interests been better served through the use of the joint institutions than they would have been had the discussions and negotiations been conducted through other governmental channels? This, obviously, is a question that cannot be satisfactorily answered. It is, however, interesting to recall that most of the joint organizations have been set up on Canadian initiatives. That was true of the IJC, the fishery commissions, the two ministerial committees, the PJBD, and the defence production–development committees. In fact, only NORAD and two or three of the other agencies concerned with defence appear to have been created on the initiative of the United States. This suggests that at least in years past Canadian statesmen and officials assumed that their interests could be served more effectively through the use of joint organizations than through reliance on the diplomats or other means. Furthermore, there still seems to be general Canadian approval of the IJC, the IBC, the fishery commissions, and other agencies not dealing with defence or economic matters. This may be more a question of mistrust of the diplomats and their 'quiet diplomacy' than any great enthusiasm for the joint agencies. But the support of Canadian commentators for the intergovernmental machinery seems to be quite genuine. They like the joint institutions, among other reasons, because they believe that they help to denationalize and to depoliticize Canadian–American issues and to 'give symmetry to ... relations that would otherwise be heavily assymmetrical, helping to correct the top-sided pattern of smaller powers versus greater powers.'[3] They have also observed that the tendency of interest groups to join forces across the border in presenting a united front in favour of, or opposition to, proposed courses of action often causes the recommendations of the joint agencies to be focused 'more on conflict between uses and management decisions than on the conflict between countries.'[4]

Not surprisingly, Canada has fared best in the organizations staffed by the experts, who normally make decisions on the basis of ascertained facts, with a minimum of regard for national considerations. How the better of these agencies operate is illustrated by the following excerpt from a statement by Dr Sylvia Ostry, former chief statistician of Canada, explaining how the United States–Canada Trade Statistics Committee tackled the problem of reconciling the gap between the American and the Canadian trade statistics for 1970:

... for the exercise to be successful it had to be conducted in a strict atmosphere of scientific objectivity. Indeed, it required, paradoxically, that statisticians leave aside the purpose of the figures and throughout the exercise consider the differences solely as an intellectual puzzle. Had statisticians approached the problem otherwise, and attempted to explain the gap from what they understood to be their country's negotiating position, the chances of agreeing would have been seriously compromised. As it turned out, at the intellectual level it became a pure problem of statistics, with officers of both countries organized as a single research team.[5]

Interestingly enough, at times, in some of the joint agencies Canada has had not merely operational equality with the United States but has actually enjoyed certain advantages over its more populous neighbour. For years this has been true of the IJC, where the larger staff of Canada's Section enables it to amass fuller legal and engineering data than is readily available to the American Section. It has also been true, in recent years, of the International Boundary Commission, where the longer tenure and greater technical competence of the Canadian commissioner has given him an edge over his American colleague. And it probably has been true of the International Pacific Salmon Commission, in which two Canadian members each served for well nigh thirty years. In still other agencies the thorough preparations made by the Canadian representatives, compared with the often less thorough preparations of the Americans, has at times given Canada the advantage.[6] Also, the greater size of the American bureaucracy, with its larger number of government agencies, has made the preparation of a United States position immeasurably more difficult than the preparation of a Canadian position.

When, however, we turn to questions of military defence and economics we find that the Canadian view or position has been accepted less frequently than that of the United States, which is not surprising. Unlike fisheries or waterways, defence and economic questions 'are important matters of national policy wherein governments insist on exercising reasonable freedom of action.'[7] Moreover, issues of defence and economics often have broad ramifications, affecting American interests and commitments in other areas of the globe. Such issues are not easily denationalized or depoliticized. Quite the contrary, they are likely to arouse strong sentiments of self-interest, patriotism, and concern – particularly when it is believed that the failure of a policy may result in national or universal disaster. Nor can one afford to overlook the indirect influence exerted upon the discussions and decisions of the agencies concerned with defence and economics by interest groups – munitions manufacturers, the mining industry, agriculture, organized labour, and so on. These groups have very definite ideas regarding such matters as trade, the exploitation of domestic natural resources, the location of defence plants and missile bases, and the proper level of defence preparations. They are 'paying the piper'; accordingly, they insist on having at least some voice in 'calling the tune.' Under such competitive conditions, Canada, with its relatively small population, modest industrial development, and even more modest military forces, is decidedly at a disadvantage.

A Canadian nationalist might very well retort: yes, the legal equality principle works reasonably well in the IJC, the IBC, and the fishery commissions, where the stakes are relatively small, but it breaks down completely when issues of national defence, trade, and other matters of vital importance are at stake. And there is, of course, much validity to such an argument. However, it would hardly be accurate to think of either the matters handled by the IJC or the fisheries as of minor importance. Prior to the creation of the IJC, American corporations, backed by their state and national governments, pretty well had their way with boundary and transboundary waters; thereafter they had to obtain the consent of the IJC for diversions or uses that affected the water levels. Before the creation of the International Pacific Salmon Commission in 1937, Canadian fishermen were obtaining only 30 per cent of the Pacific salmons;[8] thereafter they obtained approximately 50 per cent. Prior to the introduction of the Defence Production Sharing Program in 1959, in some years Canadian sales of defence supplies and equipment in the United States were only about one-tenth American sales in Canada; by the end of 1975 Canadian sales in the United States for the preceding seventeen years exceeded American sales in Canada by $307,000,000.[9] Perhaps more significantly still, on the basis of empirical analysis of major Canadian–American issues of 1950–69, Professor Joseph S. Nye, Jr, has found that Canada more than held its own in cases handled by transnational organizations.[10]

Despite the number and variety of joint institutions used by Canada and the United States over the years, there are a number of important policy areas where no joint machinery has been set up. These include science and technology, banking, investments, health, education, agriculture, energy and resources, transportation, labour relations, coastal waters, and urban sprawl along the boundary. Furthermore, aside from the Trade Statistics Committee, formed in 1971, and various working groups, no intergovernmental organizations have been created since 1967. And yet during this same eleven-year period non-governmental, trans-national relations have continued to grow at an undiminished pace.

Through the years dozens of suggestions have been advanced for filling the gaps in the intergovernmental machinery. These have included a recommendation in 1958 by L.B. Pearson, then leader of the Opposition, that a joint raw materials board be created to concern itself with the production and allocation of raw materials on a continental basis;[11] a proposal by the Canadian delegation to the ninth meeting of the Interparliamentary Group, in 1966, that intergovernmental machinery be set up 'to stimulate increased cooperation and action to preserve water resources';[12] a proposal in 1968 by John Turner, then minister of justice, that an organization be created to regulate international corporations;[13] and a policy statement in 1973 by the Progressive Conservative Party of Canada calling for 'the establishment of a joint economic commission to conduct specialized studies and to consult on economic policies.'[14]

In spite of the calls for new joint agencies, from 1960 onward neither Ottawa nor Washington showed any special inclination to add to the existing intergovernmental machinery. Although some of the reasons are obscure, certain basic factors are easily identifiable. One was the strained relations that developed between Kennedy and Diefenbaker in 1962–3 over

Cuba, nuclear arms, and other issues. These differences occurred at a time of rapidly growing nationalism in Canada, when many Canadians were rejecting the widely held viewpoint of the forties and fifties that in foreign affairs, defence, and other areas their interests were virtually identical with those of their American neighbours and now were expressing alarm over the influx of American capital and culture and the accelerated trend towards continental integration. The Diefenbaker government, during this particular period, not only did not recommend the creation of new joint agencies but chose not to use some that were already available.

With the coming to power of the Liberals, the bilateral 'dialogue' was resumed, culminating in the Hyannisport Communiqué of May 1963, committing the Kennedy and the Pearson administrations to working towards the 'rational use of the continent's resources' and the resumption of the ministerial committee meetings. But Kennedy was assassinated before much could be done to implement the commitment. Pearson and Johnson authorized ministerial meetings and set Arnold Heeney and Livingston Merchant to work preparing 'guidelines' suitable for application by the joint institutions.[15] Very soon, however, much of the president's time and attention came to be focused on Vietnam; while the late sixties brought bitter Canadian disillusionment with American foreign and defence policies, particularly the Vietnamese involvement. Pierre Trudeau's assumption, in 1968, of the leadership of the Liberal party and of the office of prime minister led to a critical new look at many aspects of Canadian foreign and defence policies, including relations with the next-door neighbour. A year or two later came the enunciation of the Nixon Doctrine, calling upon friends and allies of the United States to become more self-reliant, followed in August 1971 by Nixon's New Economic Policy, followed in turn by the shocking revelations of the Watergate irregularities. Concluding that the United States was no longer a country with which Canada could, or should, maintain a 'special relationship,' and feeling increasing concern over Canada's economic, military, and cultural dependence on the friendly but overpowering neighbour, the authorities in Ottawa in 1972 brought forward their *Canada–U.S. Relations: Options for the Future*, calling for 'the active pursuit of trade diversification and technical cooperation with countries other than the United States' and a halt to the unthinking drift towards ever greater continental integration.[16]

During the months following the publication of *Options for the Future* a number of developments appeared to improve the environment for the creation of new joint institutions and the reconstitution of the joint ministerial committees. One of these was the ending of active American participation in the Vietnamese War; a second was the emergence of a rough new symmetry in trade and investments between the two countries; and a third was the replacement of Nixon by Gerald Ford as president. In reality the environment was less favourable than it seemed. For one thing, considerable bitterness was engendered in each country by various policies and actions of the other country. American grievances included: the moves in Saskatchewan to nationalize American-controlled potash interests; the blocking out of American television commercials from programs received in Canada; the enactment of the Foreign Investment Review Act, giving the Canadian government control over foreign takeovers and new investments in Canada; and the placing of quota limitations on imports on American beef and a tax on oil exports, both restrictive actions imposed without advance consultations. Canadian grievances included threats by Congress to retaliate against Canada for reducing oil exports; the reluctance of the authorities in Washington to approve the sale to Cuba of thirty railway locomotives by an American-controlled firm, MLW-Worthington Ltd. of Montreal; the threat of oil spills off the coast of British Columbia by American oil tankers; and the seeming unwillingness, or inability, of the American government to do anything about either the proposed flooding of the Skagit Valley by the Seattle City Light company or the threatened pollution of the waters of the Souris and Red rivers in Manitoba by the Garrison Dam diversion project in North Dakota. Instead of reconstituting the Ministerial Committee on Trade and Economic Affairs or utilizing other of the joint institutions, these and many other issues of the 1972–5 period were handled mainly by the diplomats, by exchanges of letters and phone calls by the bureaucrats, by one-to-one conferences of cabinet members, by summit conferences, and by the involvement of state and provincial representatives – especially the latter – in negotiations and problem-solving.

Recently a number of factors have combined to improve the North American political environment and to bring Canadian–American relations to a new plane of 'openness, civility and warmth.'[17] These have included Carter's demonstrated eagerness to resolve a number of long-standing issues – including the Garrison Diversion; Trudeau's much-acclaimed address to the American Congress; a noticeable waning of Canadian nationalism; less Canadian emphasis on 'Option 3' and a renewed interest in American capital and markets; a greater American understanding of Canadian national objectives and independence susceptibilities; and, possibly most important of all, a common Canadian–American concern to soft-pedal or avoid issues that might weaken English-speaking Canada's ability to counter the Parti Québécois separatist threat.[18]

Does this new benign environment foretell a revival of interest in Ottawa and Washington in joint institutions? Probably not. In recent months spokesmen for each country have praised the existing institutions – particularly the IJC, the PJBD, and the Interparliamentary Group – and have gone on record as favouring a variety of techniques in dealing with Canadian–American issues. At the same time, no government representative in a responsible position in either country has publicly recommended the reconstitution of the joint ministerial committees or the creation of other major agencies. This is partly because Canadian cabinet members seem to believe that Canadian interests in such fields as energy, trade, and investments can best be safeguarded through the ad hoc type of discussion. In these areas the joint agencies, they have concluded, promote linkages, and linkages lead to continental integration.[19] But, perhaps equally importantly, from the experiences of the past eight to ten years, cabinet members and officials of both countries are convinced that, in dealing with certain types of issues, the informal ad hoc approach not only provides for greater flexibility 'but actually works better.'[20] More than that, because 'relations are so diverse, and issues crop up so unexpectedly' and in such unpredictable ways, the new pattern frequently has greater utility.[21]

The new approach, as explained by Allan J. MacEachen in 1975, simply 'consists of analysis of the particular national interest to be served, followed by consultation, discussion or negotiation with a view to reaching a mutually acceptable settlement of the particular problem.' Of basic importance is the advance consultation. In short, if one country proposes to take an action that might adversely affect the interests of the neighbouring country, it is expected to notify that country of its intentions and, 'where appropriate, to provide an opportunity for advance consultations.'[22] Thus Russell Train, administrator of the United States Environmental Protection Agency, and Canada's environment minister, Jean Marchand, agreed in June 1976 that each country should give the other early notice of proposed engineering developments that might affect the other's environment.[23] Similarly, in 1977 the attorney general of the United States conferred with his counterpart on the establishment of an 'early warning system' to thwart any attempt by anti-trust groups to extend their operations across the boundary.[24]

The extent to which prior consultation and discussion have become a basic feature of the government-to-government relations is evinced by data compiled by the Department of State. From July 1975 through January 1976 a total of forty-two meetings and consultations – exclusive of meetings of the joint agencies – were held between Canadian and American officials. The meeting sites included not only Washington and Ottawa but also New

York City, Montreal, Brussels, Paris, and half a dozen other places. Topics discussed covered almost the entire ambit of Canadian–American affairs, as well as relations with other countries – the environment, trade, finance, tax treaties, health, cable television deletions, transportation, agriculture, NATO, satellites, UN peace-keeping, and the exploitation of the continental shelf.[25]

All indications point to an increase in the number and complexity of Canadian–American issues in the years ahead – especially with respect to energy, the environment, agriculture, and defence. Since the North American neighbours have traditionally used whatever channels of communication have seemed best suited to the needs of the moment, they may very well establish new joint institutions in the not too distant future. In recent years each has established joint institutions – mainly to deal with economic questions – with a number of other countries.[26] And both Thomas O. Enders, United States ambassador to Canada, and Vice President Walter Mondale have called attention to a number of areas where new Canadian–American arrangements might well be undertaken.[27]

However, if, as seems quite probable, the provinces become increasingly active in the foreign affairs field, some issues currently handled on a cooperative basis by the two national governments may eventually be largely dealt with by state–provincial cooperation or by the provinces working directly with the government in Washington. Already the provinces, and to a lesser degree the states, are making their influence felt in many aspects of the Canadian–American relationship. For example, it was a conference convened by Premier Robarts of Ontario in 1970, attended by representatives of Ontario, Quebec, Manitoba, and the eight Great Lakes States, that provided the impetus that led to the signing of the Great Lakes Water Quality Agreement two years later. For several years the premiers of the Maritime Provinces and the governors of the New England States have been meeting at regular intervals to discuss such matters as transportation, tourism, trade, and energy and occasionally to resolve difficult issues. Neighbouring provinces and states provide mutual assistance in the event of forest fires or natural disasters; they have entered into agreements to coordinate highway load limits and truck registrations; and they have cooperated on highway projects and the construction of bridges. Significantly, by 1974 a total of 766 state–provincial agreements and other arrangements had been effected.[28] Some of these authorized the establishment of joint institutions. For example, in 1973 the Maritime premiers and the New England governors created a permanent advisory committee of officials to compile information on the power development needs of the area. Later they set up a committee to meet from time to time throughout the year to examine various regional issues and to prepare for the annual conference.

Understandably, the authorities in each of the national capitals view with mixed feelings the active involvement of the provinces and states in trans-boundary relations. On the one hand, they recognize that state–provincial cooperation can, and does, resolve many issues. On the other hand, they are acutely aware that participation by the states and the provinces complicates the formulation of national policies and the coordination of national efforts. Since, however, the natural resources and many other matters involved in trans-boundary relations fall within the jurisdictions of the regional governments, the national governments are obliged to accept, with as much grace as they can muster, state and provincial participation.

Another development unfavourable to the creation of new binational institutions is the increasing tendency for many issues of concern to both countries to be resolved at multinational conferences or at meetings of such organizations as NATO and the UN. This is pleasing to Canada, which in disagreements with the United States frequently finds it helpful to be able to enlist the support of other countries. An international forum, a Canadian scholar argues, has the additional virtue of 'minimizing the emotion that bilateral bargaining may easily arouse.'[29]

There are, of course, still other ways of resolving Canadian–American differences and for finding cooperative solutions to common needs other than resorting to organizations or leaving the solutions to the states and the provinces. Occasionally mutual objectives can be achieved through the negotiation of a treaty, or even an informal understanding, calling for parallel actions. An example is the convention signed in 1916 by Great Britain (in behalf of Canada) and the United States for the protection of migratory birds.[30] Not infrequently the desired results can be obtained through the coordinated actions of national and/or state–provincial organizations. A striking illustration is the manner in which the St Lawrence Seaway and Power Projects were constructed and are currently being operated.[31] Some problems can best be left to the cooperative efforts of private individuals and organizations. Nor should one become so preoccupied with organizations as to lose sight of other essentials of a good Canadian–American relationship. One of these, most certainly, is a friendly, open-minded attitude: a willingness not only to listen to the views of representatives of the other country but also to make an effort to understand the problems, policies, and aspirations of that country. Another essential is, of course, mutual confidence – confidence in the basic honesty, goodwill, reasonableness, and stability of behaviour of the other representatives. Finally, and of crucial importance, are the skill, personality, industry, and integrity of the individual officials and government leaders. Joint organizations can be extremely useful, but they are only instruments and do not operate automatically. They must be used and – to achieve their full potentiality – used efficiently. 'Good machinery is better than bad machinery but men matter most.'[32]

Notes

CHAPTER I

1 Canada, Senate Standing Committee on Foreign Affairs, *Report*, No. 21 (2, 9, and 16 Dec. 1975), I, 14.
2 Ibid., 15.
3 Rufus Smith, Canada, Senate Standing Committee on Foreign Affairs, *Proceedings*, No. 5 (4 Feb. 1975), 5.
4 Eugenia M. Kelley to the author, 23 May 1978; Canada, Senate Standing Committee on Foreign Affairs, *Report*, No. 21 (1975), I, 16.
5 Gerald M. Craig, *The United States and Canada* (Cambridge, Mass.: Harvard University Press, 1969), 6.
6 Canada, Senate Standing Committee on Foreign Affairs, *Report*, No. 21 (1975), I, 18.
7 Alastair Gillespie, 'Canada–United States Trade: Towards a Balanced Understanding,' *American Review of Canadian Studies* (spring 1973), 14; *Washington Post*, 29 April 1971.
8 Allan J. MacEachen, 'Canada–United States Relations,' 23 Jan. 1975, s. and s. 75/1.
9 A.E. Safarian, 'Foreign Investment in Primary Industries,' in *Canada–United States Relations*, ed. Edward English, No. 2, Vol. 32, *Proceedings of the Academy of Political Science* (1976), 76.
10 D.C. Thomson and R.F. Swanson, *Canadian Foreign Policy: Options and Perspectives* (Toronto: McGraw-Hill Ryerson, 1971), 138–9.
11 TS (U.S. Treaty Series) 105; 1 BSP (British and Foreign State Papers) 784.
12 For discussions of the arbitrations see Manley Hudson, *International Tribunals, Past and Future* (Washington, D.C.: Carnegie Endowment for International Peace, 1944), 3–19; John Bassett Moore, ed., *International Adjudications*

Ancient and Modern (6 vols., New York: Oxford University Press, 1929), Vols. I and II.

13 Hudson, *International Tribunals*, 4.

14 For the treaty see TS 133; 61 BSP 40; for the arbitrations see Goldwin Smith, *The Treaty of Washington, 1971: A Study in Imperial History* (Ithaca: Cornell University Press, 1941); L.B. Shippee, *Canadian–American Relations 1849–1874* (New Haven: Yale University Press, 1939), chap. XV.

15 For the text of the arbitration treaty see Canada, *Treaties and Agreements Affecting Canada in Force between His Majesty and the United States of America ... 1814–1913* (Ottawa, 1915), 93–8. For the arbitration see Charles C. Tansill, *Canadian–American Relations 1875–1911* (New Haven: Yale University Press, 1943), 53–86; Robert Craig Brown, *Canada's National Policy 1883–1900* (Princeton: Princeton University Press, 1964), 60–88.

16 See H. Gordon Skilling, *Canadian Representation Abroad: From Agency to Embassy* (Toronto: Ryerson Press, 1945), 200–13; William R. Willoughby, 'The Impact of the United States upon Canada's External Relations' (PH D dissertation, University of Wisconsin, 1942), 173–9, 249–50.

17 James Eayrs, 'Sharing a Continent: The Hard Issues,' in *The United States and Canada*, ed. John S. Dickey, (Englewood Cliffs, NJ: Prentice-Hall, 1964), 57.

18 For the treaty see Canada, *Treaties and Agreements Affecting Canada in Force between His Majesty and the United States of America ... 1814–1913*, 161–78.

19 Lord Pauncefote to John Hay, 23 July 1900, Anderson Papers (Library of Congress), Box 72 (1908); Hay to Pauncefote, 29 Oct. 1900, ibid.; Hay to Gerard A. Lawther, 15 July 1901, Governor General's Numbered Files (PAC), G. 21, No. 192C, Vol. 2(a), 1900–1906; W.F. King to O.H. Tittmann, 11 Jan. 1906, Anderson Papers, Box 73.

20 For the treaty see TS 720; 121 BSP 933. For a brief description of the agency see H. George Classen, *Thrust and Counterthrust: The Genesis of the Canada–United States Boundary* (Don Mills, Ont.: Longmans Canada, 1969), 362–7.

21 See the testimony of Elihu Root, United States, Senate Committee on Foreign Relations, *Hearings and Proceedings on the Treaty between the United States and Canada concerning Boundary Waters*, 61st Cong., 2d Sess. (1910), 269–70; Alan O. Gibbons, 'Sir George Gibbons and the Boundary Waters Treaty of 1909,' *Canadian Historical Review*, XXXIV (June 1953), 124–38.

22 See William R. Willoughby, 'The Canada–United States Joint Economic Agencies of the Second World War,' *Canadian Public Administration* (spring 1972), 59–73.

23 William R. Willoughby, 'The Genesis of Canadian–American Defence Cooperation,' *Canadian Defence Quarterly*, V (winter 1975–6), 42–9.

24 Interviews with Dana Wilgress, 4 Aug. 1965, and A.E. Ritchie, 11 June 1968.

25 Thomas S. Power, *Design for Survival* (New York: Coward-McCann, 1964), 153.

26 1949 CTS (Canada Treaty Series) 8; TIAS (Treaties and Other International Acts Series, United States) 1889.

27 Canada, Department of Defence Production, *Production Sharing Handbook* (Ottawa: Queen's Printer, 1967), 2–4.

28 Ibid., B 45–8.

29 Senate of Canada, Standing Committee on Foreign Affairs, *Proceedings*, No. 1 (28 March 1974), 36.

30 1951 CTS 3; TIAS 2227.

31 1963 CTS 8; TIAS 5464.

32 1967 CTS 73; TIAS 6325.

33 1964 CTS 17; TIAS 5631; 13 Eliz 2, c 19; Stat., N.B., 1964, c 11; 78 stat. 299. See also William R. Willoughby, 'The Roosevelt Campobello International Park Commission,' *Dalhousie Review*, (summer 1974), 289–97.

34 1953 CTS 18; TIAS 2922.

35 1958 CTS 22; TIAS 4098.

CHAPTER 2

1 For the text of the Treaty see Canada, *Treaties and Agreements Affecting Canada in Force between His Majesty and the United States of America ... 1814–1913* (Ottawa, 1915), 185–95.

2 For the provisions of the treaty see United States, *Treaties and Other International Acts*, Series 7312 (15 April 1972).

3 Charles Dunlop, 'The Origin and Development of the International Joint Commission as a Judicial Tribunal' (MA thesis, Queen's University, 1959), 20–1.

4 See William R. Willoughby, 'The Appointment and Removal of Members of the International Joint Commission,' *Canadian Public Administration*, XII (fall 1969), 411–25.

5 Ibid., 421–6; Dunlop, 'Origin and Development of IJC,' 28–41.

6 Currently the chairman of the American Section is paid $50,000; the chairman of the Canadian Section is paid in the range of $45,400 to $61,200 a year and is given a generous expense account. Each of the other American members receives compensation for time actually devoted to IJC business, while each of the other Canadian members receives between $19,950 and $27,500 a year.

7 George E. Foster to Magrath, 22 Feb. 1920, Magrath Papers, PAC, Subject File 22, 'IJC Correspondence.'

8 Henry A. Powell to Sir George E. Foster, 19 Jan. 1920, Borden Papers, PAC, OC489, 'International Joint Commission.'

9 May Simpson to the Secretary of State, 8 Mar. 1933, Dept. of State file 711.42152/370.

10 See William R. Willoughby, 'The International Joint Commission's Role in Maintaining Stable Water Levels,' *Inland Seas*, 28 (summer 1972), 115.

11 Article VII. As of 3 April 1978 a total of 26 boards were reporting to the IJC. Letter of that date from D.G. Chance to the author.

12 Matthew E. Welsh, 'The Work of the International Joint Commission,' *Dept. of State Bull.*, 59 (23 Sept. 1968), 313.

13 International Joint Commission, *Report on the Pollution of Boundary Waters* (1950), 4.

14 Welsh, 'Work of the IJC,' 313.

15 *Summary of the International Joint Commission Seminar on the IJC: Its Achievements, Needs and Potential, June 20 and 21, 1974, Montreal, Quebec* (mimeographed and distributed by the IJC), 24.

16 Anthony Scott, 'Fisheries, Pollution, and Canadian–American Transnational Relations,' *International Organization*, 28 (autumn 1974), 846.

17 *Summary of the IJC Seminar*, 25.

18 F.J.E. Jordan, 'The International Joint Commission and Canada–United States Boundary Relations,' in *Canadian Perspectives on International Law and Organization*, ed. R. St. Macdonald, G.L. Morris, and D.M. Johnston (Toronto: University of Toronto Press, 1974), 540.

19 Commissioner Eugene W. Weber, *Upper Columbia River Development*, Hearings before the Committee on Interior and Insular Affairs, U.S. Senate, 85th Cong., 2d Sess. (7 May 1958), 295.

20 Memo in Root's handwriting, dated 'March 1909,' Anderson Papers, Ms. Room, Library of Congress, Letter Book, Box 69.

21 L.J. Burpee, 'An International Experiment,' in *Papers Relating to the Work of the IJC* (Ottawa, 1929), 55–6.

22 M.M. Wyvell, 'Memorandum Concerning the St. Mary and Milk River Irrigation Project,' 15 May 1915, Dept. of State File 711.4216 Sa 22/21, p. 10.

23 J.C. Chacko, *The International Joint Commission between the United States of America and the Dominion of Canada* (New York: Columbia University Press, 1932), 223–31. See also 'Resumé of St. Mary and Milk River Problem,' a memo by J.T. Johnston, Ottawa, 18 Feb. 1931, Bennett Papers, University of New Brunswick Library, W-112, Vol. 1.

24 Memo by G.H. Hackworth, 6 Aug. 1919, Dept. of State File 711.4216 Sa/65.

25 William H. Smith to the Secretary of State (Charles E. Hughes), 28 Mar. 1921, Dept. of State File 711.4216 Sa 22/70.

26 L.J. Burpee, 'Insurance for Peace,' in *Papers Relating to IJC*, 67.

27 Kellogg to William Phillips, 26 July 1927, *Foreign Relations of the United States*, 1929, II, 97–9.

28 Mackenzie King to Phillips, 23 Mar. 1928, ibid., 100–3.
29 Kellogg to Phillips, 21 June 1928, ibid., 103.
30 L.J. Burpee to R.B. Bennett, 29 Feb. 1932, Bennett Papers, w-112, Vol. 1, 'Official, St. Mary and Milk River.'
31 Order, St. Mary–Milk Rivers, 4 Oct. 1921, summarized in Robert A. MacKay, 'The International Joint Commission between the United States and Canada,' in *Papers Relating to IJC*, 88.
32 See Willoughby, 'Appointment and Removal of Members of the IJC,' 418–20.
33 Note Magrath's comment to Bryce: 'It has been a great relief to get it settled because if we had failed it seems to me it would have been the death warrant of the International Joint Commission.' Letter of 27 Oct. 1921, Magrath Papers, Subject File 21, M.G. 30, B 2, Vol. 6.

CHAPTER 3

1 For examples of the three classes of waters see Chacko, *The International Joint Commission* (New York: Columbia University Press, 1932), 82–94.
2 See 44 Stat. (U.S. Statutes at Large), 2108
3 Charles Dunlop, 'The Origin and Development of the International Joint Commission as a Judicial Tribunal' (MA thesis, Queen's University, 1959), 20.
4 See William R. Willoughby, 'The Appointment and Removal of Members of the International Joint Commission,' *Canadian Public Administration*, 12 (fall 1969), 413.
5 Dunlop, 'Origin and Development of IJC,' 64, 102, 114.
6 On the general matter of procedure in quasi-judicial cases see G. Graham Waite, 'The International Joint Commission – Its Practice and Its Impact on Land Use,' *Buffalo Law Review*, 13 (fall 1963), 100–10.
7 The old rules forbade the commission to determine important questions unless all six of its members were present. Adherence to this rule caused such great inconvenience that the less restrictive rule was adopted in 1964.
8 See *Summary of the International Joint Commission Seminar on the IJC: Its Achievements, Needs and Potential, June 20 and 21, 1974, Montreal, Quebec* (mimeographed and distributed by the IJC), 11.
9 *Globe and Mail*, 7 May 1974.
10 Dunlop, 'Origin and Development of IJC,' 42.
11 Rainy River Improvement Company, 12 Apr. 1912. See L.M. Bloomfield and G.F. Fitzgerald, *Boundary Waters Problems of Canada and the United States* (Toronto: Carswell, 1958), 69–70.
12 Watrous Island Boom Company, 2 Sept. 1913, and the St. Croix River Fishways, 3 Oct. 1923. See ibid., 71, 111–12; Chacko, *The IJC*, 119.
13 R.A. MacKay, in *Papers Relating to the Work of the IJC* (Ottawa, 1929), 74,

summarizing the commission's decision in Greater Winnipeg District, 15 Jan. 1914. See also Bloomfield and Fitzgerald, *Boundary Waters Problems*, 85, 86.

14 The St. Croix Water Power Company, 15 Nov. 1915, and Sprague's Falls Manufacturing Co. Ltd., 9 Nov. 1915. See Bloomfield and Fitzgerald, ibid., 94–5.

15 Algoma Steel Corp., 27 May 1914. See Chacko, *The IJC*, 161.

16 IJC, *Further Regulation of the Great Lakes* (1976), 28.

17 George Kyte, *Organization and Work of the International Joint Commission* (Ottawa, King's Printer, 1937), 12.

18 Ibid. The dismissed application was Rainy River Improvement Co., 1913. See Bloomfield and Fitzgerald, *Boundary Waters Problems*, 69–70. The other instance when the decision was not unanimous was in 1952 when Commissioner Roger B. McWhorter disagreed with the majority decision with respect to the proposed construction of certain works in the International Rapids Section of the St Lawrence River. See William R. Willoughby, *The St. Lawrence Waterway: A Study in Politics and Diplomacy* (Madison, Wis.: University of Wisconsin Press, 1961), 242 and 335n 45.

19 See Docket No. 38, Whiteman, *Digest of International Law* (Washington, DC: Govt. Printing Office, 1964), III, 845.

20 Canada, *Sessional Paper 230*, Vol. LIV, No. 10 (1919). See also Willoughby, *The St. Lawrence Waterway*, 87–8; Chacko, *The IJC*, 190–208.

21 *Sessional Paper 230*. See also Robert J. Buckley to William Phillips, 25 Sept. 1918, Dept. of State File 711.42157 Sa 24/17.

22 Frank L. Polk to the Secretary of War, 18 Nov. 1918, Dept. of State file 711.42157 Sa 24/9; Willoughby, *The St. Lawrence Waterway*, 88.

23 For the order of approval see *Eighth Annual Report*, Conservation Commission of Canada (1917), 263–4.

24 Order-in-Council, 12 Oct. 1918, Borden Papers, PAC, RLB 2744.

25 See Canada, House of Commons Standing Committee on External Affairs, *Minutes of Proceedings and Evidence*, 12 Dec. 1957, 248–9.

26 This limitation was included in the treaty at the insistence of Secretary Root who understood full well the ardent nationalism of the senators of his day.

27 MacKay, in *Papers Relating to IJC*, 94.

28 Peter Smedresman, 'The International Joint Commission (United States and Canada) and the International Boundary and Water Commission (United States and Mexico): Potential for Environmental Control along the Boundaries,' *New York University Journal of International Law and Politics*, VI (winter 1973), 513.

29 See Canada, *House of Commons Debates*, 10 June 1935, IV, 3456.

30 J.L. MacCallum, in a conversation with the author, 12 Oct. 1966. See also Don C. Piper, 'The Role of Inter-governmental Machinery in Canadian–American Relations,' *South Atlantic Quarterly*, LXII (autumn 1963), 555.

31 TIAS 5638, Art. XVI; 1964 CTS 2. Italics added.
32 Participants in the IJC seminar of 1974 thought the joint agency could assist in establishing the general principles of liability in pollution matters. See p. 14 of the proceedings.
33 MacKay, in *Papers Relating to IJC*, 94.

CHAPTER 4

1 On the Bryan Treaties see Norman L. Hill, 'International Commissions of Inquiry and Conciliation,' *International Conciliation*, No. 278 (1932), 89–134.
2 See Chacko, *The International Joint Commission*, 242; MacKay, in *Papers Relating to IJC*, 88.
3 See Willoughby, *The St. Lawrence Waterway*, 81–3.
4 See Frank Flaherty, 'Question of Economics is the Key to Maritime Tidal Power Project to Harness Passamaquoddy,' *Canadian Business* (June 1960), 101.
5 See Bloomfield and Fitzgerald, *Boundary Waters Problems of Canada and the United States*, 154–7.
6 G. Graham Waite, 'The International Joint Commission – Its Practice and Its Impact on Land Use,' *Buffalo Law Review* 13 (fall 1963), 115.
7 Margaret Sinclair, 'The International Joint Commission and Its Relationship with the Public,' in *Institutional Arrangements for Water Management: Canadian Experiences*, ed. Bruce Mitchell (University of Waterloo, Waterloo, Ont., 1975), 90–1.
8 The first quotation is from Resource Paper No. 2, *Perceptions and Attitudes in Resources Management*, ed. W.R. Derrick Sewell and Ian Burton (Ottawa: Department of Mines and Resources, 1971), 93; the second is from T. O'Riordan, 'Beyond Environmental Impact Assessment,' in *Environmental Impact Assessment*, ed. O'Riordan and R.D. Hay (London: Saxon House, 1976), 207.
9 See Bloomfield and Fitzgerald, *Boundary Waters Problems*, 45, 177–80; John Swettenham, *McNaughton 1944–1946* (3 vols., Toronto: Ryerson Press, 1968–9), III, 243–5.
10 F.J.E. Jordan, 'Great Lakes Pollution: A Framework for Action,' *Ottawa Law Review*, V (1971), 67; Charles R. Ross, 'National Sovereignty in International Environmental Decisions,' *Natural Resources Journal*, XII (Apr. 1972), 243.
11 IJC, *Progress Report on Pollution of Boundary Waterways* (Washington, DC, 1914). For a brief historical survey of the commission's water pollution investigations see William R. Willoughby, 'The IJC: Joint Machinery for U.S.–Canadian Cooperation,' *Limnos*, Vol. 5, No. 1 (1972), 27–31.

12 IJC, *Final Report on the Pollution of Boundary Waters Reference* (Washington, 1918), 51–2.

13 Alvey A. Adee to the IJC, 11 Mar. 1919 (Files of the U.S. Section of the IJC, Washington, DC)

14 A copy of the draft treaty, with its covering note, is in the files of the U.S. Section of the IJC.

15 IJC, *Report on the Pollution of Boundary Waters* (Ottawa, 1951), 13–14.

16 Ibid., 21–2. Water quality 'objectives' were accepted in preference to the convention suggested in some government quarters.

17 'IJC Holds Meetings on Pollution of Great Lakes Connecting Channels,' *Dept. of State Bull.*, 60 (17 Mar. 1969), 234–5.

18 *The Watertown Daily Times* (Watertown, NY), 29 July 1961.

19 Alan Edmonds, 'Death of a Great Lake,' *Maclean's Magazine*, 78 (1 Nov. 1965), 28–9, 42–4, 78; *New York Times*, 9 June, 2 Aug., 4 Dec. 1960; *Financial Post*, 18 Apr. 1964.

20 IJC, *Pollution of Lake Erie, Lake Ontario and the International Section of the St. Lawrence River* (1970), 161–2.

21 Ibid., 136–7, 140–1.

22 Ibid., 149–56.

23 Frederic O. Rouse, 'The 1972 Water Quality Agreement,' *Limnos*, 5 (summer, 1972), 6.

24 For the agreement see Canada, TIAS 7312.

25 C.B. Bourne, 'Canada and the Law of International Drainage Basins,' in *Canadian Perspectives on International Law and Organization*, ed. R. St. J. Macdonald et al. (Toronto: University of Toronto Press, 1974), 488.

26 Charles R. Ross, 'National Sovereignty in International Environmental Decisions,' 275.

27 *Globe and Mail*, 6 and 11 Apr. 1974; *Financial Post*, 28 Sept. 1974.

28 IJC, *Annual Report 1975*, 17.

29 Ibid., 15.

30 IJC, *A Special Report on Various Provisions of the Great Lakes Water Quality Agreement* (Ottawa and Washington, Feb. 1977), 2.

31 *Globe and Mail*, 6 June 1978, 4; *New York Times*, 22 Nov. 1978, IV, 19: 1.

32 Ibid.

33 IJC, *A Special Report*, 6.

34 *Globe and Mail*, 20 July 1978, 9.

35 *Summary of the International Joint Commission Seminar on the IJC: Its Achievements, Needs and Potential, June 20 and 21, 1974, Montreal, Quebec* (mimeographed and distributed by the IJC), 7–8.

36 House of Commons Standing Committee on External Affairs and National
    Defence, *Minutes of Proceedings and Evidence*, 20 Nov. 1969, 22.
37 Ibid., 23; *House of Commons Debates*, 21 May 1970, 7174.
38 See A.G.L. McNaughton, House of Commons Standing Committee on External
    Affairs and National Defence, *Minutes of Proceedings and Evidence*, 12 May
    1954, 177–8; Bourne, 'Drainage Basins,' 488–9; Arnold Heeney, *The Things
    That Are Caesars: Memoirs of a Canadian Public Servant* (Toronto: University
    of Toronto Press, 1972), 186.
39 Charles R. Ross, 'The International Joint Commission, United States–Canada,'
    Proceedings of the American Society of International Law (April 1974), 234.
40 Jordan, 'Great Lakes Pollution,' 82–3.

CHAPTER 5

1   For the press release and related documents see *Upper Columbia River De-
    velopment*, Hearings before the Committee on Interior and Insular Affairs, U.S.
    Senate, 85th Cong., 2d Sess. (1958), 22–6.
2   *Summary of the International Joint Commission Seminar on the IJC: Its
    Achievements, Needs and Potential, June 20 and 21, 1974, Montreal, Quebec*
    (mimeographed), 4.
3   IJC, *Annual Report 1975*, 33.
4   *Summary of the International Joint Commission Seminar*, 4.
5   C.B. Bourne, 'Canada and the Law of International Drainage Basins,' in
    Canadian Perspectives on International Law and Organization, ed. R. St. J.
    Macdonald et al., 493.
6   Whiteman, *Digest of International Law* (Washington, DC: Govt. Printing Office,
    1964), III, 827–8; Bloomfield and Fitzgerald, *Boundary Waters*, 72–3.
7   Bloomfield and Fitzgerald, *Boundary Waters*, 154–7.
8   William R. Willoughby, 'The International Joint Commission's Role in Main-
    taining Stable Water Levels,' *Inland Seas*, 28 (summer 1972), 117.
9   Canada, *House of Commons Debates*, 17 Apr. 1972, 1348; 8 June 1972, 2955–63;
    9 June 1972, 2995–3018; *International Canada* (June 1972), 94.
10 See William R. Willoughby, 'The International Joint Commission and Air
    Pollution References,' *ACSUS Newsletter*, II (spring 1972), 58–61.
11 See, for example, R.B. Bennett, *House of Commons Debates*, 10 June 1935, IV,
    3456. J.C.H. Bonbright to C.E. Bohlen, 4 Dec. 1935, Dept. of State File
    711.42152/461.
12 See C.B. Bourne, 'The Columbia River Controversy,' *The Canadian Bar Re-
    view* (Sept. 1959), 448–9; Canada, House of Commons, Standing Committee on
    External Affairs, *Minutes of Proceedings and Evidence*, 7 June 1956, 355–73.

13 Canadian expenditures on the Ottawa IJC Secretariat increased from $499,000 in 1970–1 to $1,940,000 in 1975–6; while American expenditures on the Washington IJC Secretariat climbed from $128,500 in 1971 to $476,000 in 1976. Combined national expenditures on the IJC Regional Office grew from $228,000 in 1973–4 to $998,500 in 1975–6. Data from IJC, *The Annual Report 1976*, 37.

14 Willoughby, 'The Appointment and Removal of Members of the International Joint Commission,' 411–26; Dunlop, 'Origin and Development of IJC,' 42–4, 56, 175.

15 Dunlop, 'Origin and Development of IJC,' 43; N.A.F. Dreisziger, 'The International Joint Commission of the United States and Canada 1895–1920: A. Study in Canadian–American Relations' (PH D dissertation, University of Toronto, 1974), 391.

16 A.D.P. Heeney, 'Diplomacy with a Difference,' *Inco*, 31 (fall 1966), 21.

17 Gibbons to Clinton, 13 July 1907, Gibbons Papers, PAC, Letterbooks, Vol. 8.

18 Joseph Barber, *Good Fences Make Good Neighbors* (New York: Bobbs-Merrill, 1958), 207–9.

19 Charles R. Ross, 'National Sovereignty in International Environmental Decisions,' in *Protecting the Environment*, ed. O.P. Dwivedi (Toronto: Copp Clark, 1974), 278.

20 F.J.E. Jordan, 'The International Joint Commission and Canada–United States Boundary Relations,' in *Canadian Perspectives on International Law and Organization*, 579.

21 See W.P.M. Kennedy, 'The International Joint Commission,' *The South African Law Times*, 2 (July 1933), 136; Dunlop, 'Origin and Development of IJC,' 195.

22 Bloomfield and Fitzgerald, *Boundary Waters*, 62.

23 D.H. Dinwoodie, 'The Politics of International Pollution Control: The Trail Smelter Case,' *International Journal*, XXVII (spring 1972), 219–35.

24 R.A. MacKay and E.B. Rogers, *Canada Looks Abroad* (New York: Oxford University Press, 1938), 131.

25 Christie to O.D. Skelton, 12 July 1927, Magrath Papers, Subject File 20, 'IJC Correspondence,' 1915–38.

26 William Hearst to Magrath, 3 May 1933, ibid.

27 T. C. Norris, *Report of an Industrial Inquiry Commission Concerning Matter Relating to the Disruption of Shipping on the Great Lakes, the St. Lawrence River System and Connecting Waters* (Ottawa: Queen's Printer, 1963), 307.

28 'Principles for Partnership,' *Dept. of State, Bull.*, III (2 Aug. 1965), 200.

29 For the report, dated 28 Sept. 1965, see *Congressional Record*, 89th Cong., 1st Sess., 25394–401.

30 *Canada–United States University Seminar 1971–1972*, a Proposal for Improving the Management of the Great Lakes of the United States and Canada. (Water

Resources and Marine Sciences Center, Cornell University, Ithaca, NY, Jan. 1973).

31 Senate of Canada, Standing Committee on Foreign Affairs, *Proceedings*, 18, Mar. 1975, 6.

32 See Norman A. Mackenzie, 'American Contributions to International Law,' *American Society of International Law Proceedings*, 33 (1939), iii; James Eayrs, in *The Growth of Canadian Policies in External Affairs*, ed. Hugh H. Keenleyside et al. (Durham, NC: Duke University Press, 1960), 63–4.

33 *The Annual Report of the International Joint Commission, United States and Canada 1974* (May 1975), 20–1; ibid., 1976, 27.

34 Ibid., 5.

35 *Annual Report 1975 International Joint Commission* (1976), 7.

36 *Summary of the IJC Seminar*, 18–20.

37 Canada, The Standing Senate Committee on Foreign Affairs, *Canada–United States Relations* (1975), Vol. 1, 42.

38 *Summary of the IJC Seminar*, 26–7.

39 *IJC Annual Report 1975*, 10.

40 *Summary of the IJC Seminar*, 17.

41 See 'IJC Holds Meetings on Pollution of Great Lakes Connecting Channels,' *Dept. of State Bull.*, 60 (17 March 1969), 234–5.

42 *IJC Annual Report 1975*, 37; Margaret Sinclair, 'The International Joint Commission and Its Relationship with the public,' in *Institutional Arrangements for Water Management: Canadian Experiences*, ed. Bruce Mitchell (Waterloo: Department of Geography, University of Waterloo, 1975), 83–116

43 *Summary of the IJC Seminar*, 21.

44 Canada, The Standing Committee on Foreign Affairs, *Canada–United States Relations*, 43.

45 *Summary of the IJC Seminar*, 8.

46 *Helsinki Rules on the Uses of the Waters of International Rivers*, International Law Association (London, 1967), 9 (article IV).

47 For the original draft see Senate Document 118, 85th Cong., 2nd Sess., 12–15.

48 For Root's position, see 'Memorandum for Mr. Root' (n.d.), signed 'G.C. Gibbons,' Anderson Papers, Letter Book 13, Vol. 68.

49 William R. Riddell, 'The International Relations between the United States and Canada: An Historical Sketch,' *Maryland Quarterly* (Feb. 1911), 26.

50 Ibid.

51 C.P. Corbett, *The Settlement of Canadian–American Disputes* (New Haven, Conn.: Yale University Press, 1937), 121.

52 Such a provision was included in the Gibbons-Clinton draft but, for reasons unknown to the author, was dropped from the final draft of the treaty.

53 John Hickerson to Messersmith, quoting some unnamed person, 12 May 1939, Dept. of State File 711.42152/525.

CHAPTER 6

1 *Attorney General for Dominion of Canada* v. *Attorneys General for the Provinces of Ontario, Quebec, and Nova Scotia*, A.C. 700 (1898). For a commentary see S.V. Ozere, 'Survey of Legislation and Treaties Affecting Fisheries,' in *Resources for Tomorrow*, Background Papers for discussion at the conference held at Montreal in 1961 (Ottawa, 1962), II, 798–9.

2 Ozere, 'Survey,' 798; A.L. Pritchard, 'Fisheries Workshop A,' in *Resources for Tomorrow*, III, 78.

3 22 Ops. Atty. Gen. 214.

4 For the decision see 252 U.S. 416.

5 See, for example, Harold C. Frick, *Economic Aspects of the Great Lakes Fisheries of Ontario* (Ottawa: Fisheries Research Board of Canada, 1965), 90.

6 House Doc. No. 315, 54th Cong., 2nd Sess. (31 Dec. 1896); report of the Joint High Commission, dated 10 Oct. 1898, the Chandler P. Anderson Papers (Library of Congress), Letter Books, Box 70 (1906–1909).

7 *Report of the Committee of the Canadian Privy Council*, 23 Apr. 1906, Governor General's Numbered Files, G 21, No. 192B, Vol. 1(a) (1906–1915); Root to Sir H.H. Durand, 6 June 1906, Anderson Papers, Box 70 (1906–1909); C.P. Lucas to J. Bryce, 27 Mar. 1908, Governor General's Numbered Files, G 21, No. 192B, Vol. 1(a) (1906–1915).

8 *Treaties and Agreements Affecting Canada, 1814–1913*, 178–81

9 For the report, signed 29 May 1909, see House Doc. No. 638, 61st. Cong., 2nd Sess. 1910, S 5834.

10 Hackworth, *Digest of International Law*, I, 798.

11 See H. Doc. 638, 61st Cong., 2nd Sess. 1910, S 5834.

12 See, for example, 'A Protest by the Salmon Fishermen of Puget Sound against Federal Control of the Fisheries of the State of Washington,' prepared by Dorr and Hadley, April 1910, Anderson Papers, Box 7 (1909–1910); British Embassy to Earl Grey, 21 Feb. 1910, Governor General's Numbered Files, G 21, No. 192B, Vol. 1(b) (1906–1915).

13 See memo by C.P. Anderson, 4 Jan. 1911, Anderson Papers, Box 75; British Embassy to Edward Grey, 16 Jan. 1911, Governor General's Numbered Files, G 21, No. 192B, Vol. 1(b) (1906–1915).

14 See *United States, Canadian Fisheries*, Hearings, U.S. Cong. H. Com. on Foreign Affairs, 63rd Cong. 2d Sess. (26 Feb. 1914); *Cong. Record*, 2 Mar. 1914, 63d Cong., 2d Sess., 4173–9.

15 See Hackworth, *Digest of International Law*, I, 799.
16 Cecil Spring-Rice to W.J. Bryan, 19 Oct. 1914, Governor General's Numbered Files, G 21, No. 192B, Vol. I(b) (1906–1915).
17 Robert Lansing to Sir Cecil A. Spring-Rice, 8 Feb. 1917, Governor General's Numbered Files, G 21, No. 202A, Vol. I(b) (1910–1923). For the diplomatic exchanges see U.S. *Foreign Relations*, 1918, 432–9.
18 *Report of the American–Canadian Fisheries Conference 1918*, ibid., 439–80.
19 Leonard L. Leonard, *International Regulation of Fisheries* (Washington, DC: Carnegie Endowment for International Peace, 1944), 110.
20 For the text see U.S. *Foreign Relations* (1919), I, 258–63.
21 H.E. Gregory and K. Barnes, *North Pacific Fisheries* (New York: American Council, Institute of Pacific Relations, 1939), 237; Leonard, *International Regulation*, 111.
22 The British Ambassador to the Secretary of State, 29 Aug. 1922, *Foreign Relations*, 1922, II, 674.
23 The Secretary of State to the British Ambassador, 14 Dec. 1922, ibid., 676.
24 US TS 701; 117 BSP 382.
25 On the signing of the convention and the unsuccessful attempts of the Senate to extend its scope to other dominions and to Britain see U.S. *Foreign Relations*, 1923, I, 472; Canada, Department of External Affairs, *Documents on Canadian External Affairs* (Ottawa, 1970), III, 650–64.
26 International Fisheries Commission, *Report* (Ottawa, 1928), 3.
27 TS 837; 1931 CTS 2.
28 TS 917; 1937 CTS 9.
29 TIAS 2900; 1953 CTS 14. For a discussion of the background of the conventions of 1937 and 1953 see *Report of the International Pacific Halibut Commission* (Seattle, 1969), 17–20.
30 *Seattle Post-Intelligencer*, 14 Mar. 1933; Canada, House of Commons Standing Committee on Marine and Fisheries, *Minutes of Proceedings and Evidence*, No. 3 (28 April 1953), 55.
31 Ruth Masters, *Handbook of International Organizations in the World* (Washington: Carnegie Endowment for International Peace, 1945), 238
32 For the statistics see Henry Reiff, *The United States and the Treaty Law of the Sea* (Minneapolis: University of Minnesota Press, 1959), 171.
33 For the draft convention and the appended regulations, see Appendix A of U.S. *Foreign Relations*, 1918, 476–80.
34 *Documents on Canadian External Affairs*, III, 628–9; J. Tomasevich, *International Agreements on Conservation of Marine Resources* (Stanford: Stanford University Press, 1943), 255.
35 See TS 918; 1937 CTS 10.

36 In a radio address delivered 4 Dec. 1930, printed in the *Congressional Record*, 9 Dec. 1930, 71st Cong., 3d Sess., 392–3.

37 James G. Rogers to Hanford MacNider, 23 Mar. 1932, Dept. of State File 711.428/1545.

38 See Charles M. Barnes to James G. Rogers, 9 June 1932, 711.428/1576; W.D. Herridge to R.B. Bennett, Bennett Papers, 29 Feb. 1932, T-31, Vol. 1 – Official, 'Sockeye Salmon Treaty 1931–1933'; Memo by W.R. Castle of Conversation with H. Wrong, 6 Jan. 1933, 711.428/1608.

39 As reported by B. Reath Riggs to the Secretary of State, 9 Mar. 1932, 711.428/1545.

40 James G. Rogers to Hanford MacNider, 23 Mar. 1932, 711.428/1545.

41 Reiff, *Treaty Law of the Sea*, 173.

42 International Pacific Salmon Fisheries Commission, *Annual Report, 1957* (New Westminster, BC, 1958), 21, 31.

43 James Sinclair, *House of Commons Debates*, 23 June 1955, V, 5185–6.

44 For the Protocol see TIAS 3867; 1957 CTS 21. For a background commentary see Canadian *House of Commons Debates*, 26 Feb. 1957, II, 1687–93.

45 Great Lakes Commission, *Great Lakes News Letter* (May–June 1972), 4; (March 1962), 4.

46 The statistics are from G.C. Toner, 'The Great Lakes Fisheries: Unheeded Depletion,' *Canadian Forum*, XIX, (Sept. 1939), 178–9, and John van Oosten, 'Doom of the Great Lakes Fisheries,' *American Forests*, 43 (Feb. 1937), 103.

47 The above paragraph is based largely on Oosten, 'Doom of the Great Lakes Fisheries,' 144–5. See also *Supplemental Report of the U.S. Members of the International Board of Inquiry for the Great Lakes Fisheries* (Washington, 1943), 31–2.

48 For the resolution, Public Resol. No. 84, signed 5 Apr. 1938, see *Cong. Record*, 75th Cong., 3d Sess., 2251. See also ibid. 2914.

49 Secretary of State Cordell Hull did in fact object. See *Supplemental Report of the U.S. Members*, 35; see also 36–8.

50 For the text see U.S. Cong., Sen., *Convention with Canada for the Development, Protection and Conservation of the Fisheries of the Great Lakes*, 79th Cong., 2nd Sess., 1946 ex. c.; 1946 CTS 13.

51 The resolution was printed in the *Congressional Record*, 28 Apr. 1947, 80th Cong., 1st Sess., 4117–18.

52 William C. Herrington, special assistant for fisheries and wildlife to the under secretary of state, informed the author, 28 July 1965, that he spent a year talking to representative fishery groups and public officials.

53 Charles B. Selak, Jr., 'The United States–Canadian Great Lakes Fisheries Convention,' *American Journal of International Law*, 50 (Jan. 1956), 126. See

also William B. Furlong. 'Killer from the Sea,' *N.Y. Times Magazine*, 5 June 1960, 91–2.

54 See TIAS 3326; 1955 CTS 19. When the president transmitted the new convention to the Senate in 1955 he requested the withdrawal of the one signed in 1946.

55 See the statements of Governor Frank L. Lausche and the Ohio Wildlife Council in *Great Lakes Fisheries Convention*, Hearings (1955), 47–9.

CHAPTER 7

1 See R.K. Tiffany to Secretary Hull, 22 July 1935, Dept. of State File 711.428/1861.

2 Secretary Hull to R.K. Tiffany, 30 Sept. 1935, Dept. of State File 711.428/1861.

3 70 *Stat.* 242. For a summary of some of the considerations that led to the inclusion of this particular clause in the enabling legislation see *Great Lakes Fishery Act of 1956*, Hearing before the Subcom. on Fisheries and Wildlife Conservation of the Com. on Merchant Marine and Fisheries, H. of Rept., 84th Cong., 2nd Sess. (1956), 33–40.

4 See statement of H.J. Robichaud (minister of fisheries), House of Commons, Standing Committee on Fisheries, *Minutes of Proceedings and Evidence*, No. 1 (25 Mar. 1966), 16.

5 Reiff, *Treaty Law of the Sea*, 283.

6 William C. Herrington, 'U.S. Participation in Conservation of International Fishery Resources,' in *Papers in Marine Biology and Oceanography* (London: Pergamon Press, 1955), 404.

7 'Periodical Report on General Conditions in Canada,' No. 1572, 27 Aug. 1937, Dept. of State File 842.00/110; *Ottawa Journal*, 13 Aug. 1937.

8 The commissioner was an American member, Edward W. Allen. The incident was related to the author by William C. Herrington, 28 July 1965.

9 Conversation with Dr William M. Sprules, 18 Oct. 1966.

10 *Canadian Annual Review 1932*, 379.

11 Masters, *Handbook of International Organizations*, 220; *Report of the International Fisheries Commission, 1947*, 10. At its 1974 annual meeting the commission also established an advisory group consisting of representatives of fishermen, vessel owners, and industry. See the commission's *Annual Report 1974*, 9.

12 For the membership of the committee in 1972 see International Pacific Salmon Fisheries Commission, *Annual Report 1974*, 5.

13 Act of 4 June 1956, 70 *Stat.* 242. The pattern fixed by the American law has also been followed by Canada.

14 For a list of the committees in 1971 see Great Lakes Fishery Commission, *Annual Report 1971 (Ann Arbor, Mich., 1973)*, 61.

15 See, for example, John L. Farley, 'The Role of the Great Lakes Fishery Commission in the Solution of Great Lakes Problems,' *Transactions of the American Fisheries Society, 1956*, 86 (1957), 427.
16 'u.s. Participation in Conservation of International Fishery Resources,' 404.
17 On the respective advantages of the staff arrangements see Francis T. Christy and Anthony Scott, *The Common Wealth in Ocean Fisheries, Some Problems of Growth and Economic Allocation* (Baltimore: Johns Hopkins Press, 1965), 206; William C. Herrington, 'How International Fishery Commissions Operate to Promote Conservation of High Seas Resources,' in *Proceedings of the Gulf and Caribbean Fisheries Institute, 12th Annual Sess.*, Nov. 1959, 19–20.
18 Farley, 'Role of the Fisheries Commission,' 425–6.
19 Both agencies employ additional workers during the summer months. Thus the Salmon Commission spent $100,000 on employees for the summer of 1971 and the Halibut Commission spent $64,000.
20 John P. Babcock to President Hoover, 26 Oct. 1931, Dept. of State File 711.428/1521.
21 John P. Babcock to W.A. Found, 20 Aug. 1932, Dept of State File 711.428/1852.
22 E.W. Allen to William Phillips, 28 June 1935, Dept. of State File 711.428/1858 and July 2, 1935, 711.428/1852.
23 William Phillips to E.W. Allen, 24 July 1935, Dept. of State File 711.428/1858.
24 The six commissions on whose behalf contracts were signed were the following: the International Pacific Salmon Fisheries Commission, at New Westminster, BC; the International Commission for the Northwest Atlantic Fisheries, at Halifax, NS; the International North Pacific Fisheries Commission, Vancouver, BC; the Great Lakes Fishery Commission, Ann Arbor, Mich.; the Inter-American Tropical Tuna Commission, La Jolla, Calif.; and the International Pacific Halibut Commission, Seattle, Wash.
25 Conversation with Dr William Sprules, 18 Oct. 1966. On staffing, pensions, and related matters see Bernard E. Skud, *Jurisdictional and Administrative Limitations Affecting Management of the Halibut Fishery* (Scientific Report No. 59, International Pacific Halibut Commission, Seattle, 1976), 16–19.
26 See, for example, *Departments of State, Justice, and Commerce, the Judiciary and Related Agencies Appropriations, 1965*, Hearings before the Subcommittee of the Committee on Appropriations, u.s. Sen., 88th Cong. 2nd Sess. (1964), Part 1, 663–82.
27 Ibid., 89th Cong. 1st Sess. (1965), Part 1, 114.
28 Statistics from ibid., 88th Cong., 2nd Sess. (1964), Part 1, 665, 681; *Report of the International Pacific Halibut Commission 1954* (1955), 25; ibid. *Report 1977*, 4; International Pacific Salmon Fisheries Commission, *Annual Report 1939*

(1940), 4; phone conversation between the author and R.W. Saalfeld, 12 Mar. 1979, and between the author and A.C. Cooper, 12 Mar. 1979.

29 Conversation with Dr William M. Sprules, Member of the Halibut Commission, Oct. 18, 1966.

30 In a report printed in the *Dept. of State Bul.*, XXXIII (Dec. 12, 1955), 986.

31 In a letter to the author dated April 18, 1966.

32 Conversations with Henry Weekly, July 29, 1965, and with William C. Herrington, Aug. 17, 1966.

CHAPTER 8

1 See, for example, J.A. Crutchfield, 'Conservation and Allocation in the Pacific Coast Fisheries,' in *Proceedings of the 30th Annual Conference of the Western Economic Association at Stanford, California, Sept. 1–2, 1955*, ed. J.J. Rasmussen (1955).

2 H. Stevens (in the general discussion), in *Proceedings of Resources for Tomorrow Conference*, held at Montreal in 1961 (Ottawa, 1962), III, 86.

3 Tomasevich, *International Agreements on Conservation of Marine Resources*, 209–10; H.A. Dunlop, 'Management Practices in the Pacific Halibut Fishery and Their Relation to the Biology of Conservation,' in *Biological and Economic Aspects of Fisheries Management*: Proceedings of a conference held under the auspices of the College of Fisheries and the Department of Economics of the University of Washington at Seattle, 17–19 Feb. 1959 (Seattle, 1960), 42.

4 See the discussions within the House of Commons Standing Committee on External Affairs, *Minutes of Proceedings and Evidence*, 16 Dec. 1957, No. 8, 295–302.

5 Tomasevich, *International Agreements on Conservation of Marine Resources*, 263–4. See also the discussions between General McNaughton and members of the House of Commons Standing Committee on External Affairs, *Minutes of Proceedings and Evidence*, 14 June 1956, No. 15, 412–15; ibid., 12 Dec. 1957, No. 6, 262–6; ibid., 13 Dec. 1957, No. 7, 273–5.

6 Christy and Scott, *The Common Wealth in Ocean Fisheries*, 204. See also Douglas M. Johnston, *The International Law of Fisheries: A Framework for Policy-Oriented Inquiries* (New Haven: Yale University Press, 1965), 375.

7 See *Report of the International Fisheries Commission Appointed under the Northern Pacific Halibut Treaty* (Ottawa, 1928), 4; William F. Thompson, 'Conservation of the Pacific Halibut, an International Experiment,' in *Annual Report of the Smithsonian Institution, 1935* (Washington, 1936), 261–3.

8 See, for example, Canada, House of Commons, Select Standing Committee on

Marine and Fisheries, *Minutes of Proceedings and Evidence* (1929), 56. But note the comment of Dr W.M. Sprules to the author, Sept. 1971: 'I have been associated with several fisheries commissions for a long time and personally have not felt that the United States got the better of me in our fisheries negotiations.'

9 *Watertown Daily Times*, 6 May 1959. See also *Departments of State, Justice ... Appropriations for 1966*, Hearings before a Subcommittee of the Committee on Appropriations, House of Representatives, 89th Cong., 1st Sess., (1965), Part I, 575.

10 Significantly, the report was printed in its entirety in *Dept. of State Bull.*, XXX (12 Dec. 1955), 986–8, and in *Upper Columbia River Development*, Hearings before the Committee on Interior and Insular Affairs, United States Senate, 85th Cong., 2nd Sess., 1958, 153–6.

11 Dr Lloyd A. Royal before the Standing Committee on Marine and Fisheries, *Minutes of Proceedings and Evidence*, 6 Mar. 1957, 18.

12 'People in the News,' *Canadian Business*, 31 (Nov. 1958), 42.

13 For the statistics see International Fisheries Commission, *Report, 1947*, 14; *Report of the International Pacific Halibut Commission, 1965*, 12.

14 International Pacific Halibut Commission, *Annual Report 1973*, 30–3; House of Commons Standing Committee on Fisheries and Forests, *Minutes of Proceedings and Evidence*, 28th Parliament, 4th Session (1972), 19–20.

15 Gregory and Barnes, *North Pacific Fisheries*, 237–8; Walter M. Chapman, 'United States Policy on High Seas Fisheries,' *Dept. of State Bull.*, XX (16 Jan. 1949), 67.

16 For statistics on the increases in cyclical catches see International Pacific Salmon Fisheries Commission, *Annual Report 1960*, 3.

17 Ibid., *Report 1965*, 3.

18 Ibid., *Report 1968*, 28–9; *Report 1974*, 12–16; *Report 1976*, 9; letter of 4 Apr. 1978 from A.C. Cooper to the author.

19 On 6 May 1965, the commission's director, Lloyd A. Royal, gave the author the following assurance: 'In the entire history of the operations under the Convention of 1930 there has never been any real conflict of interest and the relations between the two countries affected by the Convention have been completely amiable. In many respects the fishermen and the fishing industry of the two countries think and act as one unit.'

20 Canada, Department of External Affairs, *Canadian Weekly Bulletin*, 18 (12 Dec. 1963); Great Lakes Fishery Commission, *Annual Report 1966*, 8; *Annual Report 1972*, 17, 22, 25.

21 Great Lakes Fishery Commission, *Annual Report 1971*, 16; ibid., *1972*, 13–25.

22 *Globe and Mail*, 18 June 1969.

23 Masters, *Handbook of International Organizations*, 222.
24 Anthony Scott, 'Fisheries, Pollution and Canadian–American Transnational Relations,' *International Organization*, 28 (autumn 1974), 841.
25 For a vigorous commentary on this problem see Homer Stevens in *Proceedings of Resources for Tomorrow*, III, 85–6. H.L. Keenleyside (8 Mar. 1972) has noted that 'the Canadian Government has now started a rationalization programme on the West Coast. The number of vessels is already substantially reduced.'
26 For the diplomatic exchanges see *Foreign Relations*, 1937, II, 183–91. See also Gregory and Barnes, *North Pacific Fisheries*, 283–4.
27 For the text of the Convention see TIAS 2786 and 1953 CTS 3.
28 International Pacific Halibut Commission, *Annual Report 1974*, 8 and 19.
29 Herrington, Hearings before the Subcommittee of the Committee on Appropriations, U.S. Sen., 88th Cong., 1st Sess. (1964), Part 1, 780; Homer Stevens, House of Commons Standing Committee on Fisheries, *Minutes of Proceedings and Evidence*, No. 3, 5 Apr. 1966, 50; William C. Herrington in a letter to the author, 2 Sept. 1971.
30 International Pacific Salmon Fisheries Commission, *Annual Report 1976*, 1.
31 *International Canada*, Mar. 1971, 67; Oct. 1972, 166–7; May 1973, 157; U.S. Dept. of Commerce Press Release, 8 May 1973.
32 U.S. Dept. of Commerce Press Release, 8 May 1973.
33 Ibid.
34 Agreement between the Government of Canada and the Government of the United States of America on Reciprocal Fishing Privileges in Certain Areas Off Their Coasts, signed 15 June 1973.
35 See International Pacific Salmon Fisheries Commission, *Annual Report 1975*, 3; A.C. Cooper, 'Presentation to the American Fisheries Society Annual Meeting, September 1976' (mimeographed).
36 Bernard E. Skud, *Jurisdictional and Administrative Limitations Affecting Management of the Halibut Fishery*, 5–6.
37 Great Lakes Fishery Commission, *Annual Report 1971*, 10.
38 Linden A. Mander, 'The Future of International Commissions,' *The American Journal of International Law*, 37 (Jan. 1943), 129–30.
39 Ex. Rept. No. 7, 83rd Congress, 1st Session (1953).
40 A report, 'Organization and Operation of International Fishery Commissions,' printed in *Great Lakes Fisheries Convention*, Hearings 1955, 26–32.
41 Both the question and Sinclair's reply are on p. 2244, Vol. III, of the *House of Commons Debates*, 21 Mar. 1955.
42 In a letter to the author, of 2 Sept. 1971, commenting on the preceding three paragraphs, Mr. William C. Herrington asserts: 'During the 1950's, while I was in "State", I gave a good deal of thought to this question. I am convinced that a

single Commission covering all U.S.–Canadian joint fishery interests is not the best solution. It would get bogged down in bureaucratic red tape and would be increasingly dominated by government. One of the strengths of the Commissions has been the local input from able commissioners closely involved with the various regions and their fishery interests. Unfortunately, in recent years there has been some trend away from this with political consideration playing a larger part in appointments.'

CHAPTER 9

1 On these conferences of 1937–9 see Mackenzie King, *House of Commons Debates*, 12 Nov. 1940, IV, 53–60; C.P. Stacey, 'The Canadian–American Permanent Joint Board on Defence, 1940–1945,' *International Journal*, IX (spring 1954), 108–9; Roosevelt to King, 21 Dec. 1937, and King to Roosevelt, 30 Dec. 1937, Roosevelt Papers (Hyde Park), President's Secretary's Files, 'Canada 1933–41,' Box 2; Norman Armour to Sumner Welles, 8 Jan. 1938, Dept. of State File 842.00/68 1/2.

2 King, *House of Commons Debates*, 12 Nov. 1940, IV, 53.

3 John W. Holmes, *Canada and the United States: Political and Security Issues* (Toronto: Canadian Institute of International Affairs, 1970; Behind the Headlines, XXIX, Nos. 1–2), 3.

4 Paper 17–18 Jul 40, written in Ottawa, entitled 'A Programme of Immediate Canadian Action,' WPD 4330, cited in Stetson Conn and Byron Fairchild, *The Western Hemisphere: The Framework of Hemisphere Defense* (Washington, DC: Government Printing Office, 1960), 368.

5 William L. Langer and S. Everett Gleason, *The Challenge to Isolation, 1937–1940* (New York: Harper and Brothers, 1952), 703.

6 See William R. Willoughby, 'The Genesis of Canadian–American Defence Cooperation,' *Canadian Defence Quarterly* 5 (winter 1975–6), 45.

7 See J.W. Pickersgill, *The Mackenzie King Record* (Toronto: University of Toronto Press, 1960), I, 122; James Eayrs, *In Defence of Canada* (Toronto: University of Toronto Press, 1965), II, 198–9.

8 Moffat to the Acting Secretary of State (Welles), 14 Aug. 1940, U.S. *Foreign Relations*, 1940, III, 144.

9 Mackenzie King, as quoted in Pickersgill, *Record*, 130–1.

10 A. Harriman, quoting the editor of the *Ogdensburg Journal*. See 'Ambassador Harriman's Remarks at Ogdensburg, Aug. 10, 1965,' *Canadian–American Relations 1867–1967* (Ottawa: U.S. Information Service, 1967), II, 11–12.

11 See Willoughby, 'Defence Cooperation,' 47–8.

12 Stacey, 'PJBD,' 112.

13 Pickersgill, *Record*, I, 134. The two statesmen may have also been motivated by the consideration that 'by indicating a collaborative arrangement designed to

outlast the war,' they would help to 'counter any suggestion that the arrangement would hasten u.s. participation in World War II.' See Stanley Dziubian, *Military Relations between the United States and Canada 1939–1945* (Washington, DC: Government Printing Office, 1959), 26.

14 See William R. Willoughby, 'The Appointment and Removal of Members of the International Joint Commission,' *Canadian Public Administration* (fall 1969), 414–17.

15 Pickersgill, *Record*, 134.

16 Dziubian, *Military Relations*, 25.

17 J.L. Granatstein, 'The Conservative Party and the Ogdensburg Agreement,' *International Journal*, XXII (winter 1966–7), 76.

18 C.P. Corbett, 'Canada in the Western Hemisphere,' *Foreign Affairs*, 19 (July 1941), 780; J.B. Brebner, 'Ogdensburg: A Turn in Canadian–American Relations,' *The Inter-American Quarterly*, 2 (Oct. 1940), 18–24.

19 See, for example, *New York Times*, 21 Aug. 1940; 'Alliance with Canada,' *New Republic*, 103 (26 Aug. 1940), 263; 'Somewhat Mixed Up,' *New Statesman and Nation*, 20 (24 Aug. 1940), 173.

20 See F. Underhill, 'North American Front,' *Canadian Forum*, XX (Sept. 1940), 166–7, and 'Canada and the North Atlantic Triangle,' in *In Search of Canadian Liberalism* (Toronto: Macmillan, 1961), 257.

21 Underhill, 'Canada and the North Atlantic Triangle,' 257.

22 See, for example, Donald Creighton, *Towards the Discovery of Canada* (Toronto: Macmillan of Canada, 1972), 169.

23 Underhill, 'Canada and the North Atlantic Triangle,' 256.

CHAPTER 10

1 Stanley Dziubian, *Military Relations between the United States and Canada 1939–1945*, 48–51; C.P. Stacey, 'The Canadian–American Permanent Joint Board on Defence, 1940–1945,' 123–4.

2 'The Permanent Joint Board on Defence' (undated memorandum), Department of External Affairs File 703-40, Vol. I.

3 Wilgress appears to have been selected and appointed by the secretary of state for external affairs. See David Beatty, 'The Permanent Joint Board on Defense: Agency for Canadian–American Military Association' (a mimeographed paper read at the Canadian Historical Association Meeting at Winnipeg, 1970), 8.

4 On the subject of the board's secretariat see Dziubian, *Military Relations*, 33, 38; H.L. Keenleyside, 'The Canada–United States Permanent Joint Board on Defence, 1940–1945,' *International Journal*, XVI (winter 1960–1), 54.

5 John Swettenham, *McNaughton* (Toronto: Ryerson Press, 1969), III, 206–7.

6 Conversation with A.E. Ritchie, 11 June 1968.

7 Beatty, 'PJBD,' 16.

8 Keenleyside, 'PJBD,' 54.

9 Virginia Brewer, 'Canada–United States Military Cooperation Committee' (Washington, DC: Memo, Foreign Affairs Division, Legislative Reference Service, Library of Congress, 2 Dec. 1965), 1–2.

10 'Notes on Visit to Washington, 3 Feb. 1941,' Moffat Papers, Ottawa, 1940–41, Book I.

11 J.W. Pickersgill, *The Mackenzie King Record* (Toronto: University of Toronto Press, 1965), 140; Sumner Welles to Roosevelt, 25 Nov. 1940, Roosevelt Papers, Official File, Box 4090.

12 For the letter, dated 10 Mar. 1942, see Roosevelt Papers, Official File, Box 4090.

13 On rare occasions, however, a member has been known to support a proposal which he knew to be opposed by his own department. For example, Dziubian notes (footnote 16, p. 42) that the board approved a recommendation – later accepted by the two governments – which envisaged the use of surplus Canadian air training capacity for training Americans even though the War Department opposed such an arrangement.

14 Interview with J.D. Hickerson, 11 June 1968.

15 At the meeting of 10–11 Nov. 1941, the board informally agreed, 'with the exception of the Canadian Air Force member,' that certain measures were needed to speed up construction of the North West River Air Base in Labrador. See Dziubian, *Military Relations*, 41.

16 Keenleyside, 'PJBD,' 54–5; Dziubian, *Military Relations*, 217.

17 For useful summaries of the recommendations see Dziubian, *Military Relations*, 347–65, 56–74; Stacey, 'The Canadian–American Permanent Joint Board on Defence, 1940–1945,' 122–4.

18 Interview with Wilgress, 4 Aug. 1965.

19 'The Permanent Joint Board on Defence' (undated External Affairs memorandum), 7.

20 The three recommendations not accepted were numbers 27, 29, and 30. See Dziubian, *Military Relations*, 358, 361; Stacey, 'The Canadian–American Permanent Joint Board on Defence, 1940–1945,' 115–16; Heeney to Howe, 17 July 1942, Howe Papers, s 19–2, 'Cabinet War Committee,' Folder 6, Vol. 53; PJBD, *Journal of Discussions and Decisions*, 1–2 April 1943. Recommendations 26, 31, and 33 were approved by Canada with the reservation that specified conditions be met. See Heeney to Howe, 28 May 1943, Howe Papers, s 19–2, 'Cabinet War Committee,' Folders 7–8, Vol. 54; Heeney to Howe, 29 Sept. 1944, ibid., Folders 3–6, Vol. 53.

21 Beatty, 'PJBD,' 23.

22 Walter Stewart, 'Defence: Taking the Joint Approach and Doing It Their Way,'

Maclean's (Dec. 1971), 62. See also John W. Warnock, *Partner to Behemoth: The Military Policy of a Satellite Canada* (Toronto: New Press, 1970), 105–7.

23 Beatty, 'PJBD,' 7.

24 Ibid.

25 See, for example, James Eayrs, *In Defence of Canada* (Toronto: University of Toronto Press, 1972), III, 349–53.

26 Paul Martin, 'The American Impact on Canada,' in *The Star-Spangled Beaver*, ed. John H. Redekop (Toronto: Peter Martin Associates, 1971), 29.

27 C.P. Stacey, *Arms, Men and Governments* (Ottawa: Queen's Printer, 1970), 375.

28 Eayrs, *In Defence of Canada*, III, 322.

29 *Soldiers and Politicians: The Memoirs of Lt. Gen. Maurice A. Pope* (Toronto: University of Toronto Press, 1962), 166.

30 Swettenham, *McNaughton*, III, 191.

31 Keenleyside, 'PJBD,' 55. Keenleyside (8 Mar. 1972) has stated that, although LaGuardia at first was hostile towards the 'striped-pants boys,' later he became cordial.

32 Pope, *Memoirs*, 163. See also NS 1017-10-30, 23 Apr. 1941, King Papers, PAC J4 Series, Vol. 320, File 3370, MG 26 J4.

33 Excerpts from the letters are printed in Stacey, *Arms, Men and Governments*, 349–54. On the controversy see also Pope, *Memoirs*, 162–6, and Dziubian, *Military Relations*, 110–16.

34 Quoted in Stacey, 'The Canadian–American Permanent Joint Board on Defence, 1940–1945,' 119.

35 See a summary of King's conversation with Hanson, in Pickersgill, *Record,* 138.

36 Beatty, 'PJBD,' 26.

37 C. Cecil Lingard and R.G. Trotter, *Canada in World Affairs, 1941–1944* (Toronto: Oxford University Press, 1950), 25.

38 Hugh L. Keenleyside and Gerald S. Brown, *Canada and the United States* (New York: Knopf, 1952), 370.

39 A.G.L. McNaughton, 'Defence of North America,' address of 12 Apr. 1948, Statements and Speeches, No. 48/18.

40 Keenleyside, 'PJBD,' 55. See also LaGuardia to Roosevelt, 28 May 1942, Roosevelt Papers, Official File 4090.

41 Swettenham, *McNaughton*, III, 200.

42 Ibid., 205–8; Beatty, 'PJBD,' 7–9.

43 Stacey, 'The Canadian–American Joint Board on Defence, 1940–1945,' 120.

44 Pope, *Soldiers and Politicians*, 166–7.

45 Canada Treaty Series, 1944, No. 19 (27 June 1944).

46 See confidential memorandum sent by H.L. Keenleyside to Norman Robertson,

11 Dec. 1943, entitled 'Evidence Relating to United States Efforts to Obtain Post-War Advantages from Wartime Expenditures in Canada,' King Papers, PAC, J4 Series, Vol. 350, No. 241909-11, MG 26 J4.

47 Beatty, 'PJBD,' 12–13, 21. See also 'The Permanent Joint Board on Defence,' undated, External Affairs File 703–40, Vol. 1.

48 Wilgress, *Memoirs*, 183–4. See also Beatty, 'PJBD,' 5–6, 32–33; James Eayrs, *Art of the Possible* (Toronto: University of Toronto Press, 1961), 99.

49 McNaughton frequently reminded his American colleagues that they should be careful not to violate Canada's sovereignty. See Beatty, 'PJBD,' 8; Swettenham, *McNaughton*, III, 192.

50 Fred Alexander, *Canadians and Foreign Policy* (Toronto: University of Toronto Press, 1960), 36–7.

51 See below, pp. 126, 129–35.

52 See Beatty, 'PJBD,' 30–8; Melvin A. Conant, *A Perspective on Defence: The Canada–United States Compact* (Toronto: Canadian Institute of International Affairs, 1974; Behind the Headlines, XXXIII, No. 4), 29.

53 Canada, External Affairs, 'The Canada–United States Permanent Joint Board on Defence,' Reference Papers, No. 116 (Nov. 1974), 6.

54 Howe to O.M. Biggar, 17 Mar. 1941, and Biggar to Howe, 22 Mar. 1941, Howe Papers, PAC, S14-7.

55 Moffat, 'Memorandum of Conversation with Mr. Norman Robertson,' 12 May 1941, Moffat Papers, 'Ottawa 1940–41,' Book 1.

56 See F.H. Soward, *Canada in World Affairs, 1944–1946* (Toronto: Oxford University Press, 1950), 271; William L. Langer and S.E. Gleason, *The Undeclared War 1940–41* (New York: Harper & Bros., 1952), 169.

57 Lt. Gen. Guy Simonds, 'Where We've Gone Wrong on Defence,' *Maclean's Magazine*, 69 (23 June 1956), 67.

58 Donald Creighton, *Toward the Discovery of Canada* (Toronto: Macmillan, 1972), 227; John W. Warnock, *Partner to Behemoth* (Toronto: New Press, 1970), 106.

59 Ramsay Cook, 'The Canadian Dilemma,' *International Journal*, XX (winter 1964–5), 7.

60 See Gen. Charles Foulkes, 'The Complications of Continental Defence,' in *Neighbors Taken for Granted*, ed. Livingston T. Merchant (Toronto: Burns and MacEachern, 1966), 117–19. See also Swettenham, *McNaughton*, III, 176.

61 Conant, *Perspective*, 29.

CHAPTER II

1 Permanent Joint Board on Defence, 8 June 1945, King Papers, JH Series, Vol. 318, File 3368.

2 Permanent Joint Board on Defence, 3 Sept. 1945, ibid.

3 James Eayrs, 'The Military Policies of Contemporary Canada: Principles, Problems, Precepts, Prospects,' in *Contemporary Canada*, ed. Richard H. Leach (Durham, NC: Duke University Press, 1967), 237–8.
4 'Memorandum by President Truman to the Canadian Prime Minister,' enclosure to 'Memorandum by the Acting Secretary of State to President Truman,' 26 Oct. 1946, United States, *Foreign Relations*, 1946, V, 60.
5 For frank statements on this subject by King, Pearson, and Massey during the years 1942–4, see Vincent Massey: *What's Past Is Prologue* (Toronto: Macmillan, 1963), 350, 370–1, 396–7, 400–1.
6 R.J. Sutherland, 'The Strategic Significance of the Canadian Arctic,' in *The Arctic Frontier*, ed. R. St. J. Macdonald (Toronto: University of Toronto Press, 1966), 261.
7 James Eayrs, *In Defence of Canada*, III: *Peacemaking and Deterrence* (Toronto: University of Toronto Press, 1972), 341–2.
8 Ibid., 339. See also *Foreign Relations*, 1946, V, 54–6; J.W. Pickersgill and D.F. Forster, *The Mackenzie King Record* (Toronto: University of Toronto Press, 1970), III, 219, 265–6.
9 See *Foreign Relations*, 1946, V, 53–56, 62–74; Pickersgill and Forster, *Record*, III, 265–7; John Swettenham, *McNaughton* (Toronto: Ryerson Press, 1969), III, 170–6.
10 Pickersgill and Forster, *Record*, III, 219.
11 Ibid., 265.
12 Eayrs (*In Defence of Canada*, III, 340), quoting the American ambassador to Canada.
13 Pickersgill and Forster, *Record*, III, 362–3. See also *Foreign Relations*, 1946, V, 61–3.
14 For a summary of the proceedings see *Foreign Relations*, 1946, V, 65–7, 70. See also Eayrs, *In Defence of Canada*, III, 343–4.
15 On the request for new weather stations see Clifford J. Pierce, 'Sovereignty as an Issue in Canadian Defence Policy: 1940 to 1968' (MA thesis, University of New Brunswick, 1976), 53–7. On the other requests see Hume Wrong, 'Memorandum for the Prime Minister,' 26 Oct. 1946, Dept. of External Affairs files, 52-C(s). Significantly, eventually the Canadian government acceded to American requests with respect to both Goose Bay and new weather stations.
16 See Eayrs, *In Defence of Canada*, III, 344–5.
17 Ibid., 345; Pickersgill and Forster, *Record*, III, 219.
18 Pickersgill and Forster, *Record*, III, 367–8.
19 Eayrs, *In Defence of Canada*, III, 347–8.
20 F.H. Soward, *Canada in World Affairs 1944–1946* (Toronto: Oxford University Press, 1950), 274; Pickersgill and Forster, *Record*, III, 265–6.

21 For the statement see *Dept. of State Bull.*, XVI (23 Feb. 1947), 361; 1947 CTS 43.
22 Later the number was reduced to five.
23 *New York Times*, 10 and 13 Feb. 1949. See below, p. 137.
24 For a discussion of Canada's role in the creation of NATO see Escott Reid, 'The Birth of the North Atlantic Alliance,' *International Journal*, XXII (summer 1967), 426–40; William R. Willoughby, 'Canada and the North Atlantic Pact,' *Virginia Quarterly Review*, XXV (summer 1949), 429–42.
25 Charles Foulkes, 'The Complications of Continental Defence,' in *Neighbors Taken for Granted*, ed. Livingston T. Merchant (New York: Frederick A. Praeger, 1966), 117.
26 Foulkes, ibid., 117–18.
27 Ibid., 119.
28 William T.R. Fox and Annette B. Fox, *NATO and the Range of American Choice* (New York: Columbia University Press, 1967), 20, f 12; 135–6.
29 Foulkes, 'Continental Defence,' 119.
30 See below, pp. 136–45.
31 Virginia W. Brewer, 'Canada–United States Military Cooperation Committee,' (Washington, DC: Memo, Foreign Affairs Division, Legislative Reference Service, Library of Congress, 2 Dec. 1965), 2.
32 Roger Swanson, 'An Analytical Study of the United States–Canadian Defense Relationship as a Structure, Response and Process: Problems and Potentialities,' (PH D dissertation, American University, 1969), 90.
33 Lt. Col. Patrick W. Powers, *A Guide to National Defense* (New York: Frederick A. Praeger, 1964), 259; Brian Crane, *An Introduction to Canadian Defence Policy* (Toronto: Canadian Institute of International Affairs, 1964), 30.
34 *Canadian Weekly Bulletin*, Vol. 5, No. 42 (25 Aug. 1950), 5; *The Montreal Star*, 18 Aug. 1950.
35 Interviews with Dana Wilgress, 4 Aug. 1965, and A.E. Ritchie, 11 June 1968.
36 See Pierce, 'Sovereignty,' 68–70.
37 See Eayrs, *In Defence of Canada*, III, 343–4.
38 Pickersgill and Forster, *Record*, IV, 24.

CHAPTER 12

1 See, for example, General Charles Foulkes, *Canadian Defence Policy in a Nuclear Age* (Toronto: Canadian Institute of International Affairs, 1961; Behind the Headlines, XXI, No. 1), 11.
2 See above, pp. 127–31.

3 Melvin Conant, *The Long Polar Watch* (New York: Harper & Bros., 1962), 35.

4 The Pinetree Line was a joint Canadian–American effort, Canada paying $174,000,000 and the United States $377,000,000; the Mid-Canada Line was built entirely by Canada at a cost of $213,000,000; the DEW Line was an American enterprise, costing approximately $350,000,000; and the control system, called SAGE, introduced between 1959 and 1963, was a shared responsibility, Canada paying approximately one-third and the United States the remainder of the cost.

5 General Charles Foulkes, 'The Complications of Continental Defence,' in *Neighbors Taken for Granted*, 113.

6 *The Montreal Star*, 24 Sept. 1953, 29 Sept. 1954.

7 Jon B. McLin, *Canada's Changing Defense Policy, 1957–1963: The Problems of a Middle Power in Alliance* (Toronto: Copp Clark, 1967), 38.

8 'The Complications of Continental Defence,' 112.

9 Ralph Campney, *House of Commons Debates*, 2 June 1955, IV, 4346–7.

10 Ibid., 13 Nov. 1957, II, 1060–1.

11 McLin, *Defense Policy*, 40. See also Pearson's statement, *House of Commons Debates*, 13 Nov. 1957, II, 1062.

12 Peter C. Newman, *Renegade in Power: The Diefenbaker Years* (Toronto: McClelland and Stewart, 1963), 347.

13 For the announcement see *Can. Weekly Bull.*, 7 Aug. 1957, 3. On the background of events see McLin, *Defense Policy*, 39–44.

14 McLin, *Defense Policy*, 45; also interviews with John W. Holmes, 27 May 1968, and with James Eayrs, 28 May 1968.

15 Trevor Lloyd, *Canada in World Affairs 1957–1959* (Toronto: Oxford University Press, 1968), 26.

16 Interviews, Holmes, 27 May 1968, and Eayrs, 28 May 1968.

17 George F.G. Stanley, *Canada's Soldiers: The Military History of an Unmilitary People* (Toronto: Macmillan, 1960), 413–14. See also McLin, *Defense Policy*, 39; 'Canada's Defence Policy,' *Canadian Labour* 8 (Apr. 1963), 23.

18 House of Commons Special Committee on Defence, *Minutes of Proceedings and Evidence*, No. 15, 22 Oct. 1963, 510. See also 527.

19 Conant, *Polar Watch*, 88.

20 See James Eayrs, 'CONAD,' *Canadian Forum*, XXVII (Sept. 1957), 122–3.

21 See, for example, *House of Commons Debates*, 6 Nov. 1957, I, 812; 7 Nov. 1957, I, 849; 22 Nov. 1957, II, 1408–9.

22 Ibid., 22 Nov. 1957, II, 1409–10; 19 May 1958, I, 192.

23 TIAS 4031; 1958 CTS 9.

24 The agreement reached was that the pay and allowances of the Canadians at NORAD headquarters would be met by Canada, while all other costs would be

paid by the United States. See Diefenbaker, *House of Commons Debates*, 19 June 1958, II, 1423.

25 Prime Minister Diefenbaker, ibid., 10 June 1958, I, 995. See also 19 May 1958, I, 190–1.

26 Ibid., 4 Jan. 1958, III, 2861, 2863–6; 30 May 1958, I, 675–6; 10 June 1958, I, 1003–4, 1019–22, 1044–5.

27 Ibid., 11 June 1958, I, 1048.

28 Pearkes, House of Commons, Special Committee on Defence Expenditures, *Minutes of Proceedings and Evidence*, 24 June 1960, 359; Edgar McInnis, *The Atlantic Triangle and the Cold War* (Toronto: University of Toronto Press, 1959), 144; R.J. Sutherland, 'Canada's Long Term Strategic Situation,' *International Journal*, XVII (summer 1962), 207.

29 *Mike: The Memoirs of the Right Honourable Lester B. Pearson*, ed. John A. Munro and Alex I. Inglis (Toronto: University of Toronto Press, 1973), II, 32–3.

30 See Pearson, *House of Commons Debates*, 10 June 1958, I, 1005. See also Herridge, ibid., pp. 1019–20.

31 See, for example, the statements of Diefenbaker, ibid., 10 June 1958, I, 996, and Pearkes, p. 1029.

32 Ibid., 6 Nov. 1957; McLin, *Defense Policy*, 50–2.

33 For the minister's successive statements see *House of Commons Debates*, 6 Nov. 1957, I, 812; 22 Nov. 1957, II, 1411; 4 Jan. 1958, III, 2864, 2872–3.

34 McLin, *Defense Policy*, 52.

35 *House of Commons Debates*, 10 June 1958, I, 998–9. See also Sidney Smith, ibid., 19 May 1958, I, 191; and 11 June 1958, II, 1050.

36 See, for example, Pearson, ibid., 10 June 1958, I, 1014.

37 Ibid., 19 June 1958, II, 1430. The eight negative votes were cast by CCF members.

38 See below, pp. 154–5, 158, 162–3.

CHAPTER 13

1 Melvin Conant, *The Long Polar Watch*, 54–5.

2 House of Commons Standing Committee on External Affairs and National Defence, *Minutes of Proceedings and Evidence*, 6 May 1969, 1412–13.

3 See the comments of James Richardson, Canadian minister of national defence, ibid., No. 7 (18 Mar. 1975), 16.

4 Neil McElroy, 'United States–Canadian Relations: A North American Market,' *Vital Speeches*, 27 (1 Apr. 1961), 371; Richard A. Preston, *Canada in World Affairs 1959–1961* (Toronto: Oxford University Press, 1965), 146–7.

5 *House of Commons Debates*, 16 July 1958, III, 2288.

6 For useful summaries of Canadian involvement in this crisis see Peyton V. Lyon, *Canada in World Affairs 1961–1963* (Toronto: Oxford University Press, 1968), 27–64, and Robert W. Reford, *Canada and Three Crises* (Toronto: The Canadian Institute of International Affairs, 1968), 169–215.

7 Patrick Nicholson, *Vision and Indecision* (Don Mills, Ont.: Longmans Canada, 1968), 154.

8 Bruce Thordarson, *Lester Pearson: Diplomat and Politician* (Toronto: Oxford University Press, 1974), 120.

9 Letter dated 7 Feb. 1976, from Douglas S. Harkness to C.F. Pierce.

10 See Peter C. Newman, *Renegade in Power: The Diefenbaker Years* (Toronto: McClelland and Stewart, 1963), 339–40; Jon B. McLin, *Canada's Changing Defense Policy, 1957–1963* (Toronto: Copp Clark Pub. Co., 1967), 157; *Financial Post*, 3 Nov. 1962.

11 See Lyon, *Canada in World Affairs*, 39–41, and Reford, *Canada and Three Crises*, 213–14.

12 *This Game of Politics* (Toronto: McClelland and Stewart, 1965), 253.

13 On the above factors see ibid., 179–80, 205–7; Lyon, *Canada in World Affairs*, 37–8; Newman, *Renegade*, 337; John W. Warnock, *Partner to Behemoth: The Military Policy of a Satellite Canada* (Toronto: New Press, 1970), 177–9.

14 See, for example, the reaction of several members of Parliament and newspaper editors cited in Lyon, *Canada in World Affairs*, 42, 48, 50–1; Warnock, *Partner*, 178–9; Charles Hanly, 'The Ethics of Independence,' in *An Independent Foreign Policy for Canada?* ed. Stephen Clarkson (Toronto: McClelland and Stewart, 1968), 25.

15 Lyon, *Canada in World Affairs*, 59.

16 TIAS 4271; 1959 CTS 16.

17 Pearson, *House of Commons Debates*, 25 Jan. 1963, III, 3116; Lyon, *Canada in World Affairs*, 80.

18 For detailed discussions of the nuclear issue see Newman, *Renegade*, 349; McLin, *Defense Policy*, 123–67; and Lyon, *Canada in World Affairs*, 76–222.

19 Lyon, *Canada* 200. See also *House of Commons Debates*, 5 June 1963, I, 701.

20 See, for example, *Financial Post*, 2 Sept. 1962.

21 *Financial Post*, 16 Sept. 1961; McLin, *Defense Policy*, 145.

22 Lyon, *Canada in World Affairs*, 116.

23 Sevigny, *This Game*, 260.

24 See below, pp. 167–8.

25 McLin, *Defense Policy*, 217.

26 *Financial Post*, 3 Nov. and 1 Dec. 1962.

27 Dale C. Thomson and Roger F. Swanson, *Canadian Foreign Policy: Options and Perspectives* (Toronto: McGraw-Hill Ryerson, 1971), 29.

CHAPTER 14

1 Roger Swanson, 'NORAD: Origins and Operations: Choices for Canada,' *International Perspectives* (Nov.–Dec. 1972), 3.
2 See Exchange of Notes of 25 May 1964, TIAS 5587; 1964 CTS 16; Paul Hellyer, House of Commons Standing Committee on National Defence, *Minutes of Proceedings and Evidence*, 12 May 1966, 16.
3 *Globe and Mail*, 20 Mar. 1969.
4 Ibid., 26 Mar. 1969.
5 Ibid., 22 Mar. 1969.
6 The quotations are from G.R. Lindsey, *Strategic Weapons Systems, Stability and the Possible Contributions of Canada* (Toronto: Canadian Institute of International Affairs, 1969; Behind the Headlines, XXVIII, Nos. 7 & 8), 10.
7 Ibid., 10–11; Report of the Standing Committee on External Affairs and National Defence, *Minutes of Proceedings and Evidence*, No. 49 (19, 20, and 26 June 1969), 9.
8 Peter Stursberg, 'AWACS and New Defence Policy,' *Commentator*, XII (May 1969), 9.
9 House of Commons Standing Committee on External Affairs and National Defence, *Minutes of Proceedings and Evidence*, No. 3 (27 Feb. 1975), 18.
10 Ibid., No. 4 (4 Mar. 1975), 18–19.
11 See John Gellner, 'Military Aerospace,' *Canadian Aviation* 45 (1972), 8; Colin S. Gray, 'The True North Strong and Free,' *Round Table*, No. 245–248 (1972), 320.
12 Although numerous Canadian commentators continue to assert that participation in NORAD, as well as in NATO, affords Canadian representatives opportunities to influence American defence policies, some Canadians are becoming sceptical. See, for example, John W. Holmes, 'Canada: The Reluctant Power,' *Orbis*, XV (Spring 1971), 299.
13 See above, pp. 141–3.
14 John W. Warnock, *Partner to Behemoth: The Military Policy of a Satellite Canada* (Toronto: New Press 1970), 234–9.
15 See Warnock, 'On Guard For Thee,' *Canadian Dimension*, 5 (Feb. 1969), 21.
16 See, for example, James Eayrs, in *Canada: The Unknown Neighbour*, ed. J. Alex Murray (Windsor: University of Windsor Press, 1971), 7.
17 See Warnock, 'Canada and North American Defence,' in *Alliances and Illusions*, ed. Lewis Hertzman (Edmonton: Hurtig, 1969), 67–8.
18 The text of the exchange of notes was released three days after the adjournment of Parliament on 1 Apr. 1968. For the notes see TIAS 6467 and 1968 CTS No. 5.
19 For the press release, dated 3 Apr. 1969, see Dept. of External Affairs, Statements and Speeches, No. 69/7.

20 Dept. of External Affairs, *Annual Review 1975* (Ottawa, 1976), 45.
21 House of Commons Standing Committee, *Minutes of Proceedings and Evidence*, No. 3 (3 Mar. 1972), 7–8.
22 For the exchanges see 1973 CTS No. 17.
23 House of Commons Standing Committee on External Affairs and National Defence, *Minutes of Proceedings and Evidence* No. 3 (27 Feb. 1975), 11–12.
24 Ibid., No. 14 (22 Apr. 1975), 24.
25 *International Canada*, May 1975, 134–5.
26 Ibid., Mar. 1975, 65–6.
27 House of Commons Standing Committee on External Affairs and National Defence, *Minutes of Proceedings and Evidence*, No. 9 (13 Apr. 1973), 26.
28 General Charles Foulkes, 'The Complications of Continental Defence,' in *Neighbors Taken for Granted*, 131–2.
29 See, for example, John Holmes in House of Commons Standing Committee on External Affairs and National Defence, *Minutes of Proceedings and Evidence*, No. 1 (4 and 6 Nov. 1969), 29–30.
30 The poll results are cited in Bruce Thordarson, *Trudeau and Foreign Policy* (Toronto: Oxford University Press, 1972), 35.
31 Note the comment of Donald Evans in *Peace, Power and Protest* (Toronto: Ryerson Press, 1967), 60.
32 House of Commons Standing Committee on External Affairs and National Defence, *Minutes of Proceedings and Evidence*, No. 3 (27 Feb. 1975), 13.
33 Ibid., No. 10 (8 Apr. 1975), 12.
34 Ibid., No. 14 (22 Apr. 1975), 24.
35 Ibid., No. 9 (13 Apr. 1973), 19.
36 Ibid., No. 10 (12–13 Apr. 1973), 10.
37 Ibid., 9.

CHAPTER 15

1 See below, pp. 167–8.
2 John J. Kirton, 'The Consequences of Integration: The Case of the Defence Production Sharing Agreements,' in *Continental Community?* Andrew Axline et al. (Toronto: McClelland & Stewart, 1974), 119.
3 For the genesis of the statement and the circumstances of its release see J.W. Pickersgill, *The Mackenzie King Record* (Toronto: University of Toronto Press, 1960) I, 189–200; J.M. Blum, *From the Morgenthau Diaries: Years of Urgency 1938–1941* (3 vols., Boston: Houghton Mifflin, 1959), II, 249. Like the Ogdensburg Agreement of 1940, the new accord was printed in the *Canadian Treaty Series* (1941 CTS 14) but received no recognition in the United States other than publication in the *Department of State Bulletin* (26 Apr. 1941), 494.
4 On the origin, organization, and activities of the committees see R. Warren

James, *Wartime Economic Co-operation* (Toronto: Ryerson Press, 1949); S.D. Pierce and A.F.W. Plumptre, 'Canada's Relations with Wartime Agencies in Washington,' *Canadian Journal of Economics and Political Science*, XI (Aug. 1945), 402–19; William R. Willoughby, 'The Canada–United States Joint Economic Agencies of the Second World War,' *Canadian Public Administration* (spring 1972), 59–73.

5 C.D. Howe in a letter printed in James, *Wartime Co-operation*, 25.
6 1949 CTS 8; TIAS 1889. Later the word 'Planning' was inserted into the title after the word 'Mobilization.'
7 U.S. Public Law No. 429 (3 Mar. 1933).
8 See William R. Willoughby, 'Canadian–American Defense Cooperation,' *Journal of Politics*, 13 (Nov. 1951), 685–6.
9 See W.E.C. Harrison, 'Canadian–American Defence,' *International Journal*, V (summer 1950), 198–9; *Time*, 56 (7 Aug. 1950), 15.
10 1950 CTS 15; TIAS 2136.
11 *The Montreal Daily Star*, 16 Nov. 1950.
12 See ibid., 15 and 20 Nov. 1950, 29 and 30 Jan. 1951.
13 Although the committee has held no meetings since 1953, the agreement by which it was established is listed in the U.S. *Treaties in Force*, edition of 1962.
14 Jon B. McLin, *Canada's Changing Defense Policy, 1957–1963* (Toronto: Copp Clark, 1967), 176.
15 On the successive difficulties of the Arrow project see the testimony of General Charles Foulkes, House of Commons Special Committee on Defence, *Minutes of Proceedings and Evidence*, 22 Oct. 1963, 509–11.
16 For the prime minister's announcement see McLin, *Defense Policy*, Appendix II.
17 *House of Commons Debates*, 20 Feb. 1959, II, 1221–4.
18 See, for example, 'Canada's Defence Perplexities,' *The Economist*, 190 (28 Mar. 1959), 1186.
19 *Globe and Mail*, 13 Dec. 1958.
20 McLin, *Defense Policy*, 179–80.
21 Canada, House of Commons Standing Committee on External Affairs and National Defence, *Proceedings July 13–27, 1970, 11th Report to the House*, 32.
22 McLin, *Defense Policy*, 179–80. For the DOD directive see Canada, Department of Defence Production, *Production Sharing Handbook* (Ottawa: Queen's Printer, 1967), 2–4.
23 Canada, Department of Defence Production, *1965 Annual Report* (Ottawa, 1966), 23–4; Foster Lee Smith, 'Canadian–United States Collaboration for Defense,' *Public Policy*, XII (1963), 312, 325; interview with William Chandler, 22 Oct. 1966; Senate of Canada, *Proceedings of the Standing Committee on Foreign Affairs*, 28 Mar. 1974, Appendix B, 36–7.

24 See below, pp. 189–96.
25 See Canada, House of Commons Special Committee on Defence, *Minutes of Proceedings and Evidence*, 17 Nov. 1964, 825.
26 See the statement of Senator Symington, u.s. Congress, *Congressional Record*, 87th Cong., 1st Sess., 13 June 1961, 10227–8; 'Stars and Political Stripes,' *Saturday Night*, 76 (15 Apr. 1961), 5–6.
27 For the agreement see Department of Defence Production, *Production Sharing Handbook* (Ottawa: Queen's Printer, 4th ed., July 1967), B 45–8.
28 Drury, *House of Commons Debates*, 7 June 1963, 770.
29 Frank Jackman, Canadian Department of Industry, Trade and Commerce, Canada, Standing Senate Committee on Foreign Affairs, *Proceedings*, No. 30 (6 Apr. 1976), 7.
30 *Financial Post*, 30 Oct. 1971.
31 Kal J. Holsti and Thomas Allen Levy, 'Bilateral Institutions and Trans-governmental Relations between Canada and the United States,' *International Organization*, 28 (autumn 1974), 882–3.
32 Ibid., 883.
33 *Financial Post*, 30 Oct. and 25 Dec. 1971; *International Canada*, Nov. 1971, 218.
34 Kenneth McNaught, 'From Colony to Satellite,' in *An Independent Foreign Policy for Canada?* ed. Stephen Clarkson (Toronto: McClelland & Stewart, 1968), 178.
35 Eric Kierans, as quoted in Bruce Thordorson, *Trudeau and Foreign Policy* (Toronto: Oxford University Press, 1972), 46.
36 Kirton, 'Consequences of Integration,' 126–7.
37 John W. Warnock, *Partner to Behemoth: The Military Policy of a Satellite Canada* (Toronto: New Press, 1970), 243–5.
38 Gideon Rosenbluth, cited in *Financial Post*, 11 Dec. 1967.
39 T.C. Douglas, cited in Thordorson, *Trudeau and Foreign Policy*, 42.
40 See *Globe and Mail*, 28 Feb. 1975.
41 'Canada, the United States and Vietnam ...,' Pearson, 10 Mar. 1967, s. & s. No. 67/8; *Financial Post*, 21 Feb. 1970. Robert Reford, *Merchant of Death?* (Toronto: Canadian Institute of International Affairs, 1968; Behind the Head-lines, xxvii, No. 4), 19–27; *Financial Post*, 21 Feb. 1970.

CHAPTER 16

1 See J.G. Parsons to the American Chargé in Ottawa, 24 June 1943, Dept. of State File 842.20 Def./222, and M.A. Robertson to the American Chargé, 1 July 1943, 842.20 Def./227.

2 *New York Times*, 1 Oct. and 1 Nov. 1950; *Montreal Daily Star*, 9 and 20 Nov. 1950.
3 *Montreal Daily Star*, 1 Nov. 1950.
4 U.S. Statutes at Large (1951), chap. 1228.
5 TIAS 2227; 1951 CTS 3.
6 Millard F. Caldwell, Head of the American Delegation, *New York Times*, 29 Apr. 1951, 1.
7 Hubert R. Gallagher, 'Development of U.S.–Canada National Security Relationships,' (U.S. Office of Emergency Planning, May 1966, mimeographed), 5–6.
8 See above, p. 137. According to Michael Barkway ('Canada's Changing Role in NATO Defence,' *International Journal*, XIV [Spring 1959], 102), the DEW Line, authorized by President Truman in 1951, was 'inspired by civil defence authorities.' The screens, which by 1956 were viewed as 'buying time' to get the bombers in the air, were originally 'thought of as possessing primarily a civil defence purpose.' James Eayrs, *Canada in World Affairs, 1955–1957* (Toronto: Oxford University Press, 1959), 143.
9 The agreements covered such matters as the free exchange of fire-fighting equipment, hospital units, ambulances, and personnel; standardization of equipment for fire-fighting and for disinfecting areas affected by either gas or germs; and the transportation of refugees across the border in the event of an attack. See *New York Times*, 8 Aug. 1951, 19; 25 Jan. 1952, 7; 7 Aug. 1952, 6; 15 Dec. 1955, 12. See also Gallagher, 6. Some were state–provincial understandings; others were between agencies of the two federal governments; none required the approval of the American Senate.
10 Barry Commoner, *Science and Survival* (New York: Viking Press, 1963), 84.
11 See 'An Open Letter to President Kennedy and Governor Rockefeller,' *New York Times*, 19 Dec. 1961, 22.
12 *New York Times*, 22 Dec. 1957, 4; 25 Dec. 1957, 1.
13 Samuel P. Huntington, *The Common Defense* (New York: Columbia University Press, 1961), 357.
14 James Eayrs, *Northern Approaches* (Toronto: Macmillan Co., 1961), 46.
15 Ibid., 20.
16 See F.G. Robertson, *House of Commons Debates*, 28 Jan. 1955, 1, 638.
17 J.F. Wallace, 'Civil Defence in North America,' *EMO National Digest* (Canada Emergency Measures Organization), 5 (Dec. 1965), 19.
18 See Gordon Donaldson, 'Our Civil Defence Mess,' *Saturday Night*, 73 (4 Jan. 1958), 8–9, 36; James Eayrs, 'Defending the Realm: 2. Memo to General Graham,' *Canadian Forum*, 145 (Oct. 1958), 167–8.
19 In April 1957 the two governments had announced that they were abandoning

combined civil defence exercises in favour of separate exercises by each country. The official explanation was that separate exercises would afford them 'an opportunity to observe and discuss mutual problems on two, rather than one, annual occasions.' See *Canadian Weekly Bulletin*, 3 Apr. 1957, 2. A more important factor, one suspects, was the difficulty involved in formulating and conducting joint exercises.

20 C.R. Patterson, 'National Emergency Measures Planning – 1968,' *EMO National Digest*, 8 (Dec. 1968–Jan. 1969), 1–2.

21 Edward A. McDermott, 'Emergency Planning,' *Military Review*, 44 (Feb. 1964), 20.

22 Lt. Col. Patrick W. Powers, *A Guide to National Defense* (New York: Frederick A. Praeger, 1964), 24.

23 McDermott, 'Emergency Planning,' 20.

24 Gallagher, 'National Security Relationships,' 6; interview with M.R. Mackenzie, 18 Oct. 1966.

25 TIAS 5464; 1963 CTS 8.

26 The title cited is that used in the United States. The Canadian title is 'The United States–Canada Agreement on Civil Emergency Planning.'

27 Gallagher, 'National Security Relationships,' 8–10.

28 *New York Times*, 2 Jan. 1966.

29 See, for example, Major Gen. H.M. Penhale, *EMO National Digest*, 4 (Feb. 1964), 3–6.

30 *Times Journal* (St Thomas), 27 Apr. 1966.

31 See Elizabeth B. Drew, 'What Happened to Civil Defense?' *The Reporter*, 32 (8 Apr. 1965), 38–9.

32 Gallagher, 'National Security Relationships,' 10.

33 'United States–Canada Agreement on Emergency Planning – 1967,' *EMO National Digest* 7 (Oct. 1967), 1.

34 Interview with M.R. Mackenzie, 18 Oct. 1966.

35 TIAS 6325; 1967 CTS 13.

36 Italics added.

37 See Roger Frank Swanson, *State–Provincial Interaction: A Study of Relations between U.S. States and Canadian Provinces Prepared for the U.S. Department of State* (Aug. 1974), 488–9, 410–12, 125.

38 See *EMO National Digest*, 10 (Feb.-March 1970), 1–5.

39 Letter of 10 Apr. 1978, from A.M. Stirton to the author.

40 Robert Reford, *Canada and Three Crises* (Toronto: Canadian Institute of International Affairs, 1968), 196.

41 See *Globe and Mail*, 22 Feb. 1971; *The Washington Post*, 28 Feb. 1971; *Globe and Mail*, 31 Dec. 1974.

42 Mungo James, 'What Became of Civil Defence?' *Saturday Night*, Aug. 1967, 7, 8–10; *Wall Street Journal*, 20 May 1971.

43 Canada, House of Commons Standing Committee on External Affairs and National Defence, *Proceedings*, No. 20 (31 May 1977), 28.

44 *Globe and Mail*, 7 Feb. 1968, and letter of 10 Apr. 1978 from A.M. Stirton to the author.

45 'Fragmented u.s. Civil Defense Effort Hit,' *Aviation Week*, 104 (14 June 1976), 17.

46 See, for example, *Civil Defense – Title VII*, Hearings on Military Posture and H.R. 5068, Department of Defense Authorization for Appropriations for Fiscal Year 1978 before the Committee on Armed Services, House of Representatives, 95th Cong., 1st Sess., 7, 8, and 9 Feb. 1977; 'Intensified Soviet Civil Defense Seen Tilting Strategic Balance,' *Aviation Week*, 105 (22 Nov. 1976), 17; 'Can the u.s. Defend Itself?' *Time*, 3 Apr. 1978, 13–15; *Wall Street Journal*, 20 July 1978.

47 *Globe and Mail*, 14 November and 28 December, 1978.

48 Colonel William O. Staudenmaier, 'Civil Defense in Soviet and American Strategy,' *Military Review* (October 1978), 5.

49 In 1950 John Diefenbaker suggested 'that consideration be given to the financing of civil defence ... by the Dominion as a whole.' *House of Commons Debates*, 4 Sept. 1950, 1, 212.

50 Col. Horst von Zitzewitz, 'Nuclear Deterrent with Outmoded Civil Defence?' *NATO's Fifteen Nations* (Aug.–Sept. 1963), 76.

51 Significantly, the agreement of 1967 omitted the statement included in both the agreement of 1951 and that of 1963 that 'as far as possible, Civil Defense activities in the United States and Canada should be coordinated for the protection of persons and property from the result of enemy attack as if there were no border.'

52 von Zitzewitz, 'Nuclear Deterrent,' 83.

CHAPTER 17

1 Don C. Piper, 'The Role of Intergovernmental Machinery in Canadian–American Relations,' *South Atlantic Quarterly*, LXII (autumn 1963), 565.

2 For the statement see *Dept. of State Bull.*, 39 (4 Aug. 1958), 208.

3 For the notes see TIAS 4098; 1958 CTS 22.

4 See above, pp. 140–1.

5 Frederick Alexander, *Canadians and Canadian Foreign Policy* (Toronto: University of Toronto Press, 1960), 38.

6 *The Economist*, 202 (17 Mar. 1962), 1030, in a review of James Eayrs' *The Art of*

the Possible. See also Alexander, *Canadians*, 36–8; 'The Mountain Arrives,' *The Economist*, 188 (12 July 1958), 133.

7 In an address to the Pilgrims Society of New York, on 28 Oct. 1958, Diefen-baker, in referring to the committee, commented that 'in the final analysis,' it is the responsibility of the political leaders 'to decide on matters of the highest policy with respect to defence preparation.' See *Statements and Speeches*, No. 58/43, p. 4.

8 See above, pp. 139–43.

9 At the conclusion of the visit of President Eisenhower and Secretary Dulles to Ottawa on 8–11 July 1958, the prime minister stated: 'I think what has taken place illustrates the need of some continuing body to permit of a general discussion from time to time of our respective points of view.' *House of Commons Debates*, 11 July 1958, II, 2140.

10 'Co-operating with Canada,' *The Economist*, 188 (12 July 1958), 126.

11 Interviews with Dana Wilgress, 4 Aug. 1965, Paul Bridle, 5 Aug. 1965, and A.E. Ritchie, 11 June 1968.

12 Howard C. Green, *House of Commons Debates*, 14 July 1960, VI, 6297.

13 Ibid., 10 Feb. 1960, I, 936. See also similar comments of George R. Pearkes, ibid., 28 Mar. 1960, III, 2509.

14 *Memoirs of a Bird in a Gilded Cage* (Toronto: McClelland & Stewart, 1968), 109–10.

15 For the texts of the successive communiqués see *Dept. of State Bull.*, 41 (30 Nov. 1959), 789; ibid., 43 (25 July 1960), 172; ibid., 51 (13 July 1964), 45–6.

16 Paul Martin, *House of Commons Debates*, 26 June 1964, V, 4749.

17 *House of Commons Debates*, 10 Feb. 1960, I, 936; 14 July 1960, VI, 6297.

18 Ibid., 28 Mar. 1960, III, 2509.

19 See above, p. 170.

20 *New York Times*, 9 Nov. 1959, I.

21 *Dept. of State Bull.*, 41 (30 Nov. 1959), 789.

22 See 'Text of NATO Council's Communique,' *New York Times*, 23 Dec. 1959, 6.

23 Arnold Heeney, *The Things That Are Caesar's* (Toronto: University of Toronto Press, 1972), 163.

24 Ibid.

25 Ibid. See also Robert W. Reford, *Canada and Three Crises* (Toronto: The Canadian Institute of International Affairs, 1968), 158.

26 See above, pp. 151–3.

27 As quoted in Peter Newman, *Renegade in Power: The Diefenbaker Years* (Toronto: McClelland & Stewart, 1963), 345.

28 McLin, *Canada's Changing Defense Policy, 1957–1963*, 137. See also *New*

York Times, 10 Nov. 1959. Interestingly enough, the committee's joint communiqué made no specific reference to nuclear weapons.

29 For the communiqué see u.s. Information Service, u.s. Embassy, Ottawa, *Canadian–American Relations 1867–1967*, III, 18–22.

30 As read into the record by Diefenbaker, *House of Commons Debates*, 6 July 1964, V, 5099.

31 *Canadian Annual Review for 1964*, 199.

32 For Paul Martin's summary of the discussions see *House of Commons Debates*, 26 June 1964, V, 4749–50.

33 Edgar J. Benson, Canada, House of Commons Standing Committee on External Affairs and National Defence, *Minutes of Proceedings and Evidence*, 3 Mar. 1972, 20.

34 See Roger Frank Swanson, *Intergovernmental Perspectives on the Canada–U.S. Relationship* (New York: New York University Press, 1978), 145.

35 Dr Robert A. MacKay, in a letter to the author, 23 Aug. 1971.

CHAPTER 18

1 Ed Hadley, *Montreal Star*, 12 Nov. 1953. See also Raymond Daniel, *New York Times*, 12 Nov. 1953; 'Canadian–American Meeting,' *The Economist*, 176 (10 Sept. 1955), 865.

2 Hadley, *Star*. The announcement of the committee's establishment was released to the press simultaneously in Washington and Ottawa on 12 Nov., the day before the president's arrival in Ottawa for talks with Canadian cabinet members and the delivery of an address to a joint session of the Canadian Parliament.

3 *Montreal Star*, 5 Nov. 1953.

4 See 'Canadian–American Meeting,' *The Economist*, 176 (10 Sept. 1955), 865.

5 TIAS 2922; 1953 CTS 18.

6 For the amendments to the original exchanges see TIAS 5448; 1963 CTS 15.

7 J.C. Langley (assistant under-secretary of state for external affairs), House of Commons Standing Committee on External Affairs and National Defence, *Minutes of Proceedings and Evidence*, No. 3 (20 Nov. 1969), 9.

8 See, for example, *House of Commons Debates*, 7 July 1958, II, 1954.

9 Dean Rusk, u.s. Information Service Release, 4 Mar. 1966.

10 See the communiqué of the eleventh meeting, held in Montreal, 20–22 June 1967.

11 Interview with John W. Holmes, 27 May 1968; A.D.P. Heeney, *The Things That Are Caesar's: Memoirs of a Canadian Public Servant* (Toronto: University of Toronto Press, 1972), 138.

12 Interview, with Rodney Grey, 17 Oct. 1966.

13 *The Economist*, 176 (10 Sept. 1955), 866.

14 See Heeney, *Caesar's*, 138.

15 Frank M. Coffin, quoted in the *House of Commons Debates*, 16 Mar. 1959, II, 1997.

16 Tim Creery, *Medicine Hat News*, 12 Mar. 1963.

17 *House of Commons Debates*, 19 Jan. 1959, I, 50; 1 May 1964, III, 2819–20.

18 Mitchell Sharp, House of Commons Standing Committee on External Affairs and National Defence, *Minutes of Proceedings and Evidence* (24 Mar. 1970), 33; George Ball, ibid. (15 Jan. 1970), 44.

19 Standing Senate Committee on Foreign Affairs, *Proceedings*, No. 2 (5 Dec. 1974), 12.

20 Ibid., 6.

21 Department of External Affairs, Press Release, No. 15, 17 Mar. 1954.

22 'Meeting of the U.S.–Canadian Committe on Trade and Economic Affairs,' *Dept. of State Bull.*, 37 (28 Oct. 1957), 683.

23 'The Joint United States–Canadian Committee on Trade and Economic Affairs,' *Statements and Speeches*, No. 59/9, 6 Jan. 1959.

24 *Dept. of State Bull.*, 49 (7 Oct. 1963), 549.

25 *Dept. of External Affairs Press Release*, 30 Apr. 1964.

26 Sylvia Ostry, Canada, Senate Standing Committee on Foreign Affairs, *Proceedings*, No. 30 (9 May 1974), 6.

27 Gerald Wright and Maureen Appel Molat, 'Capital Movements and Government Control,' *International Organization*, 28 (autumn 1974), 683.

28 Maureen Appel Molat, 'The Role of Institutions in Canada–United States Relations: The Case of North American Financial Ties,' in *Continental Community?* Andrew Axline et al. (Toronto: McClelland and Stewart, 1974), 164–93.

29 Robert Schaetzel, Standing Senate Committee on Foreign Affairs, *Proceedings* (5 Dec. 1974), 6.

30 In Ibid. (4 Feb. 1975), 9.

31 Swanson, *Intergovernmental Perspectives on the Canada–U.S. Relationship*, 145.

32 In *Proceedings* (10 June 1975), 8.

33 *Proceedings*, No. 21 (2, 9, 16 Dec. 1975), 33.

34 Ibid.

35 Ibid.

36 Ibid. (5 Dec. 1974), 6.

CHAPTER 19

1 L.B. Pearson, *House of Commons Debates*, 16 Mar. 1959, II, 1972.
2 This was a point strongly emphasized by Dr David Abshire, former assistant secretary of state for congressional relations, as a witness before the Canadian Senate Standing Committee on Foreign Affairs. See *Proceedings* of the committee, 22 May 1975, 17–18.
3 Jacob Viner, *Canada and Its Giant Neighbour* (Alan B. Plaut Memorial Lectures, Carleton University, Ottawa, 30 Jan. and 1 Feb. 1958), 48.
4 See L.B. Pearson, House of Commons Standing Committee on External Affairs and National Defence, *Minutes of Proceedings and Evidence*, 21 Apr. 1970, 31.
5 Of scores of examples that could be mentioned, it suffices to recall the passage in 1930 of the Smoot-Hawley Tariff Act, with its prohibitively high duties on many Canadian exports; the rejection by the American Senate of three successive treaties for the preservation of the Fraser River salmon; and the release by a Senate Internal Security Subcommittee of a press release accusing Herbert Norman, Canadian ambassador to Egypt, of Communist connections, contributing to his suicide in 1957.
6 'Canada Gains Congress Ear,' *Financial Post*, 17 Jan. 1959. See also *Mike: The Memoirs of the Rt. Hon. Lester B. Pearson* (Toronto: University of Toronto Press, 1972), I, 209–10.
7 See *House of Commons Debates*, 30 Jan. 1942, I, 180; 7 July 1943, V, 4426–7; *Congressional Record*, 78th Cong., 1st Sess. (1943), 6268, 6898, 7036.
8 See Norman P. Lambert, Canada, *Senate Debates*, 8 July 1958, 276–7; Robertson, ibid., 3 July 1958, 260–1.
9 *Report of the Special Study Mission to Canada*, House Report No. 1766, 85th Cong., 2d Sess. (22 May 1958); U.S. Senate, *Review of Foreign Policy*, 1958, Part 3, 85th Cong., 2d Sess. (16 May 1958).
10 Dr Percy E. Corbett, *Review of Foreign Policy, 1958, 706–7.*
11 *Report of the Special Study Mission to Canada*, 3.
12 Ibid., 13–15.
13 *Review of Foreign Policy*, 1958, Part 3, 702, 703, 704, 713.
14 In a speech given at Wesleyan University, Middletown, Conn., 8 June 1958. See *Statements and Speeches*, No. 58/21.
15 See Senate Report No. 2231, 85th Cong., 2d Sess., (7 Aug. 1958).
16 'Canada–United States Inter-Parliamentary Group,' *External Affairs*, 2 (Aug. 1959), 210.
17 See House Committee on Foreign Affairs, Committee Print: *Summary Report of the First Meeting of the Canada–United States Interparliamentary Group,*

Washington, D.C., January 1959 (GPO, 1964); *External Affairs*, II (Aug. 1959),
209–13.
18 *Cong. Record*, 86th Cong., 1st Sess. 2598.
19 See ibid., 6027–30.
20 *House of Commons Debates*, 16 Mar. 1959, II, 1972.
21 Interviews with A.D.P. Heeney, 5 Aug. 1965; A.E. Ritchie 3 Aug. 1965; Senator
   E.S. Muskie, 29 July 1965; and Representatives E.F. Kelly and C.E. Gallagher,
   26 July 1965.
22 Italics added. See *Summary Report of the First Meeting of the Canada–United
   States Interparliamentary Group, Washington, D.C., January 1959*, House
   Committee Print (1964), 3.
23 House Report No. 730, 86th Cong., 1st Sess., 3.
24 Interview with Senator S.J. Smith, 21 Oct. 1966.
25 Report of the Canadian Co-chairmen, *House of Commons Debates*, Appendix
   (1959), IV, 3273.
26 At the sixth meeting, for example, held at Ottawa and Montreal, 28 Feb. to
   4 Mar. 1962, only 16 American and 23 Canadian members participated; in
   Quebec in 1975 only 15 Americans and 22 Canadians participated.
27 For example, 29 members of the American Congress, along with 24 members
   from the Canadian Parliament, participated in the 10th meeting of the group.
28 Matthew John Abrams, *The Canada–United States Interparliamentary Group*
   (Ottawa: Parliamentary Centre for Foreign Affairs and Foreign Trade, 1973),
   36.
29 *Memoirs of a Bird in a Gilded Cage* (Toronto: McClelland and Stewart, 1969),
   14.
30 Except that this restriction was not to apply during the first session of the 86th
   Congress or to meetings held in the United States.
31 Senator Muskie, in an interview with the author, 29 July 1965, pointed out that
   he missed eight roll-call votes during a two-day period he was in Ottawa.
32 Speech of Alan A. Macnaughton, *Senate Debates*, 8 July 1975, 1137–8.
33 Canadian Section, Canada–United States Inter-Parliamentary Group, 'Report
   of the Sixteenth Meeting' (Xeroxed, 1975), 4.
34 Ibid.
35 *The Toronto Daily Star*, 12 Mar. 1970, 1.
36 Interviews with Albert C.F. Westphal, 9 Sept. 1970; Norvill Jones, 11 Sept.
   1970; Ian Imrie, 20 Oct. 1966; A.E. Ritchie, 3 Aug. 1965; and letter of 25 Aug.
   1965 to the author from G.M. Carty.
37 Canada, *Senate Debates*, 14 Mar. 1972, 135.
38 Abrams, *Interparliamentary Group*, 58.
39 See William T. Murphy, *Cong. Record*, 87th Cong., 1st Sess., (16 Mar. 1961),

4228; *Globe and Mail*, 12 Mar. 1970. On general differences between Canadian and American members see Pauline Jewett, 'The Menace is the Message,' in *An Independent Foreign Policy for Canada?* ed. Stephen Clarkson (Toronto: McClelland and Stewart, 1968), 53.

40 *Financial Post*, 14 Apr. 1973, 10.

41 *Financial Post*, 8 Apr. 1961; interviews with A.E. Ritchie, 3 Aug. 1965, Arnold Heeney, 5 Aug. 1965, and Rufus Z. Smith, 10 June 1968. See also the Merchant-Heeney Report of 28 June 1965, *Dept. of State Bull.*, 2 Aug. 1965, 8.

42 Abrams, *Interparliamentary Group*, 104.

43 Ibid., 89, 117.

44 Ibid., 84.

45 House of Commons Standing Committee on External Affairs and Defence, *Minutes of Proceedings and Evidence*, 5 May 1970, 22.

46 *Financial Post*, 26 Sept. 1959, 10 Sept. 1960; Howard Green *House of Commons Debates*, 14 July 1960, VI, 6297.

47 *Financial Post*, 8 Apr. 1961.

48 Canada, *Senate Debates*, 7 Apr. 1970, 807; *House Report of the Thirteenth Meeting of the Canada–United States Interparliamentary Group, March 10–15, 1970*; Abrams, *Interparliamentary Group*, 86.

49 Abrams, *Interparliamentary Group*, 86, 87, 105.

50 *Proceedings*, 50.

51 Canada, *Senate Debates*, 12 Apr. 1973, 529.

52 The statistics are from a speech by Senator Alan A. Macnaughton. Canada, *Senate Debates*, 12 Feb. 1969, 1019. American law provides that the four members from the Senate Committee on Foreign Relations and the four from the House Committee on Foreign Affairs be appointed for two years. Furthermore, since there is less competition in the American Congress than in the Canadian Parliament for places on a delegation, American legislators – unlike Canadian – who want to return for other conferences generally are able to do so.

53 Macnaughton, Canada, *Sen. Debates*, 12 Feb. 1969, 1019.

54 Prior to 1969 the Foreign Relations Committee of the Senate had such a committee, but in that year it was merged with the Latin American subcommittee to form the Western Hemisphere Affairs Committee. Senator Macnaughton has recommended that each of the Canadian houses create 'some continuing group' for the study of Canadian–American problems. See ibid., 12 Feb. 1969, 1019.

55 Fourteenth Meeting of the Canada–United States Interparliamentary Group, 16–20 Feb. 1972, Print of House Committee on Foreign Affairs, 92d Cong. 2d Sess., 3.

56 Letter of 8 Apr. 1978, from Ian Imrie to the author.

57 See, for example, Canada, *Senate Debates*, 12 Nov. 1968, for a description of

the extensive social and travel activities of delagates and their spouses in March 1968.

58 Canada, *Senate Debates*, 6 May 1970, 996.

59 Donald Cameron, Canada, *Senate Debates*, 12 Feb. 1969, 1024; Imrie to the author, 8 Apr. 1978.

60 Gordon Fairweather, in an interview of 26 May 1965.

61 Macnaughton, *Senate Debates*, 8 July 1975, 1138.

62 *Senate Debates*, 16 Apr. 1970, 867.

CHAPTER 20

1 See William R. Willoughby, 'The Appointment and Removal of Members of the International Joint Commission,' *Canadian Public Administration* (fall 1969), 411–26.

2 See E. Lester Jones to Wilbur J. Carr, 30 June 1924, Dept. of State File 711.42153/324; Canada, *House of Commons Debates*, 7 Apr. 1924, II, 1107.

3 Maxwell Cohen, Canadian Standing Senate Committee on Foreign Affairs, *Proceedings* (18 Feb. 1975), 6. See also Mitchell Sharp, *House of Commons Debates*, 24 Mar. 1970, 32; Standing Senate Committee on Foreign Affairs, *Report: Canada–United States Relations*, No. 21 (2, 9, 16 Dec. 1975), I, 42.

4 Anthony Scott, 'Fisheries, Pollution and Canadian–American Transnational Relations,' in *International Organization*, 28 (autumn 1974), 845.

5 Canada, Standing Senate Committee on Foreign Affairs, *Proceedings*, No. 4 (9 May 1974), 7.

6 Interview with James Eayrs, 28 May 1968.

7 Don C. Piper, 'The Role of Intergovernmental Machinery in Canadian–American Relations,' *South Atlantic Quarterly*, LXII (autumn 1963), 565–6.

8 Memorandum by W.A. Found, 17 May 1929, W.L. Mackenzie King Papers, PAC, MG 26, J4, Vol. 167.

9 Frank Jackman, Canadian Department of Industry, Trade and Commerce, Canada, Standing Senate Committee on Foreign Affairs, *Proceedings*, No. 30 (6 Apr. 1976), 7.

10 'Transnational Relations and Interstate Conflicts: An Empirical Analysis,' in *International Organization*, 28 (autumn 1974), 961–96, especially 991.

11 *House of Commons Debates*, 18 July 1958, III, 2373, 2375–6.

12 Meeting of 18–22 May 1966, *Report to the Senate* (19 Oct. 1966), 6.

13 See *CIIA Monthly Report*, Oct. 1968, 109.

14 'International Trade,' published by the party's national headquarters in Ottawa, released to the press 3 Oct. 1972.

15 For the guidelines, incorporated into the Merchant-Heeney Report, see *Dept. of State Bull.*, 2 Aug. 1965.

16 Printed as a special issue of *International Perspectives* (autumn 1972). See especially pp. 2, 22, and 201.

17 John Picton, *Globe and Mail*, 31 Dec. 1977.

18 See Louis Balthazar, 'New Atmosphere in Canadian–American Relations,' *International Perspectives* (Sept./Oct. 1977), 25–9.

19 See, for example, Don Jamieson, 'Common Challenges Confronting Canada and the United States,' Address, 29 Apr. 1977, *Statements and Speeches*, No. 77/6.

20 Letter of 7 Apr. 1978, from Carl J. Clement, Department of State, to the author.

21 Don Jamieson, Senate of Canada, Standing Committee on Foreign Affairs, *Proceedings*, No. 13, 8 Mar. 1977, 40.

22 Allan J. MacEachen, 'Canada–United States Relations,' Address, 23 Jan. 1975, *Statements and Speeches*, No. 75/1.

23 See Department of External Affairs, *Canada Weekly*, 16 June 1976, 5.

24 Balthazar, 'New Atmosphere,' 27.

25 *United States–Canadian Relations*, Hearing before the Subcommittee on International Political and Military Affairs of the Committee on International Relations, House of Representatives, 94th Cong., 2d Sess. (28 Jan. 1976), 25–6.

26 Canada, for example, has such institutions with Japan, France, Belgium, Israel, China, Tunisia, Mexico, the European Economic Community, and possibly other countries.

27 See 'An American View of the Relationship,' remarks by U.S. Ambassador Thomas O. Enders, 9 Nov. 1976, U.S. Information Service, 5–7; Speech of Vice President Walter F. Mondale, Edmonton, 18 Jan. 1978, Office of the Vice President's Press Secretary, 4.

28 Roger F. Swanson, *State–Province Interaction, A Study of Relations between U.S. States and Canadian Provinces, Prepared for the U.S. Dept. of State* (Washington, DC., Aug. 1974), 41.

29 Grant L. Reuber, *United States–Canadian Economic Relations*, Hearing before the Subcommittee on Foreign Economic Policy of the Committee on Foreign Affairs, House of Representatives, 92d Cong., 1st Sess. (7 Dec. 1971).

30 For the convention see TS 635.

31 See Willoughby *The St. Lawrence Waterway*, 264–78.

32 Max Beloff, in a review of Roger Hilsman's book *To Move a Nation*, in *International Journal*, XXIII (winter 1967–8), 160.

Index